AF841107

# Media Law in Ireland

# Media Law in Ireland

**Marie McGonagle**
**Sharon McLaughlin**
**Tarlach McGonagle**

This book was originally published as a monograph in the International Encyclopaedia of Laws/Media Law.

Founding Editor: Roger Blanpain
General Editor: Frank Hendrickx
Volume Editors: Peggy Valcke & Eva Lievens

Wolters Kluwer

*Published by:*
Kluwer Law International B.V.
PO Box 316
2400 AH Alphen aan den Rijn
The Netherlands
E-mail: international-sales@wolterskluwer.com
Website: lrus.wolterskluwer.com

*Sold and distributed in North, Central and South America by:*
Wolters Kluwer Legal & Regulatory U.S.
7201 McKinney Circle
Frederick, MD 21704
United States of America
Email: customer.service@wolterskluwer.com

*Sold and distributed in all other countries by:*
Air Business Subscriptions
Rockwood House
Haywards Heath
West Sussex
RH16 3DH
United Kingdom
Email: international-customerservice@wolterskluwer.com



*Printed on acid-free paper*

ISBN 978-94-035-0023-2

e-Book: ISBN 978-94-035-0024-9
web-PDF: ISBN 978-94-035-0025-6



Printed in the United Kingdom.

# The Authors

Marie McGonagle is a former Head of the School of Law at the National University of Ireland, Galway.* She also served as a member of the University's Governing Authority. Her research interests lie in Media and Communications Law, and she has published widely in the field of national and international levels, as well as drafting many legal and policy documents, contributing to EU and Council of Europe programmes and studies, and advising Government and media organizations. She has held visiting academic appointments at Melbourne Law School; New York Law School; University of Poitiers, France; Programme in Comparative Media Law and Practice, University of Oxford; Institute for Information Law, University of Amsterdam; University of Maastricht, The Netherlands. E-mail: marie.mcgonagle@nuigalway.ie.

Sharon McLaughlin, PhD, is a Law Lecturer in the Department of Law and Humanities at Letterkenny Institute of Technology, Ireland. Sharon's research focuses on communications law and policy. She was awarded her PhD from the School of Law at the National University of Ireland, Galway (NUIG) for her thesis, entitled 'The Protection of Children in the Online and New Audiovisual Services Environment'.

## The Authors

She holds a BA in Public and Social Policy (2001), a LLB (2003) and a LLM in Public Law (2006). She is also a member of the EU Kids Online Ireland team. E-mail: sharon.mclaughlin@lyit.ie.

Tarlach McGonagle, PhD, is a senior researcher/lecturer at the Institute for Information Law (IViR), University of Amsterdam, the Netherlands. He is also a senior researcher at the Netherlands Network for Human Rights Research and a member of the Euromedia Research Group. He specializes in and has published widely on a broad range of topics relating to international and European human rights law, media law and policy and journalism. He regularly does expert work for the Council of Europe and the Organization for Security and Co-operation in Europe. He was Rapporteur of the Council of Europe's committees of experts on protection of journalism and safety of journalists (2014-2015) and media pluralism and transparency of media ownership (2016-2017). E-mail: t.mcgonagle@ivir.nl; Website: https://www.ivir.nl/employee/mcgonagle/.

*. The authors wish to thank Bláthnaid Folan BA, LLB (NUIG), Solicitor, for editorial assistance.

# Table of Contents

# List of Abbreviations

| | |
|---|---|
| AF | Audiovisual Federation of IBEC |
| ARPF | Annual Reviews of Public Funding |
| ASAI | Advertising Standards Authority for Ireland |
| ASPC | Annual Statement of Performance Commitments |
| AVMSD | Audiovisual Media Services Directive |
| BAI | Broadcasting Authority of Ireland |
| BBC | British Broadcasting Corporation |
| BCI | Broadcasting Commission of Ireland |
| BT | British Telecoms |
| CJEU | Court of Justice of the European Union |
| ComReg | Commission for Communications Regulation |
| DAB | Digital Audio Broadcasting |
| DCCAE | Department of Communications, Climate Action and Environment (formerly DCENR) |
| DCENR | Department of Communications, Energy and Natural Resources (now DCCAE) |
| DTT | Digital Terrestrial Television |
| EC | European Community |
| ECHR | European Convention on Human Rights |
| ECtHR | European Court of Human Rights |
| EEC | European Economic Community |
| EPG | Electronic Programme Guide |
| EU | European Union |
| FTA | Free-to-air |
| GSM | Global System for Mobile Communications |
| IBEC | Irish Business and Employers Confederation |

| | |
|---|---|
| ILRM | Irish Law Reports Monthly (Journal) |
| INM | Independent News and Media |
| IPTV | Internet Protocol Television |
| IRTC | Independent Radio and Television Commission |
| MEP | Member of the European Parliament |
| MMD | Multipoint Microwave Distribution (variant of MMDS) |
| MMDS | Multipoint Microwave Distribution System/ Multichannel Multipoint Distribution Service (variant of MMD) |
| MoU | Memorandum of Understanding |
| NNI | National Newspapers of Ireland |
| ODAS | On-Demand Audiovisual Services |
| ODTR | Office of the Director of Telecommunications Regulation (now ComReg) |
| PSB | Public Service Broadcasting |
| PWC | Price Waterhouse Coopers |
| RTÉ | Radio Telefís Éireann |
| s. | Section of an Act |
| SMP | Significant Market Power |
| SRH | Scottish Radio Holdings |
| TIF | Telecommunications Internet Federation of IBEC |
| TnaG | Teilifís na Gaeilge (Irish-language television station) |
| TWFD | Television without Frontiers Directive |
| UK | United Kingdom |

# General Introduction

## §1. General Background of the Country

*1.* Ireland is an island country with a population of 4.76 million. It shares a border with Northern Ireland, which was partitioned off as part of the United Kingdom (UK) in 1920 under the Government of Ireland Act. After various periods of unrest in the early and middle decades of the twentieth century relating to partition, a long period of violence in Northern Ireland between Unionists, who supported the Union with the UK and Nationalists, who desired a united Ireland, came to an end following various attempts at settlement and two peace processes. The second of these peace processes led to the Belfast (or 'Good Friday') Agreement,[1] whereby both States agreed that the future status of Northern Ireland would be determined by a referendum of the people of Northern Ireland. Northern Ireland, therefore, remains part of the UK but since the peace process and an amendment to the Irish Constitution to give effect to the Belfast Agreement, there is increased co-operation between the Republic and Northern Ireland, and a number of cross-border State bodies are in operation.

*2.* Ireland experienced successive waves of emigration prior to and since independence in 1922, mainly as a result of unemployment and lack of opportunity. Membership of the European Economic Community (EEC), later the European Union (EU), from 1973 onwards brought a measure of prosperity particularly for agriculture and a new focus on Europe rather than on its nearest neighbour, the UK. However, emigration in large numbers continued during the downturn in the economy in the 1980s, and it was not until the late 1990s and 2000s that immigration on a significant scale began to occur. Immigrants – both asylum seekers and economic migrants – from African countries, especially Nigeria, and from Eastern Europe and other parts of the world came to Ireland as a result of an economic boom experienced during that period. The population began to rise, reaching a pinnacle of 4.76 million in 2016, according to the census figures released by the Central Statistics Office.[2] As a result, Ireland has become a more diverse and multicultural society.

1. The text of the Agreement is available at http://www.dfa.ie/uploads/documents/Anglo-Irish/agreement.pdf.
2. Central Statistics Office (CSO), 'Press Statement: Census of Population 2016 – Preliminary Results' http://www.cso.ie/en/media/csoie/census/census2016/pr/COPprelim2016.pdf, 14 Jul. 2016.

# I. Political and Legal System of the Country

## A. *Introduction*

*3.* After centuries of British rule, Ireland became a Free State with its own written Constitution in 1922. A new written Constitution was adopted in 1937 and it remains in force today. The Constitution of 1937 states that: 'Ireland is a sovereign, independent, democratic state' (Article 5). It also establishes the Irish language as the first official language and English as a second official language (Article 8). The Constitution itself is written in both languages and in the case of doubt the Irish language text prevails.

## B. *The Structure of the State*

*4.* In 1948, having ceded from the British Commonwealth, Ireland was declared a Republic. The Head of State is the President, whose role under the Constitution (Articles 12–14) is largely ceremonial but who also has certain important powers, such as the power to send proposed legislation (Bills) to the Supreme Court to test their constitutionality before s/he signs them into law. The President and the two Houses of the Oireachtas (Parliament), i.e., the Dáil (Assembly of elected representatives) and Seanad (Senate), constitute the legislature. Proposals for legislation, in the form of Bills, are introduced in one or other House, are debated in both and then, when passed by both Houses, are signed into law by the President. The Constitution provides for the structures and operation of the State and State organizations and also for fundamental rights. As well as setting out the constitution and powers of the national parliament and each of its houses, and the powers and process for making legislation, it lays down the powers and structure of government and the roles of key public officials such as the Attorney General, who is the legal advisor to government, and the Comptroller and Auditor General.

*5.* The Constitution can only be amended by referendum of the people. A number of amendments have been made over the decades, the best known of which at European level are the amendments which were required under Article 29 of the Constitution to enable Ireland to become a member of the EEC in 1973, and later amendments to enable Ireland to ratify subsequent European Community (EC) and EU treaties. The common law system, which was transported from Britain in the twelfth century with the Anglo-Norman invasion of Ireland and became the dominant legal system, has since been influenced by the Constitution. Furthermore, in 2003, Ireland passed the European Convention on Human Rights (ECHR) Act, albeit at sub-constitutional level, to make the Convention and the jurisprudence of the European Court of Human Rights (ECtHR) arguable in Irish courts. Until then, following the incorporation of the ECHR in the UK (Human Rights Act 1998), Ireland was the last 'dualist' state party to the Convention.

## C. *The Legal System*

*6.* Following the foundation of the Irish Free State, a new court system was established under the Courts of Justice Act 1924. The modern court system was introduced in the Courts (Establishment and Constitution) Act 1961, with its basis in Article 34 of the 1937 Constitution. The Courts' structure is as follows.

**Supreme Court**

*7.* The highest court in the Irish court system is the Supreme Court. It is comprised of the Chief Justice, who is President of the Court, and nine ordinary judges. Most cases are dealt with by three judges, although up to seven judges can sit in a case. The President of the Court of Appeal and the President of the High Court are ex officio members of the Supreme Court. Until October 2014, when a new Court of Appeal was established, the Supreme Court was the final Court of Appeal in all matters, civil, criminal and constitutional. Appeals may now be made to the Supreme Court only where the Court grants permission in limited circumstances as set out in the Constitution. The Court can decide on the constitutionality of a Bill if referred to it by the President under Article 26 of the Constitution. It can also determine a question of the permanent incapacity of the President if it arises. Television broadcasts of court proceedings at any court level have not been permitted in Ireland, but for the first time on 24 October 2017, as part of a pilot project between RTÉ and the Courts Service, television broadcasting of the delivery of two judgments in the Supreme Court was permitted and the footage was to be made available to other broadcasters and uploaded on the Internet.

**Court of Appeal**

*8.* The Court of Appeal was established in October 2014 to deal with civil and other matters.[3] It is comprised of a President and nine ordinary judges. The Chief Justice and the President of the High Court are ex officio judges of the Court of Appeal. This new Court of Appeal was given the appellate jurisdiction in criminal matters previously exercised by the Court of Criminal Appeal and the appellate jurisdiction in civil matters previously exercised by the Supreme Court itself. It therefore deals with appeals from the High Court in civil cases and appeals from the Circuit Criminal Court, the Central Criminal Court or the Special Criminal Court in criminal cases. Cases are dealt with by three judges.

**High Court**

*9.* On the next level is the High Court, which is called the Central Criminal Court when dealing with criminal matters. It consists of a President and (currently) thirty-six ordinary judges. It is a Court of First Instance in constitutional matters and more serious civil and criminal matters, as well as a Court of Appeal from decisions of the lower courts. It is also the court that hears judicial reviews of administrative decisions, for example a licensing decision of the Broadcasting Authority.

**Lower Courts**

---

3. The new Court of Appeal was established on 28 Oct. 2014 following a constitutional referendum, Thirty-third Amendment of the Constitution. The legislation establishing the court is the Court of Appeal Act 2014 available at http://www.irishstatutebook.ie/eli/2014/act/18/enacted/en/print.html.

*10.* The lower courts, which are courts of limited and local jurisdiction, comprise the Circuit Court, which is a regional court located in Dublin (Dublin Circuit Court) and seven other 'Circuits', with venues in each Circuit, mostly in larger urban areas. The Circuit Court deals mainly with civil and family law cases and appeals from the lowest (District) courts. When hearing criminal cases it is known as the Circuit Criminal Court. Its monetary jurisdiction in civil matters covers claims up to EUR 75,000. The lowest courts in the system are the local District Courts. There are twenty-three districts, as well as the Dublin Metropolitan District. The District Court deals with local and summary matters. The cases before a District Court fall into four categories – less serious criminal cases (also referred to as minor offences), civil cases up to a compensation level of EUR 15,000 (but not including defamation cases, which must go to the Circuit or High Courts), some family law and licensing matters.[4]

**The Doctrine of Precedent**

*11.* The system operates on the basis of the doctrine of 'precedent', which means that the lower courts are bound to follow decisions of the higher courts in similar cases and *may* follow decisions of equal courts or foreign courts, where they are of persuasive value.

**Juries**

*12.* In all criminal cases, except in minor (i.e., least serious) cases heard by the District Court and in appeals, the judge sits with a jury. Juries also serve in the High Court in a small number of civil cases, such as defamation. All courts are open to the public, in accordance with the open justice principle in Article 34 of the Constitution, except for special cases which are held 'in camera', i.e., in private, usually in the judge's chambers. These are mainly family law cases but the *in camera* rule, which prevented the media from being present and reporting, was relaxed to some extent by legislation (Civil Liability and Courts Act 2004, section 40) and more recently by the Courts and Civil Law (Miscellaneous Provisions) Act 2013, which relaxed the rule further and allows media reporting of family law cases subject to certain safeguards.[5]

**The Legal Profession**

*13.* In Ireland, those who practise law are divided into two professions. The first type of lawyer is a solicitor. Solicitors can advise clients on transactions, the conveyance of property, family law matters and prepare wills, etc. Solicitors can represent their clients in all courts since 1971, but do so mainly in the District and Circuit Courts. When a matter goes to the High or Supreme Court, a barrister will generally be retained to represent the client in court. A barrister is the second type of lawyer, who provides legal opinion and advocacy for their client in court. Senior barristers are known as Senior Counsel, as opposed to Junior Counsel, who make up the majority of the Bar. Barristers in Ireland still work independently as sole traders, rather than in chambers or groups, although legislation which is intended to overhaul the way legal services

4. The monetary jurisdiction of the lower courts was increased to the above levels under the Courts and Civil Law (Miscellaneous Provisions) Act 2013. For further information on the composition and operation of the Irish courts' system, *see* http://www.courts.ie.

5. Courts and Civil Law (Miscellaneous Provisions) Act 2013, s. 5; available at:http://www.oireachtas.ie/documents/bills28/acts/2013/a3213.pdf.

are provided, the Legal Services Regulation Act 2015 was signed into Irish law on the 30 December 2015.[6]

**Sources of Law**

*14.* The main sources of Irish law are: the written Constitution of 1937; legislation emanating from the Oireachtas, which takes the form of primary legislation (Statutes or Acts) and secondary legislation (Statutory Instruments or Ministerial Regulations, which are usually authorized by primary legislation); Common law, as elucidated in the reasoning and decisions of the courts and therefore referred to as 'case law' or 'judge-made law'; and Equity, which provides a set of principles and remedies that supplement the common law in areas such as breach of confidence, injunctions, specific performance.

## D. *Overview of the Irish Constitutional Situation in the Context of Broadcasting and Telecommunications Regulation*

### 1. Broadcasting

*15.* Both the 1922 Constitution and the current Constitution of 1937 provided for freedom of expression. The relevant provision in the current Constitution is Article 40.6.1:

> The State guarantees liberty for the exercise of the following rights, subject to public order and morality:–
>
> (1) The right of the citizens to express freely their convictions and opinions.
>
> The education of public opinion being, however, a matter of such grave import to the common good, the State shall endeavour to ensure that organs of public opinion, such as the radio, the press, the cinema, while preserving their rightful liberty of expression, including criticism of Government policy, shall not be used to undermine public order or morality or the authority of the State.
>
> The publication or utterance of blasphemous, seditious, or indecent matter is an offence which shall be punishable in accordance with law.

*16.* The text specifically refers to the media as 'organs of public opinion' and instances the media in operation at the time of the coming into force of the Constitution, namely the radio, the press and the cinema. The clause is open-ended in that it refers to organs of public opinion 'such as' the radio, press and cinema, thus leaving it open for television broadcasting and new media to be covered as and when they come on stream. The reference to the cinema indicates that artistic speech is encompassed and subsequent case law has also confirmed that commercial speech is included too.[7] In a

6. The Act is available at: http://www.oireachtas.ie/documents/bills28/acts/2015/a6515.pdf.
7. *Murphy v. IRTC* [1999] 1 IR 12; [1998] 2 ILRM 360 – *see* paras 22–23 below.

2012 case, *Cornec v. Morrice & Ors*,[8] the term 'organs of public opinion' was interpreted by the High Court to include bloggers. Furthermore, the reference to the importance of the 'education of public opinion' for the common good in Article 40.6.1 was applied to the blogger concerned, whose activities were deemed to 'fall squarely within' it, with the result that there was 'a high constitutional value in ensuring that his right to voice' his views on the subject at issue was protected.

*17.* Other rights, including the right to privacy, although not specifically referred to in the Constitution, were identified in a similar way by the courts. The right to privacy must not be unreasonably encroached upon by broadcasters and the media generally. Among the specified rights in the Constitution is the right to one's good name. This is protected by the law of defamation, which has its origins in the common law of tort. Civil actions for defamation arise frequently against all the media, including broadcasters, often resulting in substantial damages (financial compensation) and costs. Defamation law is discussed in paragraphs 248–260.

*18.* Cases involving broadcasters, which have raised constitutional issues, have mainly concerned content. They include *The State (Lynch) v. Cooney*,[9] a challenge to section 31 of the Broadcasting Authority Act 1960, as amended in 1976, which enabled the Minister to direct RTÉ, the public service broadcaster (and sole broadcaster at the time), by Order, to refrain from broadcasting a particular matter or any matter of a particular class if in his opinion it would be 'likely to promote, or incite to, crime or would tend to undermine the authority of the State'. A Ministerial Order made under section 31 placed a ban on broadcast interviews with spokespersons for and representatives of specified organizations involved in or linked to the political violence or 'troubles' in Northern Ireland, including Sinn Féin. The Order was used to deny Sinn Féin, the political wing of the Irish Republican Army (IRA),[10] airtime for party political broadcasts in the run-up to a General Election in 1982 in which it was fielding candidates. Sinn Féin was not an unlawful party, membership of which would have been an offence; rather, it was a registered political party under section 13 of the Electoral Act 1963.

*19.* However, the Supreme Court considered the evidence adduced by the Minister of Justice, which was uncontroverted and which indicated that Sinn Féin was 'an integral and dependent part of the apparatus of the Provisional IRA, an illegal terrorist organization which, by both its avowed aims and its record of criminal violence, is shown to be committed to amongst other things the dismantling by violent and unlawful means of the organs of the State ….' (per Mr Justice Henchy). The Supreme Court considered that this evidence fully justified the Minister's opinion that a broadcast made on behalf of or inviting support for Sinn Féin, or broadcast by a person purporting to represent that organization, would have been likely to promote or incite to crime or would have tended to undermine the authority of the State.

*20.* While acknowledging that 'the fundamental rights of citizens to express freely their convictions and opinions cannot be curtailed or prevented on any irrational or capricious ground', the Court found that it was 'clearly the duty of the State to intervene to prevent broadcasts on radio or television which are aimed at … or which in any way would be likely to have the effect of promoting or inciting to crime or

8. 2012 IEHC 376, at §66; judgment of Hogan J., High Court, 18 Sept. 2012.
9. [1982] I.R. 337; [1983] ILRM 89.
10. The IRA was a paramilitary organisation involved in the violence.

endangering the authority of the State'. It therefore found the ban to be constitutional, based *inter alia* on the presumption of constitutionality of legislation passed by the Oireachtas post-1937, i.e., after the coming into force of the Constitution, and on the requirement in the Constitution that the right to freedom of expression may not be used by the media to 'undermine the authority of the State' (Article 40.6.1i). The ban remained in force and was later extended to commercial broadcasters.

*21.* A challenge to the ban in *Purcell v. Ireland* was found to be 'manifestly ill-founded' by the European Commission of Human Rights in 1991.[11] Lawyers for the applicants believed that, despite the Commission's finding, the taking of the case was worthwhile in that it forced the Government to publicly defend the ban. The ban was eventually lifted in January 1994 during the first Peace Process in Northern Ireland, and it was finally repealed by the Broadcasting Act 2001.

*22.* A later case, *Murphy v. IRTC*,[12] concerned an advertisement for a religious event, which the broadcasting regulator found to be in contravention of the ban on religious advertising contained in the Broadcasting Acts. The High Court relied on the right to communicate under Article 40.3 of the Constitution but found that there were good public interest reasons for restricting the advertisement in that religious advertising could be offensive and religion had been a divisive factor in Northern Ireland. Besides, the impugned section of the Act enjoyed the presumption of constitutionality attaching to all post-1937 legislation enacted by the Oireachtas.

*23.* The Supreme Court in turn considered that religion was both a private and a public affair and that the impugned provision was a restriction of the applicant's right freely to communicate (Article 40(3) of the Constitution) and of his right to freedom of expression (Article 40(6)(1) of the Constitution), rights which could nonetheless be limited in the interests of the common good. The key question for the court, therefore, was whether the limitation imposed upon the various constitutional rights was proportionate to the purpose which parliament wished to achieve. Applying the test for proportionality, the court found that the restriction was 'minimalist' in that all it prevented the applicant from doing was to advance his views by means of a paid advertisement on radio or television. The decision of the Supreme Court, upholding the ban, was later considered by the ECtHR, which applied the margin of appreciation and found unanimously that the State's reasons for the ban were 'relevant and sufficient'.[13] Nevertheless, the case clearly established that commercial speech came within the scope of the right to communicate under Article 40.3 and the freedom of expression guaranteed in Article 40.6.1 of the Constitution.[14] The prohibition on religious advertising has since been clarified and narrowed firstly in the Broadcasting Act of 2001 and more recently the Broadcasting Act of 2009.

---

11. Purcell *v*. Ireland, Application No. 15404/89, [1991] ECHR 77 (16 Apr. 1991), available at: http://www.bailii.org/cgi-bin/format.cgi?doc=/eu/cases/ECHR/1991/77. html&query=(purcell)+AND+(v)+AND+(ireland). *See* further discussion atpara. 180 below. A challenge to a similar but later ban in the UK also failed: Brind *v*. UK, Application No. 18714/91, 9 May 1994; (1994) D.R. 42.
12. [1999] 1 I.R. 12.
13. *Murphy v. Ireland*, Application No. 44179/88, judgment of 10 Jul. 2003,§82.
14. [1999] 1 IR 12; [1998] 2 ILRM 360; Barrington J. It may be noted, however, that the ECtHR distinguished between commercial and religious advertising at §70.

## 2. Telecommunications

*24.* Telecommunications are not specifically mentioned in the Constitution but the courts have identified in the Constitution an unspecified right to communicate, as one of the personal rights of the citizen. As stipulated by the Constitution itself, the High Court and the Supreme Court on appeal are the guardians of the Constitution and interpreters of its provisions. Only they can deal with the question of the validity of any law having regard to the provisions of the Constitution (Article 34.3.2). The High Court first enunciated the right to communicate in the context of a law regarding a monopoly in the postal services, and in explaining its scope and the fact that it was a qualified right, the High Court judge specifically referred to communication by radio contrary to wireless telegraphy regulations.[15] The right was identified by reference to Article 40.3.1 and Article 40.3.2 of the Constitution. The former pledges the State 'to respect and, as far as practicable, by its laws, to defend and vindicate the personal rights of the citizen'. The latter then goes on to list certain of those personal rights which the State shall defend and vindicate 'in particular'. The courts determined that the words 'in particular' meant that the list of rights specified was not exhaustive. The act of communication was deemed to be 'the exercise of such a basic human faculty that the right to communicate must inhere in the citizen by virtue of his human personality and must be guaranteed by the Constitution'.[16]

# II. Geography and Population

*25.* Ireland is a small island situated on the periphery of Europe next to the UK, which has a population of 60 million, almost fifteen times that of Ireland. English is the common language and the language of the vast majority of the media. The British print media circulate in Ireland and many have special Irish editions. British television broadcasting services have also been available in Ireland since broadcasting began, initially due to spill-over in areas that border Northern Ireland. There is a long-established pattern of emigration to the UK from Ireland and therefore a close affinity with British media. Similarly, there are close trade links. As a result, consumption of British media in Ireland is high but, given the difference in scale (e.g., large circulation figures of print media, numbers and variety of broadcasting channels in the UK), it is difficult for the small media outlets in Ireland to compete. Many family-owned local newspapers and small radio stations were bought over by British media organizations, such as Scottish Radio Holdings (SRH). Overseas investment was necessary to enable the commercial television station, TV3, to compete with the longer established public service broadcaster, RTÉ. The British-based Sky television channels became widely availed of in Ireland. Indeed, Sky is the dominant satellite operator in Ireland, with more than 40% of households subscribed to it, while the cable market is dominated by UPC Ireland (Liberty Global) with 20% of homes.[17] Attempts to bring in Digital

---

15. *A.G. v.Paperlink* [1983] IEHC 1, §32, 15 Jul. 1983 (available at www.irlii.org).
16. *Ibid.*
17. *See* Database on TV and on-demand audiovisual services and companies in Europe: http://mavise.obs.coe.int/.

Terrestrial Television (DTT) in Ireland were stymied by the limitations of the Irish market and after a number of interested players pulled out in the belief that it would not be viable, the Government had to rule out commercial DTT and amend legislation to authorize RTÉ, the public service broadcaster, to build and operate the multiplexes.[18] As of July 2016, Irish terrestrial DTT only homes represented 11.9% of all TV homes (although 43% of TV homes receive Irish DTT). Cable/satellite platforms represented the remaining 88.1% of all TV homes in Ireland.)[19]Internet Protocol Television (IPTV) showed a slight growth in 2015 but still reached less than 4% of homes. The launch of a new service by telecoms operator Eircom (since re-branded as 'EIR') in 2013, and a further IPTV service from Vodafone in 2016 may lead to further increases. The main on-demand services established in Ireland are the catch-up services of the main broadcasters, such as the RTÉ Player. The main distributors also provide on-demand services (UPC, Sky and Eircom).

## III. Social and Cultural Values

*26.* Ireland places a high value on culture. It has a proud tradition of distinction in music and the arts, boasts several Nobel Prize winners in poetry and literature and has a distinctive oral tradition in the Irish language, including a strong tradition of oral laws up to the seventeenth century, which were known as the 'Brehon laws' and implemented by 'Brehons', giving the modern Irish-language term 'breitheamh' for judge. Irish, or Gaelic (Gaeilge), was the original language of Ireland, spoken by all but the British settlers ('planters'), who had ousted the Gaelic speakers in most of Ireland, particularly the capital (Dublin) and the provinces of Leinster and Ulster, by the seventeenth century. The language has survived mainly along the western coast in areas known as Gaeltachtaí (Irish-speaking areas and communities). As a result of the need for so many Irish people to emigrate to earn a living, the Irish language was regarded by many as a hindrance and English became the dominant language. However, Irish has experienced a revival of interest in recent decades, especially in the cities and areas where there would not have been a strong tradition of fostering the language. Irish-language schools (Gaelscoileanna) have mushroomed. Under the Constitution, Irish is the first official language and English the second (Article 8).

*27.* Since independence in 1922, concerted efforts have been made by successive governments to foster the use of the Irish language. It became a compulsory subject in schools and until recent decades was necessary for entry to the civil service and to the national university. The Broadcasting Act 1960, under which RTÉ was established, provided (section 17): 'In performing its functions, the (RTÉ) Authority shall bear constantly in mind the national aims of restoring the Irish language and preserving and developing the national culture and shall endeavour to promote the attainment of those aims.' The current broadcasting legislation requires the regulator, the Broadcasting

18. Broadcasting Act 2009; and S.I. No. 67 of 2011: Broadcasting Act 2009 (s. 26(5) (Conferral of Additional Functions – Broadcasting Services) Order 2011.
19. ComReg, Second Quarterly Report for 2016, citing Nielsen TV Audience Measurement Establishment Survey on behalf of TAM Ireland, available at: https://www.comreg.ie/publication/quarterly-key-data-report-q2-2016/ or at comreg.ie, under 'news' and searching 'publications'.

Authority of Ireland (BAI) *inter alia* to endeavour to ensure 'that the number and categories of broadcasting services made available in the State by virtue of this Act best serve the needs of the people of the island of Ireland, bearing in mind their languages and traditions and their religious, ethical and cultural diversity' and to 'promote and stimulate the development of Irish-language programming and broadcasting services'. (Broadcasting Act 2009, section 25(1) (a) and 25(2) (h).) An Irish-language radio station, Raidió na Gaeltachta, was established in 1973, under the auspices of RTÉ, the national public service broadcaster. Other independent and community radio stations broadcasting in Irish were subsequently established and in 1996 an Irish-language television station, now named TG4, was established, initially under the auspices of RTÉ but later on an independent basis.

## §2. The Media Landscape

### I. Overview of Media Markets and Main Actors

#### *A. Introduction*

*28.* The Irish broadcasting landscape is characterized by a strong radio sector, with public service and commercial national, quasi-national, regional and local radio stations, as well as community and community of interest stations. The public service broadcaster, RTÉ, still dominates the sector, with its two national radio stations, Radio One and 2FM, its arts and music service RTÉ Lyric FM, and an Irish-language station, Raidió na Gaeltachta. RTÉ is dual funded by virtue of a licence fee and advertising and had a monopoly of the airwaves and of advertising up until 1989 when the commercial sector was established. As a result, the newly established commercial stations found it difficult to compete. Indeed, the first licensed commercial national station collapsed after less than two years but since then Today FM has filled the gap. The sector generally benefited from the economic prosperity of the later 1990s and early 2000s but suffered in the recent downturn.

*29.* In television also, RTÉ had a monopoly – except in areas bordering Northern Ireland where UK television stations could be received – until a national commercial television station, TV3, began to broadcast in 1998. RTÉ, therefore, had virtually all of the television advertising spend and little competition for audiences apart from the UK services until then. From 2000 onwards, with TV3 broadcasting as a terrestrial service and BSkyB offering digital satellite services in Ireland, viewers began to have a greater choice but RTÉ remained and still remains a strong player in the market, RTÉ and RTÉ2 had a combined market share of 31.7% of the television market in 2011, 29.6% in 2012, falling to 27% in 2014.[20] As with the radio sector, the television sector experienced the highs and lows of the economic situation in recent years. The switchover to DTT proved difficult, with potential commercial players declining to enter a small market at high cost that did not appear to them to be viable. As a result,

20. For further data, *see* http://mavise.obs.coe.int/; Reuters Institute Digital News Reports: www.digitalnewsreport.org.

the switchover was achieved by requiring RTÉ to build and operate the multiplexes, with the result that only the public service stations and TV3 are currently operating via the multiplexes. In January 2015, Ulster Television (UTV), which previously operated only in Northern Ireland as one of the British ITV channels, launched a new television station in Dublin, UTV Ireland. It has since been bought over by TV3 owner, Virgin Media, a subsidiary of Liberty Global.

*30.* Ireland also has a long tradition of print media with a strong footing in the advertising market.[21] Newspapers are still widely read in hard copy and online, although circulations are falling. Indigenous newspapers have to compete with British newspapers which circulate widely in Ireland. Since the 1990s, a number of British titles have established offices in Ireland and produce Irish editions. The umbrella organization of the national newspapers, originally called National Newspapers of Ireland (NNI) and NNI Local and Regional Newspapers – represented fifteen national daily, Sunday and weekly newspapers and twenty-four local and regional newspapers with a combined weekly circulation of almost 5.8 million copies. NNI is now called NewsBrands Ireland[22] and represents sixteen national newspapers. Until the 1990s most regional and local newspapers were still family-owned and some had been in existence since the nineteenth century. However, as the Irish economy improved, regional newspapers, like local radio stations, were regarded as attractive investments and were bought over by major media groups, both Irish and British.[23]In addition to traditional newspapers, new online newspapers, such as <TheJournal.ie>, have emerged.

## B. *Television Broadcasting*

*31.* As a result of the difficult economic situation that pertained in the 1940s and 1950s, television broadcasting did not begin until 1961 under the Broadcasting (Authority) Act of 1960. Again, only one public station, RTÉ, was licensed and no further television stations were permitted to enter the market until 1989, under the Radio and Television Act of 1988.

*32.* The current broadcasting regulator is the BAI, established under the Broadcasting Act 2009. BAI regulates the independent commercial sector and the community sector. It also regulates public broadcasting media, RTÉ and TG4, in some respects, for example with regard to their Annual Statement of Performance Commitments (ASPC) and Annual Reviews of Public Funding (ARPF), although both stations are established as companies with their own Boards of Directors and the RTÉ Authority. The BAI licenses fourteen television and sixty radio services and regulates the three national TV and four national radio services. It also licenses three satellite content television services (Setanta Sports Channel Ireland, Setanta Sports 1 and Setanta Sports

---

21. *See* Athena Media, *Irish Broadcasting Landscape: Economic and Environmental Review for the Broadcasting Authority of Ireland (BAI)*, 31 Aug. 2010, p. 133. However, total spend declined over the past few years. In 2012, both television and print revenues were down 10% over the year, with the radio market declining 8% and outdoor down 7%, according to Accenture Media Management Ireland – *see* The Irish Times 10 Jan. 2013.
22. http://newsbrandsireland.ie.
23. *See* Michael Foley, 'Media Landscapes: Ireland', http://www.ejc.net/media_landscape/article/ireland/.

North America), seven Cable/MMD content television services (3e, UPC, City Channel Dublin, City Channel Waterford/South East, City Channel Galway, Munster, Hungary) and 3 community content television services (DCTV, P5TV and Cork Community TV CCTV).[24] BAI also has responsibility for the licensing of multiplex services and Electronic Programme Guide (EPG) licences. It is essentially, however, a content regulator.

## 1. Public Service Broadcasting: Television

*33.* RTÉ, the national public service broadcaster, which previously operated a radio station only, was established as a television broadcaster under the Broadcasting Authority Act 1960. Following the report of the Television Commission in 1959, the legislature enacted the Broadcasting Authority Act 1960, which invested in a semi-state body, the RTÉ Authority, the sole right to operate broadcasting services. In order to avoid a drain on the exchequer, RTÉ was dually funded from the outset by means of a licence fee and revenue from advertising.

*34.* The Broadcasting Authority Act 1960 established the structures for television broadcasting and provided for the regulation of programming in terms of both operation and content. It imposed what are now referred to as 'public service obligations' on broadcasters, including requirements of fairness and impartiality, regard for the privacy of the individual and a number of cultural aims and objectives, which have been carried through to the present day. While providing a large measure of independence to the new service, the Act gave the Minister the right to direct the RTÉ Authority to refrain from broadcasting certain matter (section 31). This provision proved controversial when invoked in the 1970s.[25] Under the 1960 Act, the government was also given the power to appoint the members of the Authority and to dismiss individual members or the Authority as a whole. The 1960 Act thus combined statutory autonomy with a measure of government control. The ministerial and governmental powers were later curtailed, however, by amending legislation in 1976 (Broadcasting Authority (Amendment) Act 1976) and safeguards for the independence and autonomy of the Authority were put in place.

*35.* Initially, the RTÉ service was black and white and, while RTE transmitted in colour for the first time in 1969, it was another six years before it was fully in colour.[26] RTÉ began with one television channel and then for many years it operated two television channels, RTE1 and 2, which remain the most prominent television channels in Ireland and still attract a large viewership. An Irish-language television station (Teilifís na Gaeilge–TnaG), with a name change to TG4, was added to RTÉ's

---

24. For further information and updates, *see* http://www.bai.ie/en/broadcasters/.
25. It was used, for example, to prevent broadcast interviews with spokespersons for or representatives of Sinn Féin, a registered political party which was also the political wing of the IRA, one of the organisations involved in the violence in Northern Ireland from the late 1960s onwards. The section was amended in the Broadcasting Authority (Amendment) Act 1976 and was eventually allowed to lapse in 2004 during the first peace process in Northern Ireland. It was finally abolished in the 2001 Broadcasting Act.
26. *See* 'Irish TV – the story of Irish Television' at www.irish-tv.com/hist70s.asp.

stable in 1996, although it was later put on an independent footing (Broadcasting Act 2001).

*36.* The Broadcasting (Amendment) Act 2007 required (*inter alia*) RTÉ to provide its broadcast services as far as was reasonably practicable, to Irish communities outside the island of Ireland (section 3(1)(b)). RTÉ now has, in addition to its previously established services, a number of new digital services, including RTÉ News Now, RTÉ 1 + 1, RTÉ jr, as well as RTÉ digital teletext and a website www.rte.ie and i-player, the RTÉ player.

## 2. Commercial Television

*37.* Provision was made for the first time in the Radio and Television Act 1988 for commercial radio and television but, while commercial radio developed very quickly, the first national commercial television station, TV3, experienced problems and did not begin to broadcast as a terrestrial service until 1998. The Radio and Television Act, 1988 gave the Independent Radio and Television Commission (IRTC) responsibility for the development of the independent radio and television sector in the State. The Broadcasting Act 2001 renamed the regulator the Broadcasting Commission of Ireland (BCI) and increased the remit to allow it to license content on digital, cable, MMD and satellite systems. Before the BCI became the BAI under the 2009 Act, it licensed thirteen television services: one independent national terrestrial television service; three satellite content television services and two pay-per-view satellite content television services (section 36 of 2001 Act), along with five Cable/MMD content television services (section 41 of 2001 Act) and two Community content television services (section 39 of 2001 Act).

*38.* All national, regional, local, special interest and television content services are now licensed by the broadcasting regulator, BAI (established by the Broadcasting Act 2009), for a period of ten years, i.e., all broadcasters apart from the public service broadcaster, RTÉ, which was licensed under a pre-existing scheme. Community, community of interest and institutional services are licensed for five years. Temporary services are licensed for thirty days in a twelve-month period. RTÉ, TV3 and 3e (owned by TV3) are available on the digital platform, Saorview.

## 3. Digital Television

*39.* Digital television was first provided for in the Broadcasting Act 2001. It was intended that a commercial entity would deliver DTT services in Ireland and make the national Irish channels available free-to-air but the proposed system proved to be too ambitious and cumbersome and failed to attract the commercial sector. The Government's Department of Communications then decided to launch its own digital trial and further legislation amending the original 2001 proposal was introduced in 2007 (Broadcasting (Amendment) Act 2007). Further attempts to license commercial stations failed, and the 2007 Act gave way to the Broadcasting Act 2009, which placed the onus on RTÉ to establish and operate multiplexes.[27] In response, RTÉ launched a pilot DTT service, called Saorview, to 94% of the population on 29 October 2010. Subsequently, a memorandum of understanding (MOU) was entered into with Northern Ireland in a bid to coordinate the digital switchover in the two parts of the island of Ireland. Among the benefits of the MOU was that the Irish-language station, TG4, and RTÉ would be carried on the DTT network in Northern Ireland.

*40.* A Statutory Instrument, S.I. No. 67 of 2011, made provision for additional functions for RTÉ in relation to multiplexes. RTÉ then sought and received approval for five new RTÉ TV channels and services and formally launched Saorview in May 2011. A year later, in May 2012, 76.8% of Irish TV households received digital television and 7% of TV households were receiving DTT services. These figures increased to 97.7% and 12%, respectively in 2013.[28]Thus, despite the difficulties mainly associated with the cost factor of establishing new services in a small market, and the fact that digital was readily available via cable and satellite, the switchover from analogue to digital television was achieved on 24 October 2012 but without any new commercial broadcasters. The existing commercial television station, TV3 and its digital station, 3e, however, are also on Saorview. For those who cannot receive Saorview, RTÉ established a satellite TV service called SAORSAT, which is available to 100% of the population. SAORSAT carries RTÉ One, RTÉ Two (HD), TG4, RTÉ One+1 (from 7pm), RTÉjr (to 7pm), RTÉ News Now, together with the RTÉ radio channels and Digital Aertel. Commercial broadcasters, TV3 and 3e, are not carried on SAORSAT. Ireland falls within the footprint of the equivalent UK free-to-air (FTA) digital satellite service, Freesat, so, as a result of the spill-over, UK channels can be viewed in Ireland via Freesat with the appropriate digital receiver equipment.

## C. *Radio*

### 1. Public Radio Broadcasting

*41.* Although Marconi carried out some of his trials in Ireland, radio broadcasting began rather late in Ireland because of the Civil War and its aftermath in the early 1920s. The Wireless Telegraphy Act was enacted in 1926 and established a licensing system both for transmission and for receipt of radio programmes. Only one radio station was licensed, and successive governments refused to license any other stations until the 1980s. Initially called 2RN, the station was operated as part of the Government's Department of Posts and Telegraphs. By the early 1930s the station could be received nationwide, and in 1939 the name of the station was changed to Radio Éireann but it remained in the control of the government. Soon afterwards, attention began to turn to television but, given the small size of the market and the weakness of the economy, it was nearly a decade before the decision was finally taken to establish a national television broadcasting service. Radio Éireann, however, continued to operate as the only licensed radio broadcaster in the State and that monopoly continued until legislation

27. For details of the various attempts made to encourage commercial DTT operators into the market, *see* BAI atwww.bai.ie/.../bai-publishes-review-of-potential-for-commercial-dtt-in-ireland-3/.
28. http://mavise.obs.coe.int/country?id=17.

– the Wireless Telegraphy Act of 1988 and the Radio and Television Act of the same year – was passed with a view to opening up the market to commercial radio operators. The only other operators in the intervening period were unlicensed, so-called pirate radio stations, which were constantly under threat of closure and threat of monetary and other sanctions provided for in the Wireless Telegraphy Act of 1926.

*42.* Nowadays, RTÉ, the public service broadcaster, still holds the main share of the market and operates RTÉ Radio 1, RTÉ 2FM, Lyric FM (a classical music station), and an Irish-language station, Raidio na Gaeltachta, as well as seven exclusively digital stations: RTÉ Radio 1 Xtra, RTÉ Pulse, RTÉ Chill, RTÉ Gold, RTÉ 2XM and RTÉ Junior. The main channels are available on FM, on digital radio (Digital Audio Broadcasting (DAB), on satellite, on mobile and online; digital stations are available on digital radio and online. RTÉ Radio 1 is also available on long wave Radio 1 Extra). It may be noted that DAB was slow to take off in Ireland but RTÉ now has a number of stations available on a DAB system.[29]

*43.* The RTÉ Board is the governing authority of RTÉ. It replaced the former RTÉ Authority, following the enactment of the Broadcasting Act in 2009. The broadcasting regulator, the BAI, has some overarching competences with regard to RTÉ under the 2009 Act. For instance, BAI codes of programme standards, commercial communications and so forth apply to all broadcasters, including RTÉ. BAI also is required (section 26(1)(l)) of the Act) to prepare and issue guidance to RTÉ as to the fulfilment of their obligations under the Act with regard to audits and accounts (section 109) and a code of fair trading practice (section 112(2)). BAI is also responsible for reviewing RTÉ's funding (section 124).

*44.* In addition to RTÉ's channels, there are a number of licensed community radio stations. These are stations operated by members of the community who are representative of, and accountable to, the community concerned (Broadcasting Act 2009, section 64(a)). In supplying programme material to the community, their sole objective must be to specifically address the interests of and seek to provide a social benefit to, the community concerned. They are non-profit and must achieve 'a monetary reward of no greater amount than is reasonably necessary to defray the expenses that will be incurred in effecting that supply' (section 64(b)).

## 2. Private/Independent Commercial Radio Broadcasting

*45.* Independent/commercial radio broadcasting began in 1989 in accordance with the Radio and Television Act 1988, which established the IRTC as the regulator. The IRTC later became the Broadcasting Commission of Ireland (BCI, Broadcasting Act 2001) and later still the Broadcasting Authority of Ireland (BAI, Broadcasting Act 2009). Commercial radio consists of local, regional and national stations. The BCI regulated a national radio service (Today FM), a quasi-national service (Newstalk), two regional radio services (Beat FM & Spin South West) and a total of fifty-two local, community, and community of interest and institutional radio services. The Commission also issued temporary licences allowing applicants to broadcast for thirty days in any twelve-month period. The BAI currently licenses one national, one quasi-national, three regional, two multi-city, one city and commuter belt and twenty-six local stations,

29. For up-to-date information and list of channels *see* www.rte.ie.

twenty-two community radio/community of interest services, six institutional radio services and a number of temporary radio services.[30]

*46.* Following a slow start, when newly licensed radio stations found it difficult to compete with the public service stations of RTÉ, which had had a monopoly of audiences and advertising until then, the commercial radio sector began to prosper and remains vibrant today. As the new stations gained listeners and advertising revenue they became targets of large, mainly British, media corporations, such as SRH and Ulster Television, which is part of the British ITV network and were bought over. A major player in the market is Communicorp, established in 1989, when the licensing process began, by Irishman, Denis O'Brien. Based in Dublin, Communicorp has grown and become a major player in the Irish media market. It now owns a number of prominent radio stations in Ireland, including a quasi-national station Today FM; a national news and sports news station Newstalk 106–108FM; and Dublin based music station 98FM. When he bought the radio stations owned by SRH, then Emap (Today FM, FM104 and Highland Radio), O'Brien was required by the then broadcasting regulator, BCI, to sell FM 104 within three months of the decision, as otherwise he would have owned the two best-established radio stations in Dublin.[31] He also owns radio stations in the UK and Bulgaria.[32] The Competition and Consumer Protection Commission,[33] which was established under the Competition and Consumer Protection Act of 2014, found in a decision of May 2016 that Communicorp was now large enough to exert competitive constraints on RTÉ radio. The complaint before the CCPC was made by the Independent Broadcasters of Ireland (IBI) against RTÉ's 2FM.[34]

## 3. Telecoms

*47.* Until 1983, telephone and postal services in Ireland were under the control of the government's Department of Posts and Telegraphs. As already indicated, the Department of Posts and Telegraphs also had control of radio broadcasting from 1926, under the Wireless Telegraphy Act of that year, up until the establishment of Radio Telefís Éireann (RTÉ) in 1961, under the Broadcasting Act of 1960. Indeed, the Minister

30. *See* www.bai.ie for updates to figures.
31. The Competition Authority http://www.tca.ie/ 7 Dec. 2007 cleared the sale by SRH to Communicorp based on the advertising market. BCI, the then broadcasting regulator, decided on the basis of its ownership and control policy, to clear the sale of two of the three stations owned by SRH in October 2007 but not FM104 (*see* http://www.independent.ie/ 8th Oct. 2007). *See* Helen Shaw, 'O'Brien bidding to rule the airwaves', *The Irish Times* 24 Jul. 2007, available at: http://www.irishtimes.com/opinion/o-brien-bidding-to-rule-the-airwaves-1.951125; http://www.athenamedia.ie/admin/report_images/Irish_Times_Radio_Takeover.pdf. Ultimately, Communicorp was allowed to buy the three stations but was required to sell FM104, as stated above. The station was sold to UTV. In a subsequent decision of 27 Jul. 2009, BCI found that under the provisions of its Ownership and Control Policy (2008), Mr. O'Brien did not have control of, or substantial interests in, an undue amount of communications media in any of the relevant franchise areas. http://www.bci.ie/news_information/press229.html.
32. *See* www.communicorp.ie.
33. *See* www.ccpc.ie.
34. *See* '"O'Brien as powerful as RTÉ" in radio', *The Sunday Times* 15 May 2016. http://www.thetimes.co.uk/edition/ireland/obrien-as-powerful-as-rte-in-radio-2l6lqhchk.

for Posts and Telegraphs had a role in relation to both radio and television broadcasting even after 1960 until such time as the Department became known as the Department of Communications in 1983, under the Ministers and Secretaries (Amendment) Act 1983. Regulation of telecommunications eventually moved from the Department to the government-established Office of the Director of Telecommunications Regulation (ODTR). Later, under the Communications Regulation Act 2002, the ODTR was replaced by the Commission for Communications Regulation (ComReg), which became the regulator of telecoms and postal services.

*48.* Telecommunications were provided for many years by the state-owned company, Telecom Éireann, which was established under the Postal and Telecommunications Services Act 1983, and had a monopoly from 1983 until the late 1990s. The Government then decided to privatize it, placing it on the stock market and renaming it Eircom. Eircom, which has since been rebranded as 'EIR', remains the major telecoms operator in Ireland, offering fixed line, mobile (formerly Meteor but rebranded as part of 'EIR' mobile network), Internet and broadband services, as well as its 'Eircom Phonewatch' (now 'Phonewatch'), a property protection burglar alarm system. Other major players include UPC, which provides cable television, digital and broadband services; and Vodafone, which acquired Eircom's mobile subsidiary, Eircell, in 2001.

*49.* Esat Telecom, which was founded by Denis O'Brien in 1990, was granted a limited telecommunications licence in 1993 and began operating in 1994. It was, therefore, the first company to provide competition in the Irish market, albeit to a limited extent. It became Esat Digifone when it acquired, in controversial circumstances, the second Global System for Mobile Communications (GSM) mobile telecommunications licence in a competitive bid in 1996. It was a joint venture between Esat Telecom and the Norwegian company, Telenor. The consortium, led by Denis O'Brien, became a major player in the telecommunications market. The Irish telecommunications market was by then fully deregulated, despite a derogation that would have lasted until 2000.[35] Esat Digifone was designated in 1999, however, as having Significant Market Power (SMP) in the mobile market by the then telecommunications regulator, the ODTR.[36] Indeed, Esat Digifone had 40% of the Irish market by the time it was sold to British Telecom in 2000, following disputes between Esat Telecom and Telenor.[37] In 2006, the company was acquired by the Spanish company Telefónica, which is a subsidiary of Telefónica Europe. It became known as O2 and subsequently as 'Three Ireland' following its acquisition by Hutchison 3G.[38]

*50.* The awarding of the second mobile phone licence to O'Brien in October 1995 became the subject of a public inquiry, known as the Moriarty Tribunal, established in 1997 to inquire into payments to politicians. The Tribunal found that it was beyond doubt that the Minister for Communications at the time imparted substantive information to Denis O'Brien which was 'of significant value and assistance to him in securing

35. On 1 Dec. 1998, telecoms were deregulated in Ireland, one year ahead of schedule. This was done despite a derogation which would have lasted until January 2000. *See* IRIS 1999-3:14/27, available at http://merlin.obs.coe.int.
36. ODTR Decision Notice 15/99.
37. *See: The Telegraph* 7 Feb. 2001.
38. The European Commission approved the acquisition by Hutchison 3 under the EU Merger Regulation in 2014: *see* http://europa.eu/rapid/press-release_IP-14-607_en.htm.

the licence'.[39] Subsequently, however, the Supreme Court held unanimously that the findings of tribunals of inquiry are not admissible in court proceedings.[40] However, the Court did give leave for two of the competing consortia to go ahead with their legal actions against the then Minister who awarded the licence, Michael Lowry, and also against East Telecom, Denis O'Brien, Ireland and the Attorney General.[41] The first set of proceedings concerned the decision of the Minister to extend the deadline for receipt of tenders one week before the original deadline. The second set of proceedings raised serious concerns about the decision of the Minister to award the licence to Esat Telecom, and the third involved a claim for damages (including exemplary damages) for misfeasance in public office, breach of duty, including statutory duty, breach of contract, breach of legitimate expectations of Persona Digital Telephony Ltd (one of the unsuccessful bidders), breach of constitutional rights of Persona Digital Telephony Ltd, breach of rights under EU law, and a declaration that the European Communities (Mobiles and Personal Communications) Regulations 1996, contravene EU law.

*51.* As the plaintiffs had not instituted proceedings until 2005 (which the plaintiffs said was due to the fact that they were monitoring events at the Moriarty Tribunal which was inquiring into the issue),[42] the High Court found that the delay was inordinate and inexcusable and that the balance of justice favoured the dismissal of the proceedings. Reliance was also placed on Article 6 of the ECHR, particularly the right to fair procedures and to a hearing within a reasonable time.

*52.* The Supreme Court, however, in an appeal from the decision of the High Court pointed out *inter alia* that this was not an appeal relating to a criminal trial, and thus the law as to delay and a criminal trial did not apply (§12). In relation to the reasonable time element under Article 6 ECHR, the Court cited *Price and Lowe v. The United Kingdom*[43] and the criteria laid down in it by the ECtHR, namely: the complexity of the case; the conduct of the applicant; the conduct of the relevant authorities; and the importance of what is at stake for the applicant in the litigation. The judges pointed to the uniqueness of this case:

> This case is absolutely unique, without precedent or parallel in the ninety year history of the State. It will be profoundly worrying, indeed alarming, in its implications for Irish public administration if the allegations made by the plaintiffs turn out to be true.[44]

---

39. Moriarty report available at www.moriarty-tribunal.ie/.
40. *In re Bovale Developments DCE v. Bailey & anor* [2011] IESC 24. O'Brien's company, Digicel, is the largest mobile telecommunications operator in the Caribbean and is now operating in the Central American mobile market also.
41. *Comcast Int. Holdings v. Minister for Public Enterprise & ors and Persona Digital Telephony Ltd v. Minister for Public Enterprise & ors*[2012] IESC 50, Supreme Court 17/10/2012, available at: http://www.bailii.org/ie/cases/IESC/2012/S50.html.
42. The first plenary summons was issued in 2001, notice of intention to proceed in 2004, and following attempts by Mr O'Brien to have the proceedings struck out, the statement of claim was delivered in 2005 (Comcast) and 2006 (Persona) – *see* full list of dates in the judgment of McKechnie, J. at §13 and §14.
43. Application No. 43185/98, ECtHR 29 Jul. 2003.
44. Per Hardiman, J.; *see also* Denham, J. at §39–§47; Fennelly, J. at §2, §63; McKechnie, J. at §45 and Clarke, J. at §6.6–§6.7.

Each of the five Supreme Court judges delivered a judgment setting out their reasons, but the decision to allow the cases to proceed was unanimous. In the recent case of *Persona Digital Telephony Ltd & another v. The Minister for Public Enterprise & others*[45] Persona Digital Telephony Ltd, who were unable to fund the case, tried to rely on another company for funding but this was disallowed.

*53.* Various other court cases involving a number of telecoms operators have arisen over the years. Some involved decisions of the telecoms regulator, ComReg. An example is ComReg's decision to designate certain companies, such as Eircom (now rebranded as 'Eir'), as having SMP, and Vodafone and O2 (now 'Three Ireland') as being jointly dominant in the telecoms market.[46] Other cases involved copyright and data protection issues, such as the 'three strikes rule' in relation to illegal downloading.[47]

## *D. Print Media*

### 1. Newspapers

*54.* A short account of the composition of the Irish newspaper market is given in the General Introduction above. Independent News and Media (INM) is the biggest group with the largest circulation daily, evening and Sunday newspapers in Ireland. It publishes five market-leading national newspapers (*Irish Independent, Sunday Independent, Evening Herald* (called simply *TheHerald* and marketed as a morning paper since March 2013), *Sunday World* and *The Star*), thirteen regional newspapers (in counties Cork, Kerry, Dublin, Louth, Wexford, Wicklow, Carlow and Sligo) and a daily free newspaper *Metro Herald*.[48] It is also Ireland's largest newspaper and magazine wholesaler and distributor.[49] The Group also has major newspaper and publishing interests in Australasia, South Africa and Northern Ireland. The overall Group publishes over 200 newspapers and magazines, has over 100 websites, 130+ radio stations and 75,000+ outdoor panels.[50] Given its dominance in the newspaper market, the group has been the subject of Competition Authority reports and media mergers and acquisitions decisions under the Competition Act 2002.[51] One of the major shareholders in the group is now Denis O'Brien, who – as detailed above – has very substantial interests in the media market, particularly radio and telecoms. His prominent position in the leading newspaper group has raised issues concerning concentration of ownership and the threat to pluralism.

---

45. [2016] IEHC 187.
46. *See* IRIS 2005-10:15/27, which refers also to the establishment of an appeals body, ECAP, to fast-track appeals by the telecommunications industry against decisions of ComReg. The existence and role of ECAP, however, only delayed the process further and was not effective, with the result that is was short-lived.
47. For example, *EMI Records (Ireland) Limited & ors v. The Data Protection Commissioner* [2013] IESC 34.
48. For data and updates on circulation and readership figures, *see* http://newsbrandsireland.ie/data-centre/media-centre/.
49. *See* www.inmplc.com/operations/Ireland.
50. *See* www.inmplc.com.
51. *See* further para 524 below.

*55.* The other major group in Ireland that owns newspapers and radio stations is Crosby Holdings, a family concern in Cork. Until early 2013 they owned the *Examiner* and *Sunday Business Post* (national newspapers), an evening title (*Evening Echo*) and several regional and local newspapers, as well as three commercial local radio stations. In March 2013 the group went into liquidation but all of the titles (with the exception of the *Sunday Business Post*), as well as the radio stations and digital and new media business were acquired by a new company (Landmark Media)comprising members of the same family who were the original owners; only the printing operation ceased trading.[52] An interim examiner was appointed to the *Sunday Business Post*. It was later reported that a corporate finance firm, Key Capital, and former Irish Daily Star managing editor Paul Cooke had formed a consortium which bought the paper.[53] The other major influential Irish newspaper, the *Irish Times*, operates – like the *Guardian* in England – on the basis of a Trust. In December 2017, it was announced that the *Irish Times* had agreed to buy the publishing and media interests of the Landmark Media group. At the time of writing, the deal is being examined by the Competition and Consumer Protection Commission in accordance with media merger procedures under the Competition and Consumer Protection Act 2014 (*see* below paragraphs 121–126).[54]

## 2. Magazines

*56.* There is also a small indigenous magazine publishing presence in Ireland, competing with the large circulation UK publications. Of the 60 million magazines bought in Ireland each year, 12 million are Irish. The trade association of magazine publishers, Magazines Ireland, represents 38 Irish publishers who together produce over 185 magazines, both consumer and business to business titles and contribute EUR 250–EUR 300 million to the Irish economy annually.[55] Like the national and regional newspapers, Magazines Ireland is represented on the Press Council of Ireland, which handles complaints against the print media based on its code of practice (*see* further below paragraphs 166–168).

## 3. Book Publishing

*57.* Ireland also has a relatively small but vibrant book publishing industry. The representative organization of book publishers, Publishing Ireland, which was originally called CLÉ – the Irish Book Publishers' Association, was founded in 1970.[56] (CLÉ are the initials of the Irish-language term for Irish Book Publishers.) Publishing Ireland is a cross-border organization with members in Northern Ireland as well as the Republic of Ireland. Some of the members are or were family-owned and dated back to the middle of the nineteenth century. One such company is Gill's, which later became Gill

52. *See* http://www.independent.ie/irish-news/statement-from-thomas-crosbie-holdings-on-restructuring-29114179.html (6 Mar. 2013).
53. *See* http://www.irishexaminer.com/business/deal-agreed-for-sunday-business-post-233598.html> (8 Jun. 2013).
54. *See* http://www.thejournal.ie/irish-times-examiner-sale-2-3735612-Dec2017/.
55. http://www.magazinesireland.ie/about-magazines-ireland.html (3 Oct. 2016).
56. *See* http://www.publishingireland.com/.

& Macmillan. The link with Macmillan was discontinued in 2016 and the company, which is also a prominent distributor, is now M.H. Gill & Co., trading as Gill. Mercier Press, based in Cork, was founded in 1944 and family-run. Most of the publishers have a particular specialism such as children's, religious, academic, Irish language and so forth. Book publishers, although part of the print media, are not members of the Press Council of Ireland at present. In the past, book publishers were affected by the very strict censorship system that operated in Ireland (*see* further below paragraphs 81–88).[57] Nowadays their concerns with the law are more with defamation and copyright. The fact that the main remedy for defamation in Ireland is financial compensation weighs heavily on small book publishers in particular. Legal costs are also high and many cases are settled out of court as a result.[58]

## *E. Concluding Remarks*

*58.* All of the media in Ireland have been adversely affected by the economic downturn in the last decade. Circulations, audiences and advertising have all been affected by the financial bailout of the banks and the austerity programme imposed by international bodies such as the International Monetary Fund, the European Central Bank and the World Bank. There have been some media casualties like the *Sunday Tribune* newspaper, which had been supported financially by INM for a number of years. The *Examiner* group recently restructured, sold its printing operations and put its national Sunday newspaper, the *Sunday Business Post*, into examinership. The *Sunday Business Post* survived[59] but all forms of media are struggling for market share in a shrinking market. Most are surviving so far and are trying to find avenues to generate other sources of revenue. There are some indications that the situation is stabilizing.[60]

*59.* Most, if not all, media outlets now have an online presence, which is being constantly developed. RTÉ, *Independent* newspapers, *TheJournal.ie*, and the *Irish Times* have the strongest presence online.[61] Citizen journalism and user-generated content have also become an increasing presence and feature of traditional media, particularly online.

57. For the history of book publishing in Ireland, *see* Clare Hutton and Patrick Walsh, eds, *The Oxford History of the Irish Book,* Vol. V, Oxford University Press, 2011.
58. *See* further below under 'Defamation' and *see* generally, Marie McGonagle, *Media Law,* 2003, Ch. 4.
59. *See* RTÉ, 'Sunday Business Post to exit examinership', 19 Jun. 2013: http://www.rte.ie/news/business/2013/0619/457507-sbp-examinership-court/.
60. *See* the Reuters Institute, Digital News Report – Ireland, 2016, available at: http://www.digitalnewsreport.org/survey/analysis-by-country/2016/ireland-2016/.
61. Changes in media ownership and output, usage and engagement, particularly news consumption, can be tracked in the annual reports on Ireland by the Reuters Institute (Jane Suiter and Niamh Kirk. 'Overview of key developments'). *See* : http://www.digitalnewsreport.org/survey/analysis-by-country/2016/ireland-2016/.

## II. Infrastructure

### *A. Cable Penetration*

*60.* Cable television began in the 1970s under the Wireless Telegraphy (Wired Broadcast Relay Licence) Regulations 1974, as amended in 1988. Urban areas, which had suitable density and size of population, were cabled. Rural areas, which were less populated, relied instead on MMDS (Multipoint Microwave Distribution System, later referred to in certain contexts as 'MMD service'). This system was governed by the Wireless Telegraphy (Television Programme Retransmission) Regulations 1989. Two types of MMDS licence were introduced: initially licences were issued under the 1974 regulations and later under the Wireless Telegraphy (Programme Services Distribution) Regulations 1999, which covered both cable and MMDS and were directed towards the introduction of digital television. MMDS (under the title Multichannel Multipoint Distribution Service) has been included under cable/satellite in the official data issued by the communications regulator (ComReg) and in market surveys. The Broadcasting Act 2009 section 76 deals with MMDS and includes a requirement that the holder of an MMDS digital licence distributes the national broadcast channels, RTÉ, TG4 and TV3. However, in 2016, the Department of Communications, Climate Action and Environment (DCCAE) announced that the MMDS service was closing down. The licence, acquired in 2004–2005 by Virgin Media on buying the two companies that previously held it, expired in April 2016.[62]

*61.* In certain areas of the country, and in particular in areas where multichannel was not available through overspill or via a pay-TV service provider, community multichannel services developed. These community-based deflector services offered access to the UK channels. The 'Deflector' systems worked by receiving the UK analogue TV broadcast signals, and amplifying and re-broadcasting them so that they would be received by an aerial at the TV viewer's home. They were generally subscription-based with the fee being used to fund the service. They operated at a fraction of the MMDS price. Cable and MMDS operators, who had apparently obtained exclusive licences for their franchise areas, objected and several court cases ensued.[63]The issue was resolved by issuing licences, subject to annual renewal, under the Wireless Telegraphy (UHF Television Programme Retransmission) Regulations 1999,[64] pending the restructuring of broadcasting under the 2001 Broadcasting Act. They then operated under a spectrum licence received from the communications regulator, ComReg. The ComReg Deflector licensing scheme expired in 2012 with the switchover to digital.

*62.* It may be noted in this regard that ComReg has responsibility for the radio spectrum and allocation of frequencies.[65] In relation to broadcasting, its main role is

62. *See* www.dccae.gov.ie under 'Communications' 'Broadcasting and Media'.
63. For example, *Southcoast Community Television Broadcasting v. Ireland* (*The Irish Times*, 11 Nov. 1995) and *Carrigaline Community Television Broadcasting v. Minister for Transport, Energy and Communications* [1997] 1 ILRM241.
64. S.I. No. 348 of 1999. The Regulations provided for annual renewal of the licences and permitted a maximum of four frequency channels in respect of any single location.
65. ComReg's 'Radio Management Spectrum Strategy 2016–2018' is available at: https://www.comreg.ie//media/2016/03/Radio-Spectrum-Management-Strategy-2016-2018.pdf.

in relation to licensing of radio and television distribution, by cable and satellite, as well as until recently MMDS, and previously the aforementioned deflector services. ComReg may, therefore, be said to be the infrastructure regulator for communications in the State, while the broadcasting regulator, BAI, is the content regulator for broadcasting and related services.

### *B. Pay-TV using Cable, Satellite or via Broadband*

*63.* Irish TV channels were also made available along with many other channels as part of a Pay-TV offering using cable, satellite or via broadband. Sky Digital began offering subscription digital satellite television services in Ireland in 1998 and thus Irish television viewers began to have extensive choice, with the majority of viewers having a minimum of twenty television services by 2004–2005.[66] By May 2012, Pay-TV households had reached 81.2%, divided between satellite and cable/MMDS.[67] Sky is now a major player in the Irish market, with over 600,000 Irish subscribers. Its success has largely been due to its early entry into the market and the lack of any alternative for reception of digital television (and/or Pay-TV) outside of the main cities and towns. In 2012, Sky also struck a wholesale deal with British Telecoms (BT) Ireland to offer Sky Broadband and Sky Talk services across Ireland. After a number of mergers, the cable market is now controlled by one operator, UPC Ireland (Liberty Global). In October 2015, UPC Ireland (Liberty Global) rebranded to Virgin Media.[68] Virgin Media reported a total of 462,000 cable customers in June 2016. Of these over 90% were digital cable customers. One of the last remaining smaller cable companies, South Coast TV, closed down in July 2010.

*64.* According to ComReg, approximately 21% of TV homes had Irish DTT as of November 2012, while homes with Irish terrestrial DTT only represented 13.3% of all TV homes. Cable/satellite platforms represented the remaining 86.7% of all TV homes in Ireland. The comparable figures for 2014 were 41% and 10%, respectively. Cable/satellite platforms represented the remaining 90% of all TV homes in Ireland in 2014. Reception by other/local supplier (deflector/relay services), and IPTV methods was relatively low. Homes with a pay-TV (cable, satellite and IPTV homes) service have generally been stable since 2009 at 70%, on average, of all TV homes.[69]

*65.* A specific problem in the Irish market arises from the fact that the British channels, with the exception of the British Broadcasting Corporation (BBC), carry advertising. BSkyB's decision to carry advertising targeted specifically at Irish audiences

---

66. *See* Athena Media, *Irish Broadcasting Landscape:* Economic and Environmental Review for the.
Broadcasting Authority of Ireland, available at: http://www.bai.ie/en/news-and-information/publications/.
67. http://mavise.obs.coe.int/country?id=17, citing data from ComReg; *see* Commission for Communications Regulation (ComReg) – 'Market Review: Broadcasting Transmission Services in Ireland' (2012), available at http://www.comreg.ie/_fileupload/publications/ComReg12121.pdf.
68. *See* 'http://www.libertyglobal.com/oo-ireland.html'.
69. Commission for Communications Regulation (ComReg), 'Document 12/134: Quarterly Report on the Irish telecommunications market for the period 1 July to 30 September 2012 (Q3 2012)' (Dublin: ComReg, 2012), pp. 65–66 and Quarterly Report (Q3 2014) p. 75; available at: https://www.comreg.ie/search-results/?q=Quarterly+report+Q+3+2014.

led to major disquiet on the grounds that it would be eating into a small advertising cake for which all the terrestrial broadcasters and print media were vigorously competing. In addition, because BSkyB was established in the UK, under the country of origin rule of EU law they were regulated in the UK and therefore not subject to the advertising codes which governed broadcasters established in Ireland. This issue became a major one for Ireland during the review of the Television without Frontiers Directive (TWFD) and subsequent drafting of the Audiovisual Media Services Directive (AVMSD).[70] This issue, along with similar concerns in other small EU Member States, led to the inclusion in AVMSD of a provision (Article 4.2–4.5), which enables Member States to contact the Member State having jurisdiction with a view to achieving a mutually satisfactory solution to any problems posed. It provides the procedures and time-frame for such contact and the option for either Member State to ask the Contact Committee to examine the case. It also sets out the conditions under which the first Member State may take measures against the broadcaster concerned. These provisions have been used by the British regulator, Ofcom, to contact its Dutch counterpart concerning adult chat channels, which were licensed in the Netherlands but broadcast widely FTA on the DTT service, Freeview, in the UK overnight. Ofcom was concerned that they could be accessed by children in their bedrooms.[71] Thus, although originally intended to address problems encountered by small states, the provisions have proven useful to larger states. At the time of writing they have not yet been availed of by Ireland.

*66.* Regardless of that provision, published figures showed that Sky received EUR 382 million in subscriptions and advertising in 2011, which represented 43% of all television revenues (EUR 789 million) in the State in that year.[72] This compares to EUR 225 million received by RTÉ, although RTÉ had a 50% share of television advertising. Indeed, 19% of all advertising revenues went to twenty-four foreign channels carried on cable and satellite, which ironically RTÉ and TV3 have to pay to carry their channels. These figures raised worrying issues in a small market such as Ireland. A separate study, which was carried out by Price Waterhouse Coopers (PWC), revealed that TV advertising spends for 2011 was down by 5.8%. The PWC Study also revealed that the shift in advertising spend to online services grew in the previous year by 12%.[73] Figures for 2014 indicated that it had reached over 30% and mobile advertising was also growing.[74]Some 30% of users now avail of ad-blockers to protect against unwanted commercial intrusions, one of the highest levels in Europe. Despite this, the level of digital advertising across the sixteen NewsBrands Ireland titles (NBI, formerly National Newspapers Ireland, digital and print titles) is growing steadily in

---

70. *See* further below regarding EUROPEAN COMMUNITIES (AUDIOVISUAL MEDIA SERVICES) REGULATIONS 2010, S.I. No. 258 of 2010, which implements the provision of AVMSD designed to address this problem.
71. *See* www.guardian.co.uk Wednesday 7 Mar. 2012.
72. Report by Oliver & Ohlbaum (O&O) commissioned by TV3 and reported in The Irish Times: *see* Ronan McGreevy, 'Sky dominates Irish TV revenues, report finds', The Irish Times, 11 Mar. 2013, Media & Marketing.
73. Commission for Communications Regulation (ComReg), 'Irish Communications Market: Quarterly Key Data Report – Data as of Q3 2012 (Document Reference No. 12/134)' (Dublin: ComReg, 2012).
74. *See* http://www.pwc.ie/media-centre/press-release/press-release-22-07-2013.jhtml.

the past few years. Between January and September 2015 revenue from advertising was up 3.75% on the same period last year (NBI Data Centre).[75]

## *C. Mobile Market*

*67.* There is now considerable competition in the mobile market. There are three main mobile telecommunications providers (Vodafone, Three and Eir) and a number of Mobile Network Virtual Operator companies (MVNOs). Vodafone has the highest market share including and excluding mobile broadband (38.5% and 37.8%), followed by Three Group (35.1% and 32.3%), Eir Group Mobile (18.2% and 20.2%) and Tesco Mobile (5.9% and 7.0%).[76] The newest market entrants are Virgin Mobile (the mobile brand of Virgin Media) and iD (established by Dixon's Carphone). These emerged from Three's purchase of O2 Ireland. The EU, in approving the purchase, laid down conditions including that the mobile operator would have to provide network capacity to two mobile virtual network operators (MVNOs) in order to facilitate competition in the market.

*68.* While there is competition in the telecoms market generally and in the mobile phone market in particular, there are areas where the market uptake has been slow. Despite early interest from a few operators, Eircom, (now Eir), which introduced eVision in 2013 (now Eir Vision), is now the only company providing IPTV services in Ireland.[77]In January 2011, ComReg published Document 11/01, which gave notification of the discontinuation of the process to award a Mobile TV licence in Ireland. ComReg subsequently issued a consultation in 2012 regarding the licensing of DVB-H. However, the project was abandoned as the industry did not express much interest in providing these services.[78]By 2014, there were still only around 2% IPTV households.

*69.* According to ComReg's report on the second quarter report for 2016, the estimated fixed broadband household penetration rate was 67.9% and the fixed broadband per capita penetration rate was 28.5%. The total broadband per capita penetration (including mobile broadband) was 36%. At the end of June 2016 there were 5,826,900 mobile subscriptions in Ireland, including mobile broadband and Machine to Machine ('M2M') subscriptions. If mobile broadband subscriptions (352,606) and M2M subscriptions (606,683) are excluded, the total number of mobile subscriptions in Ireland was 4,867,611. Mobile subscriptions for 4G rose to 33.8% in the second quarter of 2016, while 3G fell slightly to 51.1%. 4G services were rolled out from 2013. Eircom, now 'Eir', began the introduction of quadplay with the launch of eVision

75. Reuters Institute, Digital News Report, Ireland, 2016, available at: http://www.digitalnewsreport.org/survey/analysis-by-country/2016/ireland-2016/.
76. Commission for Communications Regulation (ComReg), 'Quarterly Key Data Report' (Q2 2016), 4.7; *see also* Q4 2016, 4.7.
77. *See* generally, MAVISE <www.mavise.obs.coe.int/country?id=17>. Magnet networks formerly offered 'Aertv'. 3Play Plus provided 'HomeVision'. A third company, Smart Telecom, was taken over by Digiweb. Vodafone cancelled their TV services in July 2010: *See* Commission for Communications Regulation (ComReg), 'Discontinuation of licence award for Mobile TV in Ireland (Document Reference No. 11/01)' (Dublin: ComReg, 2011).
78. ComReg annual Report 2010–2011, available at http://www.comreg.ie/_fileupload/publications/COMREGAR10-11.pdf.

television in October 2013, followed by eVision on Demand in September 2014. The iOS share of traffic in Ireland (53.64%) is higher than Android (43.34%) and Windows Phone (2.63%), according to figures at the end of 2015.[79]

*70.* Large increases have been reported in the use of tablets and smartphones.[80] The first Irish report of the 'Net Children Go Mobile' project, published in 2014, showed that smartphones were the most commonly used devices by young people going online. The report found that 40% of children aged 9–16 and over 60% of teenagers in Ireland owned a smartphone. Of these, 35% used it daily to go online, while 27% owned a tablet and used it on a daily basis to access the Internet.[81] Recent services, such as Netflix, which allow customers to watch films and television programmes on a variety of devices including their phones, are also widely used.

## III. Technological and Economic Developments on the Media Markets

### *A. Digital Television*

*71.* DTT is well established, following the switchover from analogue to digital in October 2012, the background to which is discussed above (paragraphs 29, 40). The level of digital TV households reached 90.9% of the 1.5 million households in 2014. By 2016, digital TV homes represented 98.8% of all TV homes, compared to 78.6% in May 2012, although the overall number of TV homes had decreased. The percentage of TV homes with digital cable/satellite in 2016 was also down slightly to 86.9%.[82]Satellite was the most important distribution platform, with more than 40% of homes subscribed to the services of Sky plc. Cable television is used by almost 24% of homes. The main player is UPC (Liberty Global) in 20% of homes.[83] The only development anticipated or desired in the near future is for commercial broadcasters to establish multiplexes, as previously envisaged, and thus become available on DTT platforms. This is unlikely in the current economic situation following the recent period of recession.

### *B. Convergence of Media Products*

*72.* The traditional distinctions between print media, broadcasting and other media have become blurred in Ireland, as elsewhere, as a result of technological developments, which have greatly increased the range of platforms, forms of content creation, production and distribution. The rise of social network media such as Facebook, Twitter and YouTube, and the growth of user-created content, has transformed the way

79. *See* https://deviceatlas.com/blog/5-facts-about-mobile-market-in-ireland.
80. The figure for 2013 was over 1.6 million.
81. The 'Net Children Go Mobile' report was launched on 10 Feb. 2014; available at:http://www.dcya.gov.ie/docs/10.02.2014_Minister_Fitzgerald_welcomes_first_Irish_report_o/3092.htm.
82. ComReg Key Data Report Q3 2016, available at: https://www.comreg.ie/media/dlm_uploads/2016/12/ComReg-16108.pdf.
83. *See* http://mavise.obs.coe.int/country?id=17.

traditional media engage with readers and audiences.[84] The increasing convergence of broadcasting and telecoms services, and consequent availability of bundled offers including phone calls (land line and mobile), broadband access and television access, all for a fixed price, such as initially 'triple play', and more recently, 'quadplay', has led to an abundance of choice and flexibility for media consumers. The platforms they are using to access media are constantly changing. Traditional media are experiencing an increase in their online traffic and a downturn in their traditional operations. Ireland has one of the highest penetrations of smartphones in the world, the highest in Europe, according to Statcounter, fuelled in part by adoption by younger demographics.[85]

*73.* An important factor in these developments was the introduction of broadband technology. By 2010, over 65% of households had access to the Internet, and 91% of those using the Internet had a broadband connection.[86] The National Broadband Plan (NBP), which was launched in 2012, was aimed at delivering reliable high-speed broadband throughout Ireland, through a combination of State and commercial investment.[87] State intervention was necessary because commercial operators made it clear that there are large parts of the country (hard to reach rural areas) where they could not make high-speed broadband services available commercially. An updated NBP Intervention Strategy was published in December 2015, following a public consultation. The National Digital Strategy (NDS) document 'Phase 1 – Digital Engagement' was launched in July 2013. The Strategy set out a vision and a number of practical actions and steps to encourage and assist more citizens and small businesses to get online. The estimated fixed broadband household penetration rate by 2016 was 69.6%, while access to high-speed broadband had increased to 61% of homes.[88] The 2017 report on Ireland by the Reuters Institute showed Internet penetration at 77%.[89]

*74.* Achieving interoperability of devices for accessing media was also crucial. The interoperability of digital interactive television services, for example, was provided for by statutory instruments implementing the relevant EU regulations: S.I. No. 333 of 2011 European Communities (Electronic Communications Networks And Services) (Framework) Regulations 2011, section 29, regarding use or compliance with an open application program interface; and S.I. No. 334 of 2011 European Communities (Electronic Communications Networks And Services) (Access) Regulations 2011.

84. Reuters Institute, Digital News Report, Ireland, 2017, available at: http://www.digitalnewsreport.org/survey/analysis-by-country/2016/ireland-2016/ or http://fujomedia.eu/wp-content/uploads/2017/06/BAI_FuJo_digital_news_2017_WEB.pdf follow the link from http://www.oecd.org/sti/broadband/oecdbroadbandportal.htm#map.

85. http://www.digitalnewsreport.org/survey/analysis-by-country/2016/ireland-2016/.

86. Helen Shaw, Robert Picard, Hessel Abbink Spaink, Athena Media, *Irish Broadcasting Landscape-Economic and Environmental Review for the Broadcasting Authority of Ireland,* 31 Aug. 2010, available at www.athenamedia.ie/reports.jsp.

87. *See* http://www.dccae.gov.ie/communications/en-ie/Broadband/Pages/Connecting-Communities.aspx.

88. *See* Comreg Key Data Report Q.2 2016, available at https://www.comreg.ie/media/dlm_uploads/2017/03/ComReg-1715r-1.pdf; Comreg Key Data Report Q.2 2017, available at: https://www.comreg.ie/publications/ showed a significant increase in the quality of broadband services and that 70% of all fixed broadband services to homes were a high-speed service.

89. Reuters Institute, Digital News Report, Ireland, 2017, available at: http://fujomedia.eu/wp-content/uploads/2017/06/BAI_FuJo_digital_news_2017_WEB.pdf.

### C. Interactive and On-Demand Services

*75.* In May 2012, UPC became the first provider of on-demand television in Ireland via its set-top box and without the need for broadband. In October 2012, one week before the digital switchover, Sky followed suit announcing its on-demand service, which required a broadband connection for access to content from up to fifty channels. The company's alliance with BT gave it 90% coverage of the Irish residential broadband market. In March 2013, UPC stated that there had been nearly 17 million views of its On Demand service since its launch the previous year.[90] The service offers programmes from the RTÉ and TV3 i-players as well as over 1,300 hours of popular television series. The main on-demand services established in Ireland are the catch-up services of the important broadcasters, such as the RTÉ Player. The main distributors also provide on-demand services (UPC, Sky and Eir). There are local versions of Netflix, iTunes, Xbox Live, and Mubi. The Irish service Volta (with Irish films and International independent feature films) provides a VOD rental service. Sky's Now TV has been available in Ireland since April 2017, and the streaming service, Amazon Prime, has been available since the end of 2016.[91]

*76.* The broadcasting regulator BAI does not regulate on-demand services but it did have a role with other bodies in drafting a voluntary code for on-demand operators, and it also has a role in handling complaints against them – *see* further below (paragraph 313).

## §3. Sources of Media Law

*77.* In Ireland, the Constitution is the fundamental law of the land and therefore is the most important source of media and other laws. Legislation must be compatible with the Constitution and legislative provisions may be challenged in the courts on the basis that they are unconstitutional. The Constitution as a source of Media law is therefore considered first here, before legislation.

## I. Legislation: Ireland

### A. Constitution

*78.* As indicated above, the media are specifically referred to in the constitutional protection of freedom of expression. The relevant Article (Article 40.6.1), quoted in the General Introduction (paragraph 15), makes clear that the guarantee of freedom of expression is not absolute but rather is subject to restrictions on the grounds of

90. *See* http://businessetc.thejournal.ie/upc-on-demand-viewership-827517-Mar2013/ The company said in February 2013 that it had a total of 988,700 subscriptions by the end of last year (2012), representing 11% year-on-year growth – *see* http://businessetc.thejournal.ie/upc-broadband-tv-phone-subscribers-795214-Feb2013/.
91. *See* http://mavise.obs.coe.int/country?id=17#section-6. The extension of Amazon Prime to Ireland was reported in *The Irish Times* 14 Dec. 2016.

public order and morality, which were dominant concerns in the 1920s and 1930s, the period from which the Constitution dates. As reference is made to 'the radio, the press, the cinema' – the media in existence at the time – in the context of the 'education of public opinion' and in their capacity as 'organs of public opinion', their right to freedom of expression is an instrumental one. The text acknowledges their right but places an obligation on the State to 'endeavour to ensure' that they do not exercise it in such a way as to 'undermine public order or morality or the authority of the State'. The State, therefore, is empowered to introduce legislation or other measures to that purpose.

*79.* The rider at the end of the text referring to blasphemous, seditious and indecent matter may be considered to be simply a spelling out of the public order, morality and authority of the State concerns but it is notable that the rider goes further and requires ('shall') that the publication or utterance of such matter be criminalized. This is an unusual feature to find in a Constitution and has been the subject of calls for its removal by referendum.[92] As long as the reference remains in the Constitution, however, there must be laws in place criminalizing the publication of utterance of such matter. That is the reason that an offence of blasphemy, for example, was inserted in the Defamation Act 2009.[93] All legislation must be compatible with the Constitution and can be struck down by the courts if found not to be compatible. However, legislation passed after the Constitution came into force in 1937 carries a presumption of constitutionality, and if challenged in the courts, the courts will only intervene if no reasonable interpretation compatible with the Constitution can be established.

*80.* The Constitution refers specifically to radio and therefore broadcasting, the words 'such as' later incorporating television broadcasting when it began in 1961. The freedom of expression of the media is recognized in the text, and it is expressly stated to include the right to criticize Government policy. It shall not, however, be used to undermine public order or morality or the authority of the State. The constitutional situation regarding broadcasting is set out above (paragraph 15), as is some of the case law involving broadcasters that raised constitutional issues (paragraphs 18–23).While it is possible to take court cases based on the provisions of the Constitution itself, claiming infringements of constitutional rights or preventing breaches of constitutional guarantees, there is also specific legislation governing broadcasting. The main Act at present is the Broadcasting Act 2009.

**Print Media**

*81.* The print media in Ireland also have the benefit of the constitutional guarantee of freedom of expression, subject to the limitations set out in Article 40.6.1. For

---

92. *See* , for example, the Consultation Paper (1991) and Report of the Law Reform Commission on the Crime of Libel (LRC 41-1991); the Concluding Observations of the United Nations Human Rights Committee on Ireland, 8 Aug. 1993: CCPR/C/79/Add.21, §21; and the Report of the Special Rapporteur on the promotion and protection of the right to freedom of opinion and expression, submitted in accordance with commission Resolution 1999/36; ADDENDUM, Report on the Mission to Ireland 1999, E/CN.4/2000/63/Add.2 §87. Following a recommendation from the Constitutional Convention established by the Government in 2012 (https://www.constitution.ie/), the Government announced that it would hold a referendum to remove the reference to blasphemy in the Constitution but at the time of writing, a date has not yet been given.
93. *See* below paras 112–113, 259–260.

instance, an interesting and unusual constitutional case, *A.G. for England and Wales v. Brandon Book Publishers Ltd.*,[94] occurred in 1986, when the Attorney General for England and Wales sought an injunction in the Irish High Court to prevent the sale and distribution of a book *One Girl's War*. The book, which was published in Ireland, concerned the author's recollections of the Second World War and the activities of the British Intelligence Agency MI5 some forty years earlier. The Irish High Court refused the injunction because the content of the book did not pose any threat to the Irish state, which under the Irish Constitution ('shall not be used to undermine … the authority of the State') was the only justifiable reason for restricting freedom of expression in the circumstances.

*82.* Nevertheless, the print media have been subject to the Censorship of Publications Acts 1929–1967, which led to a notorious censorship regime throughout most of the twentieth century. The Acts remain in place, although they have rarely been invoked in the last ten years or more. Their concern was mainly with public morals, which is one of the areas of restriction recognized by the Constitution.

*83.* The censorship of books and periodicals was operated by the Censorship of Publications Board, which was established under the 1929 Act, as amended in 1946, and was vigorous well into the 1980s. Books and periodicals could be referred to it by Customs officials wishing to prevent importation or by complaint from any member of the public. Under the legislation, the Board was to have regard to the literary, artistic, scientific or historic merit of the particular publication, its language and general tenor, the nature and extent of publication, the class of reader addressed and any other matter it considered relevant. However, if the Board reported that a particular publication was in its general tendency indecent, obscene or – in the case of a periodical – unduly devoted to crime, the Minister for Justice could make an order prohibiting its sale and distribution within the State. While the Board itself came into existence under the 1929 Act, an Appeal Board was not provided for until the Act of 1946. Also prohibition orders, once made, if not lifted on appeal, lasted forever until the 1967 Act provided a twelve year limit in respect of books that were banned on the grounds that they were indecent or obscene. Books or periodicals that carried advertisements for abortion clinics or otherwise 'advocated' abortion were not covered by the twelve-year limit and remain banned unless successfully appealed. The system became notorious as many books, including important works of literature, were banned in the early decades by the Board, often on the basis of marked passages or even single sentences or phrases. Few decisions were appealed, however, often because the publisher was from outside the State, the Irish market was tiny anyway, and besides, to be banned in Ireland could be used as a sales pitch.

*84.* Until 1979, when the Health (Family Planning) Act was passed, books and periodicals could be banned on the basis that they advocated contraception, and the printer, publisher, seller or distributor could be prosecuted. One of the few cases taken against the decisions of the Board, *Irish Family Planning Association v. Ryan*,[95] concerned the banning by the Board of an information booklet on birth control that was in use in family planning clinics. The case was decided on natural justice principles rather than freedom of expression. The Supreme Court said that the Board ought to

---

94. [1986] I.R. 597.
95. [1979] I.R. 295.

have exercised their discretion to communicate with the publisher, as the publisher was readily contactable, and the book was purely factual, not advocating any course of conduct and not obscene. Following this case, the Censorship of Publications Regulations, 1980 (S.I. No. 292 of 1980) set out the procedures for making a complaint in writing, the forms to be used, and the procedures for the Board to consult with the publishers if it decided to do so.[96]

*85.* The censorship of publications that addressed or advocated abortion, on the other hand, remained unchanged until 1995, when the Regulation of Information (Services outside the State for Termination of Pregnancies) Act 1995 was passed to regulate abortion information. The 1995 Act section 3(1) (a) allows for the publication of information – as defined in the Act – provided 'the information is truthful and objective and does not advocate or promote, and is not accompanied by any advocacy or promotion of, the termination of pregnancy'.

*86.* As Irish society became more liberal in the latter part of the twentieth century, censorship gradually waned and in recent years the Board has banned very few publications. There have been very few cases since *In Dublin* magazine was the subject of a six months' ban imposed by the Board in 2000. The Board had received a complaint with regard to advertisements for escort agencies and massage parlours, which were a front for brothels and prostitution. The publisher initially challenged the ban but subsequently criminal charges were brought and the case was dealt with under the Criminal Justice (Public Order) Act 1994.[97]

*87.* Although the censorship of publications has waned and there have been calls for abolition of the Boards,[98] a Censorship of Publications Board and a Censorship of Publications Appeal Board continue to be appointed by the Minister for Justice every three years. Previously, they were appointed in secret and few details of the members were made public. Now, however, public notices inviting applications are issued.[99] A public register of banned books exists and can be consulted at the Board's

---

96. *See* http://www.irishstatutebook.ie/1980/en/si/0292.html.

97. *DPP v. Hogan and Hoson Publications Ltd.*, unreported, Dublin Circuit Criminal Court, 19 Oct. 2000. On this case and the operation of the Censorship laws generally, *see* McGonagle, M. *Media Law* (2nd ed., Dublin: Thomson Round Hall, 2003), Chs 8 and 9. *See also Melton Enterprises v. The Censorship of Publications Board*, [2003] 3 I.R. 623; [2003] IESC 55, available at http://www.bailii.org/ie/cases/IESC/2003/, a case that raised questions as to the validity of certain provisions of the Censorship of Publications Act 1946 having regard to the provisions of the Constitution.

Censorship was particularly rampant during the Second World War – *see* Ó Drisceoil, *Censorship in Ireland 1939–1945: Neutrality, Politics and Society* (Cork University Press, Cork, 1996).

98. *See* , for example, Eoin O'Dell, 'Why do we need a Censorship of Publications Board?' available at www.cearta.ie 7 Nov. 2010 and 18 Dec. 2010; and John Byrne, 'What a shocker: no more books to ban', The Irish Times, 18 Dec. 2010, available at: http://www.irishtimes.com/culture/tv-radio-web/what-a-shocker-no-more-books-to-ban-1.688191.

99. The most recent notice appeared in February/March 2013.

office or on the website of the Department of Justice.[100] In 2014 a new Board had to be constituted, and jurisdiction had to be handed over to the Minister of Arts, Culture and the Gaeltacht, when a complaint was made about a novel written by the then Minister for Justice some twenty-five years previously.[101]

*88.* In addition to regulation of the print media under other general laws, the Press Council and Press Ombudsman now exercise independent oversight of press standards (newspapers and magazines, but not books) based on a Code of Practice. The role of Press Council and Press Ombudsman role is recognized in statute (Defamation Act 2009) and might best be described, therefore, as a form of co-regulation. Their role is discussed further later (paragraphs 299–309). Other laws that apply to the print media, such as defamation, contempt of court and privacy, are also discussed in later sections (paragraphs beginning 248, 275 and 261, respectively). Issues contained in Article 40.6.1 of the Constitution such as blasphemy will also be discussed in relation to the print media in the context of the legislation that addresses them.

**Audiovisual Media**

**Cinema**

*89.* Cinema is expressly referred to in the Constitution and therefore enjoys the freedom of expression guarantee, subject to the stated restrictions. However, the Censorship of Films Acts 1923–1992 established the office of Film Censor and a Censorship of Films Appeals Board, and films for showing in cinemas had to be submitted to the Censor in order to get a certificate for the public showing of a film. As well as a general certificate (there were no age categories), the Act permitted the Censor to grant a limited certificate, i.e., a certificate to which restrictions or conditions are attached, to any picture deemed unfit for general exhibition in public.[102]The Censor could refuse to grant a certificate, however, on the grounds that the film or part of it was indecent, obscene or blasphemous or would tend to inculcate principles contrary to public morality or would otherwise be subversive of public morality (section 7(2)). The 1923 Act was amended in 1925 to include promotional material, posters, trailers, and such like and was amended again in 1930 to extend to the sounds in so-called talkies or talk movies.

*90.* In the late 1950s and early 1960s, film reviewers became increasingly disillusioned with the Censor's treatment of British 'new wave' cinematic films and

---

100. The Register reveals that on 31 December 2010 there were no books prohibited solely on the grounds that they were indecent or obscene. The Register is available at http://www.justice.ie/en/JELR/qsearch. A large number of magazines are listed, some of them dating back as far as the 1930s. At the time of writing, the Register for 2012 is available at http://www.justice.ie/en/JELR/Register%20of%20Prohibited%20Publications%202012.pdf/Files/Register%20of%20Prohibited%20Publications%202012.pdf The Censorship of Publications Regulations 1980 (S.I. No. 292/198 set out the procedures for making complaints to the Board and Appeal Board.

101. *See* http://www.independent.ie/irish-news/censor-panel-appointed-for-alan-shatters-steamy-novel-30104614.html and http://www.independent.ie/irish-news/politics/shatters-novel-is-cleared-by-the-censor-30258684.html. In 2016, a book (Jean Martin, *The Raped Little Runaway*) containing graphic descriptions of the rape of a minor was banned: *see* https://www.irishtimes.com/news/ireland/irish-news/censorship-board-bans-book-for-the-first-time-since-1998-1.2571029.

102. *Ibid.* at s. 7(2). For example, restrictions on the audience to which the film may be shown.

began to demand changes to the system.[103] They argued that the introduction of some form of grading system would protect children from 'adult narratives' and, more particularly, from 'adult drama and horror films, even when these had been severely cut by the Censor'.[104] The reviewers believed that the absence of grading failed to protect children from 'films which had been produced with an adult audience in mind but which might prove disturbing even in their cut form'.[105] In 1962, cinema owners also called for the grading of films, arguing that the introduction of such a system would go some way towards ameliorating the downturn in cinema attendance.[106] Eventually, in 1964, the then Minister for Justice introduced four limited certificates for cinematic film: under-12s accompanied by an adult, over-16s, over-18s, and over-21s (issued on only four occasions).[107] The mid-1960s, then, saw the beginning of a shift away from strict film censorship to age-appropriate film classification in Ireland.[108]

*91.* From then on, age classifications, as a guide for parents on the suitability of content of films, were displayed in the Censor's certificate and advertising of films. The system of banning and cutting scenes from films, which was pursued until the early 1970s, up to which time in excess of 3,000 films were banned and scenes cut from 8,000 others, was gradually relaxed. Very few films are banned nowadays. Indeed, in 2008, the Civil law (Miscellaneous Provisions) Act, section 71 changed the name of the Censor's office to the Irish Film Classification Office and the title of the Film Censor to Director of Film Classification.

*92.* In 2008, an additional criterion – 'likely to cause harm to children' – was added to the list of criteria to be considered by the Director of Film Classification under section 7 of the 1923 Act. Section 7(2) of the 1923 Act, as amended, provides that the Director shall certify that a picture is fit for public exhibition unless, having viewed the work, the Director is of the opinion that the work is unfit for general exhibition in public:

(a) by reason of it being – (i) likely to cause harm to children, (ii) indecent, obscene or blasphemous, or,
(b) because the exhibition thereof in public – (i) would tend to inculcate principles contrary to public morality, or (ii) would be otherwise subversive of public morality.[109]

---

103. Kevin Rockett, *Irish Film Censorship: A Cultural Journey from Silent Cinema to Internet Pornography* (Dublin: Four Courts Press, 2004), 187. According to Rockett, at 189, '[w]ith such widespread banning and cutting of films in the early 1960s, it was inevitable, especially within the context of the process in train of modernizing and internationalizing of the Irish economy (if not of the culture and society), that resistance to the general certificate policy would emerge'.
104. *Ibid.* at 189–190.
105. *Ibid.* at 193.
106. *Ibid.* at 194–195. However, the then Minister for Justice – Charles Haughey – rejected this assertion, stating that the decline in cinema audiences was happening worldwide and thus the problem could not be attributed to the system of film censorship in Ireland.
107. *Ibid.* at 200. *See alsoDáil Éireann Debates* 219 Col 34, 24 Nov. 1965.
108. *Ibid.*
109. Censorship of Films Act 1923 s. 7(2), as amended by the Civil Law (Miscellaneous Provisions) Act 2008, s. 70.

The age classifications have been changed on a number of occasions since they were first introduced. In 2005, for instance, they were amended following discussions with parents, educators, the public, film distributors, and cinema managers. The changes also reflected the findings of a nationwide survey of parental usage and attitudes to film classification.

*93.* Prior to the changes made in the 2008 Act, an interesting issue arose following the film Censor's decision in October 1994 not to grant a certificate to Oliver Stone's controversial film 'Natural Born Killers', a decision which was upheld by the Censorship of Films Appeal Board in January 1995. Four years later, TV3, the national commercial broadcaster, planned to broadcast an edited 'made for television' version of the film late at night (10:45 p.m.) in January 2000. That version had removed the most offensive sequences and was to be preceded by regular warnings to viewers. The day before the planned broadcast, the Department of Justice threatened to seek a court injunction to prevent it. TV3 reluctantly decided to withdraw the film.

*94.* However, as the Censorship of Films Acts apply only to the exhibiting of films 'in public by means of a cinematograph or similar apparatus', it appeared that the Minister for Justice had no authority to intervene. Instead, the appropriate authority, since it related to broadcasting, was the then broadcast regulator, the IRTC. The Radio and Television Act 1988, which established the IRTC, and was still in force in the year 2000, required the IRTC to ensure that broadcasters did not broadcast anything which might reasonably be regarded as offending against good taste or decency, or likely to incite to crime. The IRTC had already established procedures and practices for considering certain television programme material. Following the 'Natural Born Killers' incident, the IRTC adopted additional procedures and practices for the assessment of 'exceptional' television programme material. TV3 was advised of the new procedures and it was then a matter for it to decide whether to proceed with the broadcast. In any event, the original ban by the Film Censor was lifted and the film was finally broadcast on TV3 late on Saturday 25 August 2001.[110]

*95.* The Office of Film Classification now provides current age classifications, symbols and detailed guidelines on its website. The guidelines provide information on the theme/content of films in each category, as well as the presence of violence/threat, sexual content/nudity, language and drugs. Its aim is to provide the public and parents in particular with a modern and dependable system of classification that protects children and young persons, has regard for freedom of expression and has respect for the values of Irish society.[111] In 2016, IFCO classified 829 cinema works (features, shorts and trailers) and 3830 DVD/Video Works.[112]

**Video Recordings**

*96.* The restrictions on freedom of expression in the Constitution refer specifically to the cinema and the public showing of films but extend also to the newer form of video film available for personal viewing. The Video Recordings Act 1989 gives effect to the constitutional concerns with public order and morals in particular. The Act extended the remit of the Director of Film Classification (then known as the Official

110. *See* McGonagle, M., op cit. 2003, Ch. 9, and *IRIS* 2001-8:11.

111. *See* http://www.ifco.ie.

112. *See* IFCO, Annual Report if the Director of Film Classification 2016, available at: http://www.ifco.ie.

Censor) to cover video works.[113] Under section 7(1) of the Act, the Director is empowered to issue an order, referred to in the Act as a prohibition order, proscribing the supply of a 'video work' if, having examined the work, he is of the opinion that the work is unfit for viewing because:

(a) the viewing of it:

> (1) would be likely to cause persons to commit crimes, whether by inciting or encouraging them to do so or by indicating or suggesting ways of doing so or of avoiding detection, or
> (2) would be likely to stir up hatred against a group of persons in the State or elsewhere on account of their race, colour, nationality, religion, ethnic or national origins, membership of the travelling community or sexual orientation, or
> (3) would tend, by reason of the inclusion in it of obscene or indecent matter, to deprave or corrupt persons who might view it, or,

(b) it depicts acts of gross violence or cruelty (including mutilation and torture) towards humans or animals … .

The criteria in section 7 thus reflect those in the Censorship of Films Act 1923 but add the concerns prevalent in the 1980s in relation to incitement to hatred and the gross violence and cruelty depicted in the so-called video nasties that had begun to appear in that period.

*97.* Unlike the Censorship of Films Acts, however, the age classifications for video/DVD are expressly stipulated in the Video Recordings Act 1989. Section 4(1) of the Act established four age classifications for video works: fit for viewing by persons generally; fit for viewing by persons generally but where a child is under 12 years old, only where accompanied by a responsible adult; fit for viewing by persons aged 15 years or more; and fit for viewing by persons aged 18 years or more. As was the case also in relation to age categories introduced for films, the precise ages were amended on a number of occasions. In 2008, the Civil Law (Miscellaneous Provisions) Act (section 69 (b)) amended section 4 of the Video Recordings Act, setting out five age certifications for video works:

> (a) fit for viewing by persons generally, (b) fit for viewing by persons generally but, in the case of a child under the age of 12 years, only under parental guidance, (c) fit for viewing by persons aged 12 years or more, (d) fit for viewing by persons aged 15 years or more, (e) fit for viewing by persons aged 18 years or more.

*98.* Very few videos have been banned under the legislation. However, a re-release on DVD of the horror film, 'I Spit on Your Grave', first released in 1978, was refused a certificate for sale in September 2010 by the Irish Film Classification Office (IFCO) for depicting acts of gross violence and cruelty towards humans.[114]A 7%

---

113. Video Recordings Act 1989.
114. *See* www.bbc.co.uk/news/uk-northern-ireland-11377869.

increase in the number of DVDs submitted for classification to IFCO in 2015 was welcomed by IFCO as it was regarded as reinforcing 'the desire of our business partners to have their product classified by IFCO for distribution in Ireland. Consequently it affords the consumer the opportunity to make informed choices based on a consistent level of classification'.[115]

*99.* It is an offence to supply or offer to supply a video without a supply certificate (Video Recordings Act 1989, section 5). A licence is also required from IFCO authorizing persons to sell video recordings by wholesale or to let them on hire (Video Recordings Act 1989, section 18). It is an offence for a person to have in his possession a video recording for the purpose of selling it or letting it on hire without a licence (section 20). The few court cases that have arisen have concerned adult shops challenging decisions of IFCO to ban the sale of specific adult videos. *Byrne v. The Official Censor and Censorship of Films Appeals Board*, for example, concerned a challenge on the basis of principles of constitutional and natural justice.[116] The owner of an adult shop complained that the Censor did not give reasons for refusing to certify the sale of a particular video. The Censor had simply quoted the precise provisions of the Video Recordings act under which he had made the decision. The High Court judge took the view that sufficient information was conveyed to the applicant as to why a certificate was refused to enable her to decide whether or not to appeal the decision.

**Video Games**

*100.* Video games are an important part of the audiovisual industry in Ireland and generate considerable revenue and employment.[117] Video games are expressly exempt from the classification procedure established by the Video Recordings Act 1989 Act unless they come under one or more of the criteria listed in section 7(1) of the Act, as set out above (paragraph 96). Instead, video games are classified using the Pan European Game Information (PEGI) classification system. However, while it is not expressly stated in the 1989 Act itself, any video game which, because of its content, is brought within the remit of the legislation, must be submitted to the Irish Film Classification Office (IFCO) for approval.[118] Additionally, the Director of Film Classification will investigate any video game which is the subject of a complaint made by a member of the public.[119] The regulatory system pertaining to video games in Ireland may therefore be described as co-regulatory in nature, based on an agreement as to rating and labelling between the video games industry and IFCO, which retains the power to carry out its own assessment in certain cases.[120]

---

115. *See* the Annual Report of the Director of Film Classification 2015 at http://www.ifco.ie.
116. [2007] IEHC 464, available at http://www.bailii.org/ie/cases/IEHC/2007/H464.html.
117. The revenue from Video Games in Ireland in 2016 was $139 million and is expected to show an annual growth rate of 7% over the next five years. *See* https://www.statista.com/outlook/203/140/video-games/ireland#.
118. Sharon McLaughlin, 'The Protection of Children in the Online and New Audiovisual Services Environment' (PhD Thesis, NUI Galway, 2010).
119. *Ibid.*
120. Marie McGonagle, 'Co-operative Regulatory Systems in the Media Sector of Ireland' in *Final Report Study on Co-Regulation Measures in the Media Sector*, (Hamburg: Hans-Bredow Institut, 2006) at 219–221.

*101.* In June 2008, IFCO issued a prohibition order in respect of the video game '*Manhunt 2'* under section 7 (1) (b) of the 1989 Video Recordings Act.[121] This was the first video game to be banned under the Act, and IFCO cited the 'high level of gross, unrelenting and gratuitous violence' in the game as the reason for its proscription.[122] Recognizing the seriousness of its action, IFCO acknowledged that 'in certain films, DVDs and video games, strong graphic violence may be a justifiable element within the overall context of the work; however, in the case of *Manhunt* 2, the IFCO believes there is no such context, and the level of gross, unrelenting and gratuitous violence is unacceptable'.[123]During 2016 IFCO examined twenty-six games rated eighteen by the Pan European Games Information System (PEGI) to ensure compliance with provisions of The Video Recordings Act 1989.[124]

## *B. Legislation*

*102.* There is wide-ranging legislation specifically directed at the media in Ireland and also general legislation which has specific provisions either directed at the media exclusively or of broader application but encompassing also the media. Some of the legislation giving effect to constitutional guarantees and restrictions has been discussed in the previous section. Likewise, reference has been made above to the fact that the Constitution sets out the requirements for the enactment of legislation (Articles 20–27). First of all, under the Constitution, the Oireachtas (national parliament) has 'the sole and exclusive power of making laws for the State' (Article 15.2.1). Draft legislation takes the form of 'Bills', which are prepared and drafted in the relevant government department or the Attorney General's office and introduced into each House of the Oireachtas for debate. The stages of debate, which they must go through, are set out, and the role of each House in the process, culminating in a final vote that 'This Bill do now pass'. The Bill, once passed by both Houses, is called an Act, and is sent to the President to be signed into law, with a notice to that effect then being published in An Iris Oifigiúil, the State's official publication. The Act as a whole, or certain provisions of it, may come into force as soon as they have been signed; other provisions of it may be stated in the Act to commence at a later date when the relevant government Minister chooses. This is usually done by means of secondary legislation (discussed below), in the form of Statutory Instruments or Ministerial Regulations.

The principal legislation (Acts of the Oireachtas) currently in force relating to the media is as follows:

---

121. *See also* IFCO, 'Manhunt 2 Video Game Prohibited', http://www.ifco.ie, 18 Jun. 2007.
122. *Ibid.*
123. Press Release from the Irish Film Censor's Office, 18 Jun. 2007, available at http://www.ifco.ie in the 'news' section. The developer of the game – the US-based 'Rockstar Games' – neither submitted a modified version of the game for classification by IFCO nor challenged the issuance of the prohibition order. Personal e-mail correspondence to this effect from Ger Connolly, Deputy Director of IFCO, to Sharon McLaughlin, 28 Apr. 2009.
124. *See* the Annual Report of the Director of Film Classification 2016 at http://www.ifco.ie.

## 1. The Broadcasting Act 2009

*103.* The Broadcasting Act 2009 is a major piece of consolidating legislation which repealed a number of previous Broadcasting and Broadcasting Authority Acts: the Radio and Television Act 1988, the Broadcasting (Major Events Television Coverage) Acts 1999–2003 and the Broadcasting (Funding) Act 2003, as well as sections of other previous legislation. It also made provision for digital television, replacing the earlier schemes provided for in the Broadcasting Acts of 2001 and 2007. It established a new regulatory authority, the BAI, with an expanded remit and new structure, replacing the former regulatory commission (BCI) and the Broadcasting Complaints Commission. The BAI has two committees, a Licence Contracts Committee and a Compliance Committee, the latter taking over the role of the Broadcasting Complaints Commission (Part 2 of the Act).

*104.* In addition, the Act sets out the obligations of broadcasters and makes provision for the drafting of codes and rules by the BAI (Part 3 of the Act). Broadcasters' duties include ensuring that news is reported in an 'objective and impartial manner' without any expression of the broadcaster's own views and, likewise, current affairs programming, with the addition that it 'is fair to all interests concerned' (section 39(1)). An exception is made for party political broadcasts, provided that a broadcaster does not, in the allocation of time for such broadcasts, give an unfair preference to any political party. Radio broadcasters are required to devote a minimum of 20% of airtime to news and current affairs programming, unless a derogation is permitted by the BAI. Echoing the Constitution, all broadcasters are required to ensure that 'anything which may reasonably be regarded as causing harm or offence, or as being likely to promote, or incite to, crime or as tending to undermine the authority of the State' is not broadcast by the broadcaster. This and a further provision relating to privacy: 'in programmes broadcast by the broadcaster, and in the means employed to make such programmes, the privacy of any individual is not unreasonably encroached upon' are not new. They address constitutionally protected rights and restrictions, and were contained in previous broadcasting legislation.

*105.* The broadcasters' obligations set out in the Act are also the subject of Codes, which the Act mandates the BAI to draft and with which all broadcasters established in the State must comply (section 42). For instance, the BAI's Code on Fairness, Objectivity and Impartiality in News and Current Affairs was published in April 2013 and became operative from 1 July 2013. Other Codes address advertising rules, both content and time/manner/place rules, set out in the Act. In accordance with AVMSD, advertising and other forms of promotion, sponsorship, etc., are now collectively referred to as commercial communications – thus the BAI's code is called the General Commercial Communications Code and, as required by the Act, there is a separate Children's Commercial Communications Code.[125] Codes are accompanied by non-binding Guidance Notes that are intended to assist broadcasters, advertisers and the general public to interpret and apply the Codes. Complaints of breaches of the Codes must be directed by the complainant to the relevant broadcaster in the first instance and if the complainant is not satisfied or the broadcaster does not reply within the stipulated time, s/he may refer the complaint to the BAI, where it will be handled

125. A full list of the Codes is available at: http://www.bai.ie/en/codes-standards/.

either at Executive level (Executive Complaints Forum) or by the BAI's Compliance Committee.[126] The Broadcasting Act also requires the BAI to draft and implement Broadcasting Rules (section 43), for example Access Rules. Codes and Rules, the broadcasting complaints system and commercial communications are discussed further below.

*106.* The Broadcasting Act also provides for a detailed right of reply scheme (section 49), as required initially under TWFD and now AVMSD. Part 5 of the Act deals with enforcement measures, including financial sanctions and termination or suspension of a broadcasting contract in cases of serious breaches but with a right of appeal to the High Court. It is to be expected that such far-reaching measures will be used only rarely. An isolated example of termination of a radio broadcasting contract under earlier broadcasting legislation can be seen in *Radio Limerick One Ltd v. IRTC.*[127]The contract was terminated by the then regulator, the IRTC, for persistent breaches of the conditions of the broadcasting contract. However, the High Court and the Supreme Court on appeal upheld the decision of the IRTC. The Chief Justice, acknowledging the seriousness of the measure, stated in his judgment that:

> As to the question of proportionality, I have already indicated that circumstances could arise in which the invocation of the drastic power of terminating a sound broadcasting contract could be regarded as a grossly disproportionate and hence unreasonable exercise of the powers vested in the Commission. In the present case, there was, in my view, abundant evidence to justify the conclusion drawn in the High Court that the invocation by the Commission of this sanction was not disproportionate to the gravity of the breaches involved.

*107.* A slightly different set of circumstances arose in the case of *TV3 v. IRTC.*[128]TV3, which had been awarded a contract for the first national commercial television station, was unable to meet the conditions imposed by the regulator, at that time the IRTC. After a very considerable delay in getting the station on air, the IRTC decided to withdraw the licence. However, the High Court quashed the decision on the grounds of natural justice, as the IRTC had not given TV3 notice of its intention to do so and did not afford it an opportunity to be heard. The Supreme Court dismissed an appeal by the IRTC and following further negotiations the licence was restored to TV3 and it began broadcasting in 1998.

*108.* Although broadcasting contracts are rarely terminated and financial sanctions were virtually unknown before 2009, the financial measures provided for in the 2009 Act (section 52–section 57) have already been used by BAI in one case. The circumstances were that an investigative team attached to an RTÉ current affairs television programme door-stepped a Catholic priest, Fr Reynolds, whom it accused of having raped a girl while serving as a priest in Africa and of having fathered her child. The priest in question had offered to take a paternity test, but the programme was broadcast regardless.

126. A list of complaints handled by the BAI is available at: http://www.bai.ie/en/news-and-information/publications/?q=complaints%20decisions.

127. [1997] 2 I.R. 291, [1997] IESC 3 (16 Jan. 1997), available at http://www.bailii.org/ie/cases/IESC/1997/3.html.

128. High Court 4 May 1992 (unreported), Supreme Court 26 Oct. 1993.

Subsequently a paternity test showed that Fr Reynolds was not the father. He sued RTÉ for defamation and accepted a settlement believed to be in the region of EUR 1 million. As the door-stepping and treatment of Fr Reynolds by the journalists amounted to a serious breach of his privacy also and led to outrage among the public and politicians, BAI appointed an external investigator and ultimately fined RTÉ EUR 200,000. The 2009 Act sets out very detailed procedures in this regard, and RTÉ could have opted to ask the High Court to decide if the proposed fine was appropriate but given the public outcry it did not do so. The incident led RTÉ to discontinue the particular investigative unit, reassign some of its staff members and issue new Journalism Guidelines.[129]

*109.* Other parts of the Broadcasting Act 2009 deal with the contracts of commercial and community broadcasters, including the terms and conditions and application processes (Part 6). This part of the Act also deals with Electronic Programme Guides (section 74) and must-carry and must-offer rules (section 77). It also creates offences for contravention of the requirements in this Part and sets out maximum fines. Part 7 deals with the structures of Public Service Broadcasting (PSB), the requirement to have audience councils, advisory committees, public service statements and annual statements of performance commitments and for public access to archives. The allocation and oversight of public money to public service broadcasters, and the establishment of new television channels, specifically an Oireachtas (Parliament) channel and an Irish film channel, also feature in this part of the Act. Part 8 deals with digital broadcasting and the analogue switch-off in 2012, while Part 9 deals with the television licence payable by all who have television sets and offences for not having a licence. As more and more people began to transfer to mobile devices rather than television sets for their viewing, the then Minister for Communications indicated in 2013 that he intended to move from the current system of collecting the licence fee through the postal service to a system whereby a levy would be placed on households in the same way as other utility bills, such as electricity and gas. However, that did not happen and the idea appeared to have been shelved indefinitely, although a 2017 report has now revisited the matter.[130] Part 10 of the Act deals with the operation by the BAI of a broadcasting funding scheme to support high-quality programming of various genres that can be said to come under the broad 'culture' or 'diversity of Irish culture and heritage' rubric. Finally, of the remaining parts, Part 11 covers major events television coverage as introduced in TWFD (amended in 1997) and subsequently in AVMSD; Part 12 sets out the necessary transitional provisions; Part 13 deals with wireless telegraphy and Part 14 has miscellaneous provisions. Issues arising from various provisions of the Act are discussed below. At the time of writing, a new Broadcasting Bill is in preparation.

---

129. The new guidelines issued in October 2012 can be found at http://www.rte.ie/documents/about/rte-journalism-guidelines-oct-2012-final.pdf (19 Jun. 2013).

130. *See* https://www.rte.ie/news/2013/0717/463069-bai-public-service-broadcasting-charge/ (17 Jul. 2013); https://www.irishtimes.com/business/media-and-marketing/analysis-broadcasting-charge-finally-shelved-after-five-years-1.2675979 (8 Jun. 2016). However, a report from the Oireachtas Joint Committee on the Future Funding of Public Service Broadcasting, launched on 28 Nov. 2017, recommends that the current model be replaced by a household-based charge to be collected by the Revenue Commissioners. The Report is available https://data.oireachtas.ie.

## 2. The Defamation Act 2009

*110.* Another major piece of legislation passed in 2009 is the Defamation Act 2009. It replaced the Defamation Act 1961, which was outdated in many respects. Defamation is essentially a common law tort, and many of the rules and principles that apply to it emanated from court cases over the centuries since the seventeenth century when the early press came into existence. Legislation, initially British Acts that applied in Ireland, and then the 1961 and 2009 Acts, clarified, amended or supplemented the common law rules. Defamation law, and hence the Defamation Act 2009, applies to all media. Much of the content of the 2009 Act is simply a repeat or update of previous provisions but there are also some new provisions. For instance, the old common law division of defamation into two separate torts, namely libel (defamation in any permanent or lasting form) and slander (usually the spoken word or another transient form) has been abolished in the Act and a single tort of defamation recognized instead. Previously, there was no statutory definition of defamation, only judicial pronouncements, but the new Act now contains a definition of both 'defamation' and 'defamatory statement', as well as 'defamation action'.

*111.* Among the Act's new and more salient features, which aim to redress issues and problems experienced by the media under the previous Act, are: a new defence of fair and reasonable publication on a matter of public interest (section 26), which is different from, but reflects and builds on, the so-called *Reynolds* defence delineated in the House of Lords' judgment of Lord Nicholls in *Reynolds v. Times Newspapers*;[131] the introduction of alternative remedies to damages (financial compensation), such as correction orders and declaratory orders, for which the court procedures are less complex and less lengthy; a provision that apologies will not constitute an admission of liability, which is an important consideration for the media, who were often reluctant to apologize, as their apology was likely to be construed as an admission of liability and would leave them unable to plead any defence.

*112.* Defamation in Ireland is almost totally civil and rarely criminal. Indeed, the Act abolishes old common law offences of defamatory libel, obscene libel and seditious libel. However, it does not abolish the old common offence of blasphemous libel outright but instead inserts a provision which replaces it. The reason given by the then Minister for Justice for including an offence of blasphemy was that the Constitution required it. Unlike the publication or utterance of indecent or seditious matter, which are also mentioned in Article 40.6.1 of the Constitution along with blasphemous matter, there was no other legislation in place – according to the Minister, on advice from the Attorney General – to establish an offence relating to blasphemy. The intention of the Minister was that there would be a referendum to change the Constitution but pending that it was considered necessary to retain a provision in the Defamation Act. Prior to the Act of 2009, blasphemous libel was considered at best to be moribund. It was a ground for refusing a certificate for the public showing of films under the Censorship of Films Act 1923 (above) and although films had been refused a licence or had scenes cut out, there had been no court cases dealing specifically with blasphemy since 1855.

131. [1999] 4 All E.R. 609.

*113.* However, a case that came before the Supreme Court in 1999 breathed some life into it but highlighted all its shortcomings. *Corway v. Independent Newspapers*[132]arose from a complaint by a member of the public who sought to have the publishers prosecuted for blasphemous libel for publishing a cartoon. The cartoon in question depicted three Catholic priests with the faces of political leaders, the middle one holding up consecrated bread for Holy Communion. The caption, which played on a slogan used in a prior referendum on divorce, was a comment on the fact that the Catholic Church in Ireland was no longer in a position of power. The Supreme Court found that there were many uncertainties and anomalies attaching to the common law offence of blasphemous libel and refused the application. It was a matter, therefore, for the legislature to introduce legislation to clarify the common law or else to hold a referendum to amend the Constitution. The new provision inserted in the Defamation Act 2009 is discussed below (paragraph 260).

*114.* The Defamation Act also includes provisions recognizing the Press Council and setting out its composition and objectives and code of practice. The Press Council is discussed below (paragraphs 299–309).[133]

## 3. The Communications Regulation Acts 2002–2007

*115.* The Communications Regulation Act 2002 established the ComReg, transferring to it the functions previously held by the Office of the Director of Communications Regulation, known as the ODTR. The functions of the Commission as set out in section 10 are:

(a) to ensure compliance by undertakings with obligations in relation to the supply of and access to electronic communications services, electronic communications net-works and associated facilities and the transmission of such services on such networks;
(b) to manage the radio frequency spectrum and the national numbering resource …;
(c) to ensure compliance by providers of postal services with obligations in relation to the provision of postal services;
(d) to investigate complaints from undertakings and consumers regarding the supply of and access to electronic communications services, electronic communications networks and associated facilities and transmission of such services on such networks; and
(e) to ensure compliance, as appropriate, by persons in relation to the placing on the market of communications equipment and the placing on the market and putting into service of radio equipment.

*116.* The Commission was also designated as the national regulatory authority for the purposes of Regulation No. 2887/2000 of 18 December 2000 on unbundled access to the local loop. The main objectives of the Commission in relation to electronic

132. [1999] 4 I.R. 484; [1999] IESC 5, available at http://www.bailii.org/ie/cases/IESC/1999/5.html.
133. A review of the Defamation Act 2009 is being carried out by the Department of Justice. *See* : http://www.justice.ie/en/JELR/Pages/Review_of_the_Defamation_Act_2009_-_Public%20 consultation.

communications were to promote competition, contribute to the development of the internal market, and promote the interests of users within the EC. The Commission was to be independent but was required to comply with policy directives from the Minister (section 13). The Minister was precluded from intervening, however, in any matters concerning individual undertakings or persons.

*117.* Under the Act the maximum number of commissioners is three. They are appointed by the Minister for a term of 3–5 years, with the possibility of one further such term, following a Civil Service competition process (section 15). One of the Commissioners acts as Chairperson. The normal disqualifications, such as election or appointment to either House of the Oireachtas or the European Parliament, apply (section 19). There is a prohibition on the unauthorized disclosure of confidential information by a Commissioner, member of staff or agent of the Commission (section 24) and an amendment to the Freedom of Information Act 1997 addresses this. Unauthorized disclosure is deemed an offence for which a monetary fine can be imposed on summary conviction. Commissioners, staff and others engaged by or with the Commission are also required to make a disclosure of interests (section 25). In order to defray its expenses, the Commission is authorized to impose a levy on providers of electronic communications and postal services (section 30). Other sections of the Act deal with public service requirements, strategy statements, annual reports, accounts and such like. Part 3 deals with enforcement powers including search warrants and the power of the Commission to prosecute for summary offences. Part 5 is an important part of the Act in that it deals with electronic communications infrastructure, road authorities and such.

*118.* Substantial changes and additions to the Act were made in the Communications Regulation (Amendment) Act 2007.[134] Additional powers were conferred on the Commission in relation to emergency call answering (section 5 and section 16, inserting a new Part 6), overcharging by undertakings (section 13) and enforcement, as well as special powers to compel evidence or produce documents (section 10). Additional functions included statistical data collection and analysis, and obtaining information from undertakings (section 6, with failure on the part of undertakings to provide information constituting an offence). Given the prohibition on disclosure of confidential information in the 2002 Act, protection from civil or criminal liability or victimization is provided in the amending Act for whistleblowers who make an 'appropriate' disclosure of information to the Commission about undertakings or associates (section 7 amending section 24 of the 2002 Act). Part 3 of the Act amended the Electronic Commerce Act of 2000, and also set out the regulatory measures and procedures for the registration of domain names. Part 4 amended the Competition Act 2002 to include *inter alia* an additional function for the Commission to investigate complaints relating to the electronic communications market; and to make provision for the formation of a co-operation agreement between the Commission and the Competition Authority.

## 4. The Competition and Consumer Protection Act 2014

*119.* Prior to the enactment of the Competition and Consumer Protection Act 2014, the Competition Act 2002 contained provisions (section 23) specifically dealing

134. For updates on further amendments *see* http://www.comreg.ie/about/legislation/.

with media mergers and acquisitions. Under the 2002 Act, the Competition Authority made a determination on any proposed merger based on competition issues. Its determination was then referred to the Minister for Enterprise, Trade and Employment for an independent review on other non-competition criteria. The procedure allowed the Minister to consider submissions or observations from interested parties, such as the BAI, when making a determination in relation to a proposed media merger.[135]

*120.* The BAI also has a role under the Broadcasting Act 2009 to ensure pluralism and diversity in the broadcasting sector. The Act requires it, when determining applications for licences, to consider a range of factors such as the character, expertise and experience of the applicant; the quality, range and type of the programmes proposed; the desirability of having a diversity of services in the area specified; the desirability of allowing any person, or group of persons, to have control of, or substantial interests in, an undue number of sound broadcasting services or an undue amount of the communications media in the area specified (section 66). In accordance with the Act, the BAI has drafted its Ownership and Control Policy, updated in 2012.[136] The media interests of Denis O'Brien, who owns six radio stations and who is now the major shareholder in Independent Newspapers – INM, were considered by the BAI in July 2012, particularly with regard to 'the desirability of allowing any person, or group of persons, to have control of, or substantial interests in, an undue amount of communications media' in an area. However, the BAI determined that 'Mr. O'Brien does not control IN&M. Rather he has a substantial interest in the Company, as that term is defined in the (Ownership and Control) Policy. In this regard, the Authority (BAI) was not obliged to review Mr O'Brien's interests in the context of an undue amount of communications media.'[137]

*121.* In March 2008 the Minister for Enterprise, Trade and Employment established an Advisory Group on media mergers to review the current legislative framework regarding the public interest aspects of media mergers. The Group reported in January 2009[138] and its recommendations led to new provisions contained in the Competition and Consumer Protection Act 2014.[139]

*122.* The 2014 Act established the Competition and Consumer Protection Commission and Part 4 (section 74) of the Act relates specifically to media mergers. The term 'media merger' itself and terms such as 'media business', 'diversity of content', 'diversity of ownership' are defined, and 'plurality of the media' is stated to include both diversity of ownership and diversity of content. The public interest in protecting plurality of the media is central to the provisions.

*123.* Notification of a proposed merger must be made by the parties (undertakings) to the Minister for Communications, Energy and Natural Resources and an initial examination is carried out by the Minister. S/he must inform the undertakings that have made the media merger notification within a stipulated time period:

---

135. For decisions of the Competition Authority *see* http://www.tca.ie/EN/Mergers--Acquisitions/Merger-Notifications.aspx.
136. Available at http://www.bai.ie/wordpress/wp-content/uploads/2012-OC-policy-Apr-2012.pdf.
137. *See* http://www.bai.ie/?p=2649.
138. Available at: https://www.djei.ie/en/Publications/Publication-files/Advisory-Group-on-Media-Mergers-Report-2008.pdf.
139. Available at: http://www.oireachtas.ie/documents/bills28/acts/2014/a2914rev2.pdf.

(a) that in his or her opinion the result of the media merger will not be contrary to the public interest in protecting plurality of the media in the State, and accordingly that the media merger may be put into effect;
(b) that, in light of proposed commitments offered by the undertakings, in his or her opinion the result of the media merger will not be contrary to the public interest in protecting plurality of the media in the State, and accordingly the media merger may be put into effect subject to the incorporation of those proposed commitments as specified conditions to be complied with; or
(c) that he or she is concerned that the media merger may be contrary to the public interest in protecting plurality of the media in the State, and accordingly that he or she intends to request the (BAI) to carry out an examination under section 28E.

*124.* The 'relevant criteria' to which the Minister must have regard in making a determination are set out and include:

(a) the likely effect of the media merger on plurality of the media in the State;
(b) the undesirability of allowing any one undertaking to hold significant interests within a sector or across different sectors of media business in the State;
(c) the consequences for the promotion of plurality of the media in the State of intervening to prevent the media merger or attaching conditions to the approval of the media merger.

*125.* Provision is made for the Minister to have regard also to any guidelines,[140] submissions, any decision of the Competition and Consumer Protection Commission or European Commission and any research published by the BAI. Timelines are set out for each stage of the process.

*126.* As indicated in (c) above, in cases where a full examination is required, the BAI also have a role. When requested by the Minister to do so, BAI must carry out an examination (referred to as a 'full media merger examination') in relation to the media merger concerned. It must publish a copy of the request on its website, invite submissions to be made within twenty working days and send a copy of the request to the Joint Oireachtas Committee and invite a submission from it also. Its report must contain a recommendation as to whether the merger should be put into effect or not. The criteria to which the BAI must have regard in drawing up its report are set out, as is the power of the Minister to establish an advisory panel to assist the BAI, where s/he deems it necessary. Fines (in serious cases up to EUR 250,000) are provided for failure to notify or provide information, and fines and periods of imprisonment are provided for contravention of a determination (in serious cases fines up to up to EUR 10,000 and imprisonment of up to two years).

140. Ministerial guidelines issued further to the Act, which are to be updated from time to time, include indicators of diversity of content and of diversity of ownership and control of media businesses that would be used in determining whether a media merger would be regarded as contrary to the public interest.

## 5. Other Legislation

*127.* Other Acts of major importance to the media, although of general application, include the Freedom of Information Act 2014, the Data Protection Acts 1988–2003 and the Copyright and Related Rights Acts 2000–2007.

**The Freedom of Information Act 2014**

*128.* The Freedom of Information Act currently in operation is the Freedom of Information Act 2014.[141] It repealed the first such Act introduced in 1997[142] and an amending Act of 2003. The 1997 Act was a strong piece of legislation that made provision for public access to a wide range of information, both personal and non-personal, held by public bodies. The presumption was that the public would have access to information (broadly defined in the Act) to the greatest extent possible subject to consideration of the public interest and the right to privacy. The Act established the office of Information Commissioner, as part of the role of the national Ombudsman, and that proved crucial to the successful operation of the Act. If information was refused by a public body within a specified time limit (four weeks), an internal review could be sought and if unsuccessful (within three weeks) an appeal could be made to the Information Commissioner.[143] A further appeal from the decision of the Commissioner could be made to the High Court. The Act is considered in more detail below in Chapter 5, Access to Public Information.

**The Data Protection Acts 1988–2003**

*129.* The Data Protection Act 1988 in Ireland enabled individuals to access personal records held on computer but not those held manually. This was rectified in an amending Act of 2003, which was introduced to transpose into Irish law the European Directive on Data Protection (Directive 1995/46). A new Bill, the Data Protection Bill 2018, which is intended to give effect to Regulation (EU) 2016/670 and to Directive (EU) 2016/680, was published in October 2017. The Regulation 'on the protection of natural persons with regard to the processing of personal data and on the free movement of such data' (the 'GDPR') takes legal effect from 25 May 2018 and the Directive 'on the protection of natural persons with regard to the processing of personal data by competent authorities for the purposes of the prevention, investigation, detection or prosecution of criminal offences or the execution of criminal penalties, and on the free movement of such data' must be transposed by 6 May 2018.

*130.* Of particular interest to the media in the existing legislation is the exemption contained in section 21 of the 2003 Act(inserting section 22(a) of the 1988 Act), which states:

> Personal data that are processed only for journalistic, artistic or literary purposes shall be exempt from compliance with any provision of this Act specified in subsection (2) of this section if–

141. Available at: http://www.oireachtas.ie/documents/bills28/acts/2014/a3014.pdf.
142. As the 1997 Act forms the basis of, and is frequently referred to in the 2014 Act, it is described here in some detail.
143. A full list of decisions of the Information Commissioner, including media-related decisions, is available at http://www.oic.gov.ie/en/Decisions/Decisions-List/.

(a) the processing is undertaken solely with a view to the publication of any journalistic, literary or artistic material,
(b) the data controller reasonably believes that having regard in particular to the special importance of the public interest in freedom of expression, such publication would be in the public interest, and
(c) the data controller reasonably believes that, in all the circumstances, compliance with that provision would be incompatible with journalistic, artistic or literary purposes.

*131.* Increasingly, the Data Protection Act is relied on in privacy cases involving the media. For instance, it was relied on, though unsuccessfully, by the defendant newspaper in *Evans v. Sunday World* in 2005 to oppose the granting of an injunction to the plaintiff, Dave Evans, 'the Edge' of U2.[144] He obtained a temporary injunction when the newspaper published details of the illness of a family member which had resulted in a delay to the commencement of U2s 'Vertigo' world tour. The newspaper claimed that the illness was a matter of public interest and already in the public domain.

*132.* Among its many other activities, the Irish Data Commissioner carried out an audit of the social networking site, Facebook, in 2011 and a review in 2012.[145] It did so by reference to the Data Protection Acts 1988–2003, along with guidance provided by the EU's Article 29 Working Party and in consultation with other data protection authorities. As Facebook, Google, Apple and many other major companies have their European headquarters in Ireland, the Irish Data Commissioner is responsible for ensuring their compliance with the Acts. The case of *Schrems v. The Irish Data Protection Commissioner*, for instance, led to a preliminary ruling of the Court of Justice of the EU in relation to his personal data being transferred to Facebook's headquarters in the United States.[146]In a later development arising out of the *Schrems* case, the Data Protection Commissioner sought, and was granted, in October 2017, a referral by the High Court to the Court of Justice of the European Union (CJEU) to determine the validity of three decisions by the European Commission insofar as they apply to data transfers from the European Economic Area (EEA) to the United States.[147]

*133.* In addition to audits and case studies, the DPC's office also provides guidance on a range of issues as they arise. For example, among the topics on which it provided guidance in 2016 were anonymization and pseudonymization, and location data.

*134.* The Communications (Retention of Data) Act 2011 is a related Act, which also comes within the remit of the Data Protection Commissioner. It deals with the retention by Governments of telephone and Internet data. The Act gives effect to

144. *Evans v. Sunday World – see The Irish Times* 31 Jan. 2005: www.irishtimes.com/news/u2-star-begins-legal-case-over-family-illness-1.1296733; and *The Sunday Times* 6 Feb. 2005.
145. Report of Audit, 21 Dec. 2011; Report of Re-Audit, 21 Sept. 2012. *See* http://www.dataprotection.ie/documents/facebook%20report/final%20report/report.pdf and http://www.dataprotection.ie/documents/press/Facebook_Ireland_Audit_Review_Report_21_Sept_2012.pdf.
146. Maximilian Schrems and Facebook (Case C-362/14), which led to the striking down of the 'safe harbour' agreement.
147. *The Data Protection Commissioner v. Facebook Ireland Ltd &Anor* [2017] IEHC 545 (3 Oct. 2017).

Directive No. 2006/24/EC.[148]Service providers are required to retain telephone and mobile data for two years and Internet access, e-mail and Internet telephone data for one year (section 3(1)). The ePrivacy Regulations 2011 (S.I. 336 of 2011)also deal with data protection for phone, e-mail, SMS and Internet use. They give effect to the EU ePrivacy Directive 2002/58/EC(as amended by Directive 2006/24/EC and 2009/136/EC).However, as a result of the EU Directive 2006/24/EC being invalidated by the CJEU in 2014 (combined case C-293/12 *Digital Rights Ireland v Minister for Communications, Marine and Natural Resources and others*, and *Karntner Landesregierung and others*), new data retention legislation is in preparation. The General Scheme of the Communications (Retention of Data) Bill 2017 was published in October 2017.

**The Copyright and Related Rights Act 2000**

*135.* The Copyright and Related Rights Act 2000 is a major piece of legislation, which replaced the Copyright Act 1963. The latter was hopelessly out of date long before the new Act was passed.[149] Given the amount of time that had elapsed and the very significant developments in technology that had occurred in the interim, it took a very long time to draft and enact the new legislation, which led to infringement proceedings being taken against Ireland in the European Court of Justice for failure to transpose the EC Directive on rental and lending rights on time.[150]

*136.* The 2000 Act had to take account of other EC Directives also, for instance the EC Term of Copyright Directive.[151] Prior to 2000 the duration of copyright in Ireland was fifty years. However the EC Directive of 2003, which had to be transposed by 1995, increased that period to seventy years. This led to a number of problems and court cases concerning the works of renowned author James Joyce, in particular. In 2001, for example, *The Irish Times* settled a copyright claim resulting from a webcast of James Joyce's novel 'Ulysses'. The webcast, to celebrate Bloomsday on 16 June 1998, involved a global reading of 'Ulysses' over the Internet by well-known personalities, which was carried on *The Irish Times* website. The preparations for the webcast were made during the interim period, 1992–5, when Joyce's work was out of copyright in Ireland, and the extracts used on the webcast were taken from an edition of the book published during that interim period. The court proceedings were settled out of court, prior to the hearing, on very far-reaching terms involving not only the payment of

148. Directive No. 2006/24/EC of the European Parliament and of the Council of 15 Mar. 2006 on the Retention of Data Generated or Processed in connection with the Provision of Publicly Available Electronic Communications Services or of Public Communications Networks and amending Directive 2002/58/EC.

149. For instance, the High Court had to decide in 1998 in *Mandarin Records Limited v. Mechanical Copyright Production Society (Ireland) Limited,* [1998] IEHC 146, whether a 'Power CD' was a 'record' for the purposes of the 1963 Act. One of the best-known cases taken under the 1963 Act was *Gormley v. EMI Records (Ireland) Ltd.* [1999] 1 ILRM 178, in which the court found that a tape-recording of schoolchildren re-telling, in their own dialect, Bible stories taught to them by their teacher was not entitled to protection as a literary work. The tape, released by EMI, later led to an animated film 'Give up yer aul sins', which was shortlisted for an Oscar for Best Animated Short at the 2001 Academy Awards.

150. ECJ, 12 Oct. 1999.

151. Council Directive 93/98/EEC of 29 Oct. 1993 harmonizing the term of protection of copyright and certain related rights, Official Journal No. L 290, 24 Nov. 1993 p. 0009–0013.

costs and damages to the James Joyce estate but also agreement to a permanent injunction, which would prevent any future webcast.[152]

*137.* Another case of use of copyright to prevent publication occurred in *Sweeney v. National University of Ireland Cork t/a Cork University Press.*[153]In this case, the High Court granted an interlocutory injunction preventing the inclusion of extracts from the works of James Joyce in an anthology of twentieth-century Irish literature. The anthology was published with blank pages and missing representation of one of the greatest writers of the period. In 2004 in order to avoid another such loss to the public, the Copyright and Related Rights (Amendment) Act 2004 was passed. A short Act, its purpose was to prevent the James Joyce estate from challenging Joyce's manuscripts being put on public display at the National Library. The State had purchased the manuscripts for EUR 12.6 million. The relevant provision (section 1, amending section 40 of the 2000 Act) states that 'no infringement of any right … in relation to an artistic or literary work occurs by reason of the placing on display the work… in a place or premises to which members of the public have access'.

*138.* Apart from extending the duration of copyright (section 24–section 26), the 2000 Act (section 107–section 114) introduced moral rights for the first time. Moral rights, emanating from the French concept of *droit moral,* are non-economic rights, independent of copyright, which derive from an author's relationship to his/her creative work. Thus they include a paternity right (the right to be acknowledged as the author of one's work), integrity right (the right not to have one's work distorted, mutilated, modified or subjected to any other derogatory action that would prejudice the author's reputation), right against false attribution (not to be associated as author with a work that is not one's own or has been altered by someone else) and the right to privacy in photographs and films. Under the Act (section 115–section 118), each of these moral rights can be waived, but cannot be assigned or alienated.

*139.* The 2000 Act also makes provision *inter alia* for fair dealing, a range of civil remedies for copyright infringement and breach of moral rights, as well as creating a number of criminal offences. However, a High Court judge subsequently found that the range of remedies under the Act was rather limited and that the Act did not provide a basis for blocking, disabling access to or cutting off Internet sites.[154] That decision meant that a previous decision he had made was wrong. He acknowledged that there was no legislative basis for his earlier blocking of the Pirate Bay website through the service provider Eircom (arrived at without hearing any evidence from Eircom because of the terms of a settlement between the parties) and that it was open to the parties to

152. *See* IRIS 2001-10:15/35. Public reading of extracts 'from a literary or dramatic work which has been lawfully made available to the public' is covered in s. 90 f the 2000 Act.

153. [2000] IEHC 70; [2001] 2 IR 6; [2001] 1 ILRM 310. *See also* the UK case *Sweeney v. Macmillan Publishers Ltd.*, Case No. CH 1997 S 3257, [2001] EWHC Ch. B66 (Chancery, 22 Nov. 2001), in which infringement was found only in relation to some manuscript usage and the Joyce estate had to pay its own costs; *see also* the U.S. case of *Schloss v. Sweeney* No. C 06-03718 JW, United States District Court for the Northern District of California, San Jose Division. F. Supp. 2d, 2007 WL 2924056. 9 Feb. 2007, which ended in a settlement and payment by the Joyce estate of the plaintiff's legal costs.

154. *EMI Records (Ireland) Ltd & Others v. UPC Communications Ireland Ltd* [2010] IEHC 377, judgment of 11 Oct. 2010.

that case, therefore, to reapply to the court if they wished.[155] As a result of this case, the EU (Copyright and Related Rights) Regulations 2012 were signed into law on 29 February 2012 to amend section 40 and section 205 of the Copyright and Related Rights Act 2000, by inserting provisions that permit the owner of the copyright or a related right in a work to apply to the High Court for an injunction against an intermediary whose services are used by a third party to infringe a copyright or related right in respect of that work.[156]A number of amendments have been made to the Act by means of secondary legislation.[157]

*140.* One interesting characteristic of Irish copyright law in general is that, as a form of intellectual property, copyright has been recognized by the courts as coming within the guarantees of private property in the Irish Constitution. In *PPI v. Cody,*[158] a case which pre-dated the 2000 Act, the High Court judge held that:

> The right of the creator of a literary, dramatic, musical or artistic work not to have his or her creation stolen or plagiarised is a right of private property within the meaning of Article 40.3.2 and 43.1 of the Constitution, as is the similar right of a person who has employed his or her technical skills and/or capital in the sound recording of a musical work … [It] is the duty of the organs of the State, including the courts, to ensure, as best they may that these rights are protected from unjust attack and, in the case of injustice done, vindicated.

The onus on the State to protect and vindicate copyright therefore applies to its enactment of legislation and other measures.

*141.* In May 2011, with a view to reviewing and updating the 2000 Act, the Government established a Copyright Review Committee. The committee was asked to examine the current copyright legislative framework in Ireland and to identify any areas of the legislation that might be deemed to create barriers to innovation. The Committee reported in October 2013.[159] Its key recommendations were for the establishment of an independent Copyright Council of Ireland, similar to the Press Council of Ireland, and specialist intellectual property tracks in the District and Circuit Courts. It also recommended introducing the full range of exceptions permitted by EU law and limited copyright exceptions for innovation and fair use. However, to date its recommendations have not been acted upon.

---

155. *Blocking of PirateBay Case EMI Records (Ireland) Ltd & Others v. Eircom Ltd* [2009] IEHC 411, judgment of 24 Jul. 2009.
156. S.I. No. 59/2012, available at http://www.irishstatutebook.ie/2012/en/si/0059.html. *See alsoEMI Records (Ireland) Ltd & Others v. The Data Protection Commissioner* [2012] IEHC 264, and Supreme Court appeal: [2013] IESC 34.
157. For an unofficial consolidated version of the Act which incorporates the amendments up to 2016, *see* https://www.djei.ie/en/Legislation/Legislation-Files/Unofficial-consolidated-Copyright-and-Related-Rights-Act-2000-as-amended-.pdf.
158. [1994] 2 ILRM 241, per Keane, J., at 247.
159. Copyright Review Committee, *Modernizing Copyright: A Report Prepared by the Copyright Review Committee for the Department of Jobs, Enterprise and Innovation* (Committee Report, 2013), available at: https://www.djei.ie/en/Publications/Publication-files/CRC-Report.pdf.

## C. *Secondary Legislation: Statutory Instruments*

*142.* As can be seen in the sections above, secondary legislation is regularly used in Ireland, often to transpose EC Directives or to update primary legislation. It is also used to give effect to provisions of primary legislation, for instance where it is more appropriate to deal with detailed procedures or policies in a separate instrument. These may be dealt with in Ministerial Regulations or local by-laws, for example. Secondary legislation may also be used to clarify a provision(s) or fill a loophole in legislation.

*143.* Secondary legislation in Ireland takes the form of Statutory Instruments (S.I.s).[160] They are much easier and quicker to introduce than primary legislation. The latter has to go through various stages of debate in both Houses of the Oireachtas and when passed by both Houses it must be signed into law by the President. S.I.s, on the other hand, can simply be signed into law by the relevant Government Minister, or other person or authority designated in the main Act, and a copy placed before the Houses of the Oireachtas.

*144.* Some specific S.I.s relating to the Acts discussed above have already been mentioned. In relation to copyright, the EU (Collective Rights Management) (Directive 2014/26/EU) Regulations 2016 and the EU (Certain Permitted Uses of Orphan Works) Regulations 2014, are recent examples. Other S.I.s that relate to various aspects of media and communications law are set out here by way of example.

*145.* Under section 14 of the ComReg (Amendment) Act 2007, for instance, the Minister for Communications was given special powers to make regulations to give effect to EC instruments relating to communications matters. Prior to that, the European Communities Electronic Communications Framework Package was also transposed via S.I.s, namely the European Communities (Electronic Communications Networks and Services) (Framework) Regulations 2003, S.I. 307 of 2003; the European Communities (Electronic Communications Networks and Services) (Authorization) Regulations 2003, S.I. 306 of 2003 (+ General Authorization, pursuant to Regulation 8, Doc. No. 03/81R3, last updated 23 March 2011) and S.I. 210 of 2006 European Communities (Electronic Communications Networks and Services) (Authorization) Regulations 2003 (Amendment) Regulations 2006; the European Communities (Electronic Communications Networks and Services) (Access) Regulations 2003, S.I. 305 of 2003; the European Communities (Electronic Communications Networks and Services) (Universal Service and Users' Rights) Regulations 2003, S.I. 308 of 2003; and the European Communities (Electronic Communications Networks and Services) (Data Protection and Privacy) Regulations 2003, S.I 535 of 2003.

### 1. Secondary Legislation Related to Broadcasting

*146.* While the transposition of AVMSD was effected mainly through the provisions of the Broadcasting Act 2009, subsequent statutory instruments were made in order to complete the process in relation to aspects of both linear and non-linear audiovisual media services. They include S.I. 258 of 2010 (European Communities (Audiovisual Media Services) Regulations 2010), which is the main legislative source

160. S.I.s can be found in the Irish Statute Book (www.irishstatutebook.ie/) by year.

of regulation of on-demand services. Another S.I., S.I. 67 of 2011 (Broadcasting Act 2009 (section 26(5)) (Conferral of Additional Functions – Broadcasting Services) Order 2011) related to digital broadcasting services on RTÉ multiplexes and gave the BAI additional functions including consultation with RTÉ about available capacity and costs of carriage of broadcast services on its multiplexes.

### *D. Common Law*

*147.* The common law, also called 'judge-made law' is an important source of media law in Ireland and therefore is discussed separately here. Its importance and centrality to the development of law and legal principles in Ireland is reflected in the discussion in many of the earlier sections of this book of cases decided in court by judges applying the common law.

*148.* Ireland is a common law country, although Irish common law has developed separately from that of the UK and has been influenced by the written Constitution and by European law. Nonetheless, case law or so-called judge-made law still forms a very important part of the legal armoury. However, common law rules and principles established in particular cases that have come before the courts and developed on the basis of precedent, have been affected to varying extents by legislation. Some have been consolidated in legislation; others have been clarified, extended, varied, repealed or replaced by legislation. The law governing contracts, for example, while retaining most of the common law rules, has been supplemented by consumer legislation, sale of goods, unfair contract terms and other such legislation. Likewise, the common law governing torts has been affected by legislation governing civil liability, occupiers' liability, industrial relations, road traffic and so forth. Of specific interest in the area of media law is the tort of defamation. Many of the common law rules of defamation, which were developed in the early days of the print media, have survived but have been clarified or altered to varying extents by legislation enacted both in Britain while Ireland was under British rule and more recently by legislation enacted by the Irish Parliament, the Oireachtas. The law of defamation is considered below (paragraphs 248–260 et passim).

*149.* Since the adoption of a written Constitution, first in 1922 and then in 1937, Irish common law can also be said to have become constitutionalized to some extent. Tort law is still regarded as a common law subject, augmented by legislation. However, it is also the mechanism used by the State to fulfil its constitutional obligation in Article 40.3.2 to protect and vindicate the good name of the citizen. Very often nowadays the pleadings in defamation actions in the High Court will refer to the constitutional right to one's good name and increasingly also to the constitutional right to freedom of expression. The concept of constitutional torts as such, however, has not developed very significantly. The courts have tended to take the view that generally speaking the law of tort provides adequate protection for constitutional rights and it is only where the law of tort does not provide a remedy in particular circumstances that a constitutional action will be taken directly.[161]

---

161. *See* generally, Gerard W. Hogan & Gerry F. Whyte, JM Kelly: The Irish Constitution, 4th ed. (Dublin: Tottel Publishing, 2003).

*150.* An example of the latter is the constitutional action taken by journalists Geraldine Kennedy and Bruce Arnold in 1987 when their home telephones were tapped by order of the Minister for Justice.[162] As there was no common law tort of invasion of privacy as such, but the courts had recognized aspects of a right to privacy protected by the Constitution, the two journalists took a constitutional action claiming that their constitutional right to privacy had been breached. While allowing for the fact that some level of interference with telephone communications was inevitable, the President of the High Court found that the deliberate and conscious intrusion by the State in this case amounted to a violation of the journalists' constitutional rights to privacy and granted them a declaration of unconstitutionality along with an award of damages. Tort law would have provided a remedy in certain circumstances involving breach of privacy, for example if there had been a trespass on the journalists' property or trespass to their goods; or if the activities complained of had amounted to the common law tort of private nuisance, i.e., interference with the plaintiffs enjoyment of their property. Equity, which was developed originally to provide a remedy where the common law was lacking, would have provided a remedy if there had been a breach of confidence.

*151.* Nowadays, Irish common law is also influenced by European law, particularly in the case of torts such as defamation, by the ECHR, which was incorporated into Irish law at sub-constitutional level by the European Convention on Human Rights Act of 2003. Indeed, it may be argued that one influence of the Convention has been to develop a general 'tort' of privacy insofar as Article 8 has been used by the courts to fashion a much broader right to privacy than the one that was emerging bit by bit under the Constitution.

*152.* Some areas of common law, however, still remain largely unaffected by legislation and only to a limited extent by the Constitution. One such area is contempt of court law. The rules and principles that apply to contempt of court remain common law rules as devised by judges in court cases. There is no Contempt of Court Act as such in Ireland. Some legislation dealing with other matters, such as tribunals of inquiry, contains isolated references to contempt of court but only to the extent of stating that certain conduct is to be treated as if it were contempt of the High Court. Contempt of court is an area of law that affects how journalists and media report court cases and is therefore important. It is the area of the common law that was found wanting in some respects by the ECtHR in the 1979 case of *Sunday Times v. United Kingdom* concerning the thalidomide drug tragedy.[163] Contempt of court is discussed in more detail below.

## *E. Equity*

*153.* The law of Equity provides remedies based on the fairness of the matter where the common law is deficient. Its main role in Media Law is in respect of injunctions. It also provides a remedy for breach of confidence, which is not as developed in the area of media law in Ireland as it is in the UK, where, in recent years, it became

---

162. [1987] I.R. 587.
163. Series A, No. 30, judgment of 26 Apr. 1979; available at: Available at: http://www.bailii.org/cgi-bin/format.cgi?doc=/eu/cases/ECHR/1979/1.html&query=(sunday)+AND+(times)+AND+(v)+AND+(united)+AND+(kingdom).

a surrogate for a right to privacy. As indicated above, the right to privacy in Ireland has developed slowly under the Constitution and in recent years in accordance with Article 8 ECHR following incorporation of the ECHR into Irish law in 2003.

## 1. Breach of Confidence

*154.* Nevertheless, breach of confidence is sometimes relied on as a cause of action in media law cases in Ireland. For instance, breach of confidence was an issue, although not the determinative issue, in *A.G. for England and Wales v. Brandon Book Publishers Ltd.*[164] In the case of *National Irish Bank v. RTÉ*, the Bank sought to stop broadcasts concerning alleged tax evasion on the grounds of client confidentiality.[165] The Supreme Court, however, upheld the High Court decision, concluding that the public interest in broadcasting the information outweighed the public interest in confidentiality in the circumstances of the case. Breach of confidence was also relied on as a cause of action along with negligence, breach of contract and privacy, in *FW v. BBC*, in which a former competitive swimmer was interviewed on a BBC radio programme about child sexual abuse perpetrated by a former swimming coach.[166] He had agreed to give the interview on condition that his identity was not revealed. When his identity was revealed, the BBC admitted liability and therefore the breach of confidence issue was not tested.

## 2. Injunctions

*155.* In each of the three cases just mentioned, breach of confidence was ahead of claim and in the first two the remedy sought was an equitable remedy, namely an injunction. Injunctions in media cases are usually sought to prevent publication before it takes place or to prevent repeat publication in the event that the material has already been published. They are therefore a form of prior restraint and as such are susceptible on freedom of expression grounds. Injunctions are rarely granted in defamation cases partly due to common law and partly for constitutional reasons.[167] They will be refused if the media defendant can demonstrate intent and ability to plead one of the defences available in defamation actions.[168] Under the Defamation Act 2009 (section 33), the court must refuse to grant an injunction (prohibition order) unless it is of the opinion that the statement is defamatory and that the defendant has no defence that is reasonably likely to succeed. This test was applied by the High Court in *Meegan v. Associated Newspapers*,[169] in 2010 and the order was refused.

*156.* Injunctions may be *interim* (temporary), usually granted ex parte (with only the party seeking it present, without notice to the other party) and lasting for a few days pending a preliminary hearing in court. They have been granted in a small

164. [1998] IESC 2; [1986] I.R. 597; [1987] ILRM 135.
165. [1998]2 I.R. 465; [1998] 2 ILRM 196.
166. Reported in *The Irish Times* 19, 20, 26 Mar. 1999.
167. *See* , for example, Kelly, J. in *Foley v. Sunday Newspapers* referring to the common law rule in *Bonnard v. Perryman* [1891] 2 Ch. 269.
168. *Xv. RTÉ,* reported in *The Irish Times*, 28, 29 Mar. 1990.
169. H.Ct. 19 Apr. 2010; reported in *The Irish Times* 20 Apr. 2010.

number of cases involving Internet sites. One such case was *Maguire v. Gill,*[170]where the court granted an interim injunction requiring the defendant to remove offending material concerning a lawyer from a website.

*157. Interlocutory* injunctions are granted occasionally in media cases. They cover a longer period pending a full hearing of the issues in the court. Notice must be given to the other party and, in defamation cases, the defendant must persuade the judge that s/he has a defence that is reasonably likely to succeed. An example of a case prior to the 2009 Act in which an interlocutory injunction was granted is *Reynolds v. Malocco t/a 'Patrick' Magazine*, which concerned an article to be published in a magazine claiming that the plaintiff permitted the sale of drugs in his night-club.[171]The court held that, in order to obtain an injunction restraining publication, the plaintiff must not only show that he or she 'has raised a serious issue concerning the words complained of' but also that 'there is no doubt that they are defamatory'.[172] As Clarke, J pointed out in *Cogley and Aherne v. RTÉ* (below) 'one of the underlying reasons for the reluctance of the courts in this jurisdiction to grant injunctions at an interlocutory stage in relation to defamation stems from the fact that if the traditional basis for the grant of an interlocutory injunction (i.e., that the plaintiff had established a fair issue to be tried) was sufficient for the grant of an injunction in defamation proceedings public debate on very many issues would be largely stifled' and 'a disproportionate effect on the conduct of public debate on issues of importance would occur'.

*158.* Apart from defamation cases, injunctions are sometimes sought to restrain publication on the grounds of breach of privacy or the right to a fair trial. In *Cogley and Aherne v. RTÉ* (Leas Cross Nursing Home case)[173] the plaintiffs sought to prevent the broadcasting of a programme where conditions in a nursing home had been secretly filmed. The first plaintiff, a nurse, whose action lay in defamation, was refused an injunction on the grounds as set out in *Reynolds v. Malocco t/a 'Patrick' Magazine* (above). The claim of the second plaintiffs, the owners, was for breach of privacy. (The privacy rights of the patients filmed were to be protected by pixilation or consent of the families, or both.) Relying *inter alia* on a New Zealand case, the court considered the context and circumstances in which the impugned methods were employed, any special public interest considerations for broadcasting the programme, and the adequacy of damages as an available remedy for any wrong proved at trial. In light of all those circumstances, the judge in *Aherne* said that the issues raised in the programme 'are those of the highest public interest and that, therefore, a very significant weight indeed needs to be attached to those matters in weighing the rights and values involved at this [interlocutory] stage'. As RTÉ had shown that there were 'very real, significant and weighty public interest issues involved', the judge refused to grant an interlocutory injunction which would have the effect of restraining the broadcast. However, the second plaintiffs had also claimed that the secret filming amounted to the tort of trespass and in that regard the trial judge took the view that the ordinary 'balance of convenience' test for granting an injunction should apply. 'Pending the establishment after a full trial of the lawfulness or otherwise of the use of such methods', he said, 'it seems to

170. Reported in *The Irish Times* 14 Sept.–24 Nov. 2006.
171. [1998] IEHC 175; [1999] 2 I.R. 203; [1999] 1 ILRM 289.
172. *Ibid*., at §19.
173. [2005] IEHC 180, Clarke, J. 8 Jun. 2005.

me that the balance of convenience would favour restraining RTE from engaging in any further trespass on the premises of the plaintiffs in the Aherne hearing'. Accordingly, an injunction to prevent any further trespass pending the hearing of the action was granted.

*159.* In *Mahon Tribunal v. Sunday Business Post*, the Tribunal, which was inquiring into planning matters, was concerned at the leaking of its documents to the media, in this instance the defendant newspaper. It therefore sought orders restraining the defendant and, in effect, all media of communication, from publishing them until such time as they would be disclosed at a public hearing. Following the granting of *interim* injunctions on an ex parte basis, the Tribunal sought interlocutory injunctions in the High Court but these were refused.[174] The High Court judge referred to the Constitution and to the jurisprudence of the ECtHR, recognizing 'the cardinal importance of press freedom. Any restriction on it must be proportionate and no more than is necessary to promote the legitimate object of the restriction'. The Supreme Court also underlined the importance of freedom of expression, acknowledging *inter alia* that:

> The media are not required to justify publication by reference to any public interest other than that of freedom of expression itself. They are free to publish material which is not in the public interest....
>
> The right of freedom of expression extends the same protection to worthless, prurient and meretricious publication as it does to worthy, serious and socially valuable works. The undoubted fact that news media frequently and implausibly invoke the public interest to cloak worthless and even offensive material does not affect the principle. (§§42-43)

*160.* On the issue of confidentiality which founded the Tribunal's claims, the Supreme Court held that such a restriction was not 'prescribed by law' as required by Article 10 ECHR, as it had not been established in Irish law that governmental or other public or statutory bodies have the right to apply for injunctions preventing the disclosure of confidential information.[175]

*161.* In deciding whether to grant an injunction, courts are guided, as seen in the cases referred to above, by equitable principles, by the fundamental rights provisions of the Constitution and by the jurisprudence of the ECtHR. Very occasionally, *permanent* injunctions are sought. It is extremely rare for them to be granted in media cases and especially in defamation cases.[176] A breach of an injunction is a breach of a court order and is treated as a form of contempt of court, which is discussed below.

174. [2005] IEHC 307.
175. [2007] IESC 15 (29 Mar. 2007).
176. *See* generally, M. McGonagle, *Media Law*, 2003, Chs 4 and 6, referring *inter alia* to *Aer Rianta v. The Sunday Business Post*, reported in *The Irish Times* 5 Dec. 1992 and 12 Jan. 1993.

## *F. Ethical Codes*

### 1. BAI Codes

*162.* The BAI is mandated to draft codes on a number of issues by the Broadcasting Act 2009. As such, BAI codes have a statutory basis and broadcasters are required to comply with them. Failure to do so can result in complaints to the Compliance Committee of BAI and the possibility of findings against them. Serious or repeated breaches of the codes can also result in fines under the Act. BAI codes dealing with programme standards, commercial communications, election and referendum coverage and other matters are discussed below.

### 2. RTÉ Code of Fair Trading

*163.* RTÉ has a number of internal Codes relating to various aspects of its activities and including, for example, a Code of Practice for the employment of people with a disability (2009) and various policies and guidelines.[177]In addition, under the Broadcasting Act 2009, section 112, each public service broadcaster, RTÉ and TG4, is required to prepare and publish a code of fair trading practice, setting out the principles that it shall apply when agreeing on terms for the commissioning of programming material from independent producers. The BAI is required, having consulted with the Minister for Communications, RTÉ, TG4, and independent producers (or their representatives) to prepare and issue guidance to public service broadcasters (PSBs) on the format of a code of fair trading practice.[178] RTÉ and TG4, having considered the guidance prepared by the BAI, must each prepare a code and submit it to the Minister for approval. The Act directs a PSB to include in its code reference to its approach to: (a) Acquisition of rights; (b) Multiannual commissioning, and (c) Timetable for contractual negotiations. Compliance with the code is part of the Compliance Committee's remit, and the code has to be reviewed every four years.

### 3. On-Demand Code

*164.* A voluntary code of conduct for providers of on-demand audiovisual services was jointly launched on 4 May 2011 by the On-Demand Audiovisual Services (ODAS) group within Irish Business and Employers Confederation's (IBEC's) Audiovisual Federation (AF) and Telecommunications Internet Federation (TIF), the Broadcasting Authority of Ireland (BAI) and the Advertising Standards Authority for Ireland (ASAI). The code sets out the minimum standards required of service providers, provides a complaints mechanism for consumers and complies with European directives. IBEC is the Irish Business and Employers Confederation.[179]

---

177. The various policies and guidelines are available at: http://www.rte.ie/about/en/policies-and-reports/policies-guidelines/.
178. *See* BAI, *Code of Fair Trading Practice: Guidance for Public Service Broadcasters*, April 2011, available at: http://www.bai.ie/en/codes-standards/.
179. www.ibec.ie. The ODAS Code is available at: http://www.bai.ie/en/codes-standards/.

*165.* The code was developed in furtherance of section 13(1) of Statutory Instrument No 258 of June 2010. The code covers all ODAS made available under the jurisdiction of the Republic of Ireland. Following the definitions section, it has sections on Audiovisual Commercial Communications (Pt. 1); Content (Pt. 2, which covers community standards, protection of minors, accessibility, rights and European works); Compliance and Complaints (Pt. 3). Complaints are handled by the ASAI. The Compliance Committee of the BAI shall accept appeals against the resolution offered by the service provider with regard to breaches of subsections 1 & 2 of PART 2 of the Code and make determinations on complaints.

## 4. Press Council Code

*166.* The Press Council of Ireland and the Office of the Press Ombudsman were set up on an independent basis to safeguard and promote professional and ethical standards in Irish newspapers and magazines. The professional and ethical standards are those set out in the Code of Practice for Newspapers and Magazines. Although independent, the Press Council of Ireland and the Office of the Press Ombudsman are given recognition in the Defamation Act 2009, which also requires them to prepare and implement a code, which shall:

> specify the standards to be adhered to, and the rules and practices to be complied with by the members of the Press Council including–

(a) ethical standards and practices,
(b) rules and standards intended to ensure the accuracy of reporting where a person's reputation is likely to be affected, and
(c) rules and standards intended to ensure that intimidation and harassment of persons does not occur and that the privacy, integrity and dignity of the person is respected. (Schedule 2, s. 10)

The Preamble to the Code adopted by the Press Council states *inter alia* that the freedom to publish is vital to the right of the people to be informed and makes clear that 'this freedom includes the right of a newspaper to publish what it considers to be news, without fear or favour, and the right to comment upon it'. It acknowledges, however, that 'Freedom of the press carries responsibilities. Members of the press have a duty to maintain the highest professional and ethical standards.' The ten principles set out in the code cover truth and accuracy; distinguishing fact and comment; fairness and honesty; respect for rights; privacy; protection of sources; court reporting; prejudice; children; and publication of the decision of the Press Ombudsman or Press Council.

*167.* Full details of the complaints procedure are published on the Council's website. Basically, a complaint can be made by anyone who feels that any article personally affects them, provided that article in question has been published within the last three months in a newspaper or magazine that is a member publication of the Press Council of Ireland. Member publications include all daily and Sunday newspapers; the Irish editions of UK newspapers; the majority of regional newspapers; and the majority of Irish-published magazines. Online-only newspapers have also sought membership and *TheJournal.ie*, for example, is now a full member. Indeed, the Defamation Act 2009, which gives statutory recognition to the Press Council, appears to envisage wider membership in that it states that the 'owner of *any* periodical in circulation in the State or part of the State shall be entitled to be a member' of the Press Council. (Second Schedule, section 4, emphasis added.) Furthermore, the term 'periodical' is defined in section 2 of the Act as:

> any newspaper, magazine, journal or other publication that is printed, published or issued, or that circulates, in the State at regular or substantially regular intervals and includes any version thereof published on the internet or by other electronic means.

*168.* Complaints must first be made in writing directly to the editor of the publication concerned. If there is no reply within the stipulated time-frame (two weeks) or the complainant is not satisfied with the reply, s/he can then complain to the Press Ombudsman. The aim is to resolve the issue through a process of conciliation if possible or, if not, the Ombudsman will make a decision or refer the matter to the Press Council.[180]If any part of the complaint is upheld, the publication concerned will have to publish that part of the Press Ombudsman's decision in accordance with the provisions of the Press Council's Publication Guidelines. An appeal from a decision of the Ombudsman may be made to the Council in writing within two weeks on grounds that an error of procedure or application of the Code has occurred or that significant new information is available that could not have been or was not made available to the Press Ombudsman before he made his decision.

## 5. The Advertising Standards Authority of Ireland Code

*169.* The Code of the ASAI is a voluntary code. It is not mandated by statute. The ASAI is an independent self-regulatory body set up and financed by the advertising industry. The ASAI, which is a member of the European Advertising Standards Alliance (EASA), comprises a Board and a Complaints Committee. Its code, the Code of Standards for Advertising and Marketing Communications in Ireland, applies to advertising in all forms and all media, including broadcasting.[181] The ASAI code covers general rules, such as truth and honesty in marketing communications; respect for the dignity of all persons; the principle of equality; responsiveness to the diversity of Irish society and taking account of people's sensitivities. It also contains sections with detailed rules on children, food and beverages, alcoholic drinks, health and beauty,

180. In 2011 and 2012, approximately a quarter of all complaints processed were resolved through conciliation, while around half led to decisions by the Press Ombudsman. The largest category of complaints is consistently that relating to 'truth and accuracy'. *See* the annual reports available at www.presscouncil.ie.

181. The ASAI code is directed at its members, whereas the BAI codes on commercial communications and children's commercial communications (http://www.bai.ie/en/codes-standards/) are specifically directed at broadcasters. The two bodies work in consultation with each other.

slimming, environmental matters, online behavioural advertising and more.[182] The Complaints Committee is responsible for considering and dealing with complaints of breaches of the code. The ASAI publishes monthly complaints bulletins on its website, and many of its decisions on complaints are also reported in the national newspapers. A decision of the ASAI, however, does not deprive a consumer or an advertiser of the right to take further action or prejudice any rights under the law.

*170.* The system, which relies on the support and commitment of the advertising industry – advertisers, advertising agencies, media specialists, direct marketing companies, sales promotion consultants and the various media – print, radio, television, cinema and outdoor interests– provides an alternative, low-cost and easily accessible means of resolving disputes. The ASAI also plays a role in relation to the ODAS code for on-demand services.

## 6. National Union of Journalists' Code

*171.* Over 90% of full-time journalists in Ireland belong to the National Union of Journalists (NUJ).[183] The NUJ operates a Code of Conduct, which has been in existence since 1936 and is updated periodically, most recently in 2011. The code sets out the main principles of journalism and all journalists joining the union must sign a declaration that they will strive to adhere to it. The twelve-point code, along with a 'conscience clause' added in the latest revision of the code, is as follows:

A journalist:

(1) At all times upholds and defends the principle of media freedom, the right of freedom of expression and the right of the public to be informed
(2) Strives to ensure that information disseminated is honestly conveyed, accurate and fair
(3) Does her/his utmost to correct harmful inaccuracies
(4) Differentiates between fact and opinion
(5) Obtains material by honest, straightforward and open means, with the exception of investigations that are both overwhelmingly in the public interest and which involve evidence that cannot be obtained by straightforward means
(6) Does nothing to intrude into anybody's private life, grief or distress unless justified by overriding consideration of the public interest
(7) Protects the identity of sources who supply information in confidence and material gathered in the course of her/his work
(8) Resists threats or any other inducements to influence, distort or suppress information and takes no unfair personal advantage of information gained in the course of her/his duties before the information is public knowledge

182. The 7th edition of the Code came into effect on 1 Mar. 2016, available at: http://www.asai.ie/asai-code/.

183. The NUJ represents journalists working all over the island of Ireland. There are over 3,500 members in the Republic and 800 in Northern Ireland.

(9) Produces no material likely to lead to hatred or discrimination on the grounds of a person's age, gender, race, colour, creed, legal status, disability, marital status, or sexual orientation
(10) Does not by way of statement, voice or appearance endorse by advertisement any commercial product or service save for the promotion of her/his own work or of the medium by which she/he is employed
(11) A journalist shall normally seek the consent of an appropriate adult when interviewing or photographing a child for a story about her/his welfare.
(12) Avoids plagiarism.

The NUJ believes a journalist has the right to refuse an assignment or be identified as the author of an editorial that would break the letter or spirit of the code. The NUJ will fully support any journalist disciplined for asserting her/his right to act according to the code.

*172.* The NUJ has a strong record of defending journalists in the face of pressure or intimidation from outside forces.[184] As is evident from the text of the two codes, the NUJ code and Press Council Code contain similar principles, though with nuanced differences. Nonetheless, the NUJ has signed up to the Press Council Code of Practice (discussed above in paragraphs 166–168) and is represented on the Press Council.

## G. *Other Codes*

*173.* Certain other voluntary codes and guidelines have been developed in relation to media reporting. Codes relating to alcohol and alcohol promotion have been agreed between the drinks industry, the Department of Health and Children and the media in relation to television, radio, cinema and outdoor/ambient media.[185]Also, the Samaritans have worked closely with the media to promote sensitive and appropriate reporting of suicide and make it a priority to respond quickly and expertly to journalists' enquiries about how to portray these deaths. The Samaritans teamed up with the Irish Association of Suicidology (IAS) to produce Media Guidelines for Reporting Suicide. The Guidelines include reporting tips, 'dos and don'ts' and other useful issues, such as the use of appropriate language. There is a section specifically geared to digital media. The Guidelines are updated regularly.[186]

---

184. For instance, the NUJ campaigned in earlier decades for the end of censorship in Ireland and the ban on broadcast interviews with spokespersons for or representatives of Sinn Féin (the political wing of the IRA), and defended journalists such as Ed Moloney (who was brought to court in Northern Ireland in 1999 in an attempt to get him to reveal sources and hand over his notes in relation to a paramilitary related murder) and in June 2013, the NUJ condemned a death threat against a journalist in Northern Ireland and expressed concern at 'the growing number of threats being made by paramilitary groups in Northern Ireland against journalists who are carrying out their work.' *See* generally, http://www.nuj.org.uk/ (13 Jun. 2013). The NUJ (UK) also has an ethics council and operates the NUJ Ethics Hotline, as an advisory service for journalists.
185. *See* Alcohol Marketing, Communications and Sponsorship Codes of Practice of 2008, available at http://asai.ie/wp-content/uploads/Alcohol-Codes-of-Practice-2008.pdf.
186. The Guidelines are available at: http://www.samaritans.org/sites/default/files/kcfinder/files/Samaritans%20Ireland%20Media%20Guidelines.pdf.

## II. Legislation: European Union

*174.* As in the case of all Member States of the EU, Ireland is bound by the legislation emanating from Brussels. While Regulations are directly binding, Directives have to be transposed into domestic law within a given period. Ireland has been tardy in respect of some Directives, particularly in the environmental field, but it has been timely for the most part in transposing directives in the media and audiovisual field. Thus, AVMSD was mostly in place in Ireland by the transposition date of 19 December 2009. Likewise, Ireland met the deadline for the switchover from analogue broadcasting to digital on 24 October 2012. It is recognized that the better option is to transpose Directives by means of primary legislation, which is now the norm in Ireland but many aspects of EU law continue to be implemented by means of secondary legislation, as can be seen in the references to Statutory Instruments or Ministerial Orders elsewhere in this text.

## III. Case Law: Ireland

*175.* A considerable amount of Irish case law decided by the domestic courts has been discussed above. This section will deal, therefore, with cases heard in Ireland and referred to the European Court of Justice, now the Court of Justice of the EU.

**Cases referred to the ECJ/CJEU:**

***Society for the Protection of Unborn Children (SPUC) v. Coogan***

*176.* A small but increasing number of cases in Ireland have resulted in references to the European Court of Justice (ECJ).[187] An early case which resulted in a referral to the ECJ was *SPUC v. Coogan,*[188] which concerned abortion information. The issue was whether an injunction granted by the Irish courts against a students' union that had distributed a handbook for students which contained information on abortion services would interfere with the right to distribute information about legally available services within the Community. The ECJ did not address the substantive issues but found that, as there was no business relationship between the students and the abortion services, there was no issue under Community law.

***Phonographic Performance (Ireland) Ltd v. Ireland & Anor***

*177.* In the case of *Phonographic Performance (Ireland) Ltd v. Ireland & Anor,*[189] the Commercial Court decided to seek a preliminary ruling on the interpretation of Articles 8 and 10 of Directive 92/100/EC on rental right and lending right and on certain rights related to copyright in the field of intellectual property, as codified by Directive 2006/115/EC. The case was taken by PPI, a licensing body which acts on behalf of phonogram producers who hold rights in sound recordings. The central issue was whether section 97 of the Irish Copyright Act 2000 was contrary to Ireland's

187. The title of the Court is now the Court of Justice of the European Union (CJEU).
188. [1989] I.R. 734; Case C-159/90, *SPUC v. Grogan* [1991] 2 CEC, 539. The issue of abortion information was later addressed in the Regulation of Information (Services outside the State for Termination of Pregnancies) Act 1995, referred to above at paragraph 85.
189. High Court (Commercial), [2010] IEHC 79, judgment of 23 Mar. 2010. *See also* IRIS 2010-7:1/27.

obligations pursuant to the Directive, as it allowed sound recordings to be heard in hotel and guesthouse bedrooms without payment, though not in areas such as nightclubs or concert areas where a discrete charge is made for admission. In its judgment, the Court of Justice first considered whether, for the purposes of Union law, a hotel operator, which in its guest bedrooms provides televisions and/or radios to which it distributes a broadcast signal, is a 'user' making a 'communication to the public' of a phonogram which may be played in a broadcast. Having considered the relevant criteria, the court concluded that a hotel operator is indeed a 'user' making 'communication to the public' and therefore is obliged to pay reasonable remuneration for the broadcast of a phonogram, in addition to that paid by the broadcaster. It was not the private nature of the use by the hotel guests that was relevant, the court said, but rather whether the use made of the work by the hotel operator itself is private or not.[190]

***Ireland v. European Parliament and Council of the European Union***

*178.* In a case concerning data retention, judgment was given against Ireland. In *Ireland v. European Parliament and Council of the European Union,*[191]Ireland had attempted to have Directive 2006/24/EC on data retention annulled on the ground that it was not adopted on an appropriate legal basis.[192]Ireland, supported by the Slovak Republic, submitted that the choice of Article 95 EC as the legal basis for Directive 2006/24 was a fundamental error, principally because the sole or main objective of the directive was to facilitate the investigation, detection and prosecution of crime, including terrorism. However, the Court concluded that 'Directive 2006/24 covers the activities of service providers in the internal market and does not contain any rules governing the activities of public authorities for law-enforcement purposes.' (at §91). Consequently, the Communications (Retention of Data) Act 2011 was passed by the Oireachtas to give effect to Directive 2006/24/EC on the retention of data. However, prior to that enactment, the European Commission, in Case C202/09, successfully took enforcement action against Ireland (and other countries) for failure to transpose the Directive.

***Digital Rights Ireland v. Ireland***

*179.* In May 2010, the High Court heard a challenge by Digital Rights Ireland concerning Irish data retention law. This case also involved a submission on the lawfulness of EU Data Retention Directive 2006/24/EC, but in this instance the focus was primarily on its implications for the right to privacy.[193] A number of questions to be referred to the ECJ were agreed. In 2014 the Court of Justice of the EU in two joined cases (C-293/12 Digital Rights Ireland and C-594/12 Seitlinger and Others)

---

190. Case C-162/10, Third Chamber, judgment of 15 Mar. 2012.
191. Case C-301/06, Judgment of ECJ, Grand Chamber, 10 Feb. 2009, OJ C 82 of 4 Apr. 2009, p. 2, concerning DIRECTIVE 2006/24/EC OF THE EUROPEAN PARLIAMENT AND OF THE COUNCIL of 15 Mar. 2006 on the retention of data generated or processed in connection with the provision of publicly available electronic communications services or of public communications networks and amending Directive 2002/58/EC.
192. Directive 2006/24/EC of the European Parliament and of the Council of 15 Mar. 2006 on the retention of data generated or processed in connection with the provision of publicly available electronic communications services or of public communications networks and amending Directive 2002/58/EC.
193. *Digital Rights Ireland Ltd v. Minister for Communication & Ors* [2010] IEHC 221 §113.

declared the data retention directive to be invalid. It held that the directive 'interferes in a particularly serious manner with the fundamental rights to respect for private life and to the protection of personal data' and that the interference 'is not sufficiently circumscribed to ensure that that interference is actually limited to what is strictly necessary'.

## IV. Case Law: Council of Europe and European Union

### Council of Europe – European Convention on Human Rights

#### *Purcell v. Ireland*

*180.* Not many Irish cases involving the media have been decided in the ECtHR or, indeed, by the Commission of Human Rights when it was in existence, and only one of them to date (*see* below paragraph 191, *Independent Newspapers v. Ireland* 2017) has been decided in favour of the applicants.[194] The case of *Purcell v. Ireland,* as noted above, which challenged the broadcasting ban (section 31 of the Broadcasting Authority Act 1960, as amended) on interviews with spokespersons for or representatives of Sinn Féin, was deemed to be 'manifestly ill-founded' by the European Commission of Human Rights in 1991. According to the Commission's report, the applicants in their affidavits claimed that the effect of the Ministerial Order imposing the ban, and the RTÉ guidelines interpreting it, had been:

> gravely to distort coverage of all news events, current affairs and social developments in Northern Ireland, to deter journalists and/or producers from choosing to put on programmes relating to any issue in Northern Ireland and to prevent journalists and producers from complying with the statutory requirement as to balance and impartiality in the programmes they produced.

*181.* The applicants also argued that section 18 of the Broadcasting Authority Act 1960 (as amended) offered a sufficient safeguard against the use of the broadcasting media to undermine the authority of the State, without the need for section 31. This section 18 provision imposed inter alia a duty of impartiality on the RTÉ Authority but also provided that no matter could be broadcast 'which may reasonably be regarded as being likely to promote, or incite to, crime or as tending to undermine the authority of the State'.

*182.* The Commission accepted that 'compliance with the section 31 Order entailed restrictions and conditions not only on the choice of the material the applicants may broadcast but also on their editorial judgment'. Considering 'the eminent role of journalists in the dissemination of information' and considering in particular that the ban applied to interviews with spokespersons of a registered political party (Sinn Féin), the Commission concluded that the Order constituted an interference with the exercise of the applicants' right to receive and impart information and ideas under Article 10 (1) of the Convention. The interference was found to be 'prescribed by law' and to

194. Application No. 15404/89, available at http://hudoc.echr.coe.int/sites/eng/pages/search.aspx?i=001-893#{%22itemid%22:[%22001-893%22]}.

have a 'legitimate aim', namely protecting the interests of national security and preventing disorder and crime.

*183.* On the question of necessity, however, the Commission took the view that in light of the Government's margin of appreciation its 'sole task' was to examine whether the reasons underlying the section 31 Order were 'relevant and sufficient under Article 10 para. 2, i.e., whether the Minister had convincing reasons for assuming the existence of a pressing social need for imposing the impugned restrictions on the applicants'. In so saying, the Commission cited *Muller v. Switzerland.*[195]However, it will be recalled that Muller concerned 'artistic' expression and public morals, where the margin of expression would be wider, rather than 'political' expression, which was the case in Purcell. Also, the acceptance that the restrictions impinged on the journalists' editorial judgment does not appear to have weighed heavily with the Commission, compared to the Court a few years later in *Jersild v. Denmark.*[196] Rather, the restrictions were dismissed by the Commission as merely causing the applicants inconvenience.

*184.* The real nub of the decision appears to be the Commission's concern that 'the defeat of terrorism is a public interest of the first importance in a democratic society'. 'In a situation where politically motivated violence poses a constant threat to the lives and security of the population and where the advocates of this violence seek access to the mass media for publicity purposes,' the Commission said, 'it is particularly difficult to strike a fair balance between the requirements of protecting freedom of information and the imperatives of protecting the State and the public against armed conspiracies seeking to overthrow the democratic order which guarantees this freedom and other human rights.'

*185.* Among the Commission's other considerations was the fact that the restrictions resulting from the Order did not refer to the contents of radio and television programmes and also that radio and television are media of considerable power and influence, whose impact is more immediate than that of the print media, and the possibilities for the broadcaster to correct, qualify, interpret or comment on any statement made on radio or television are limited in comparison with those available to journalists in the press. 'Live statements', the Commission said, 'could also involve a special risk of coded messages being conveyed, a risk which even conscientious journalists cannot control within the exercise of their professional judgment'. It concluded that 'Given the limited scope of the restrictions imposed on the applicants and the overriding interests they were designed to protect, the Commission finds that they can reasonably be considered 'necessary in a democratic society' within the meaning of Article 10 para. 2 (Art. 10-2) of the Convention'.[197]

*186.* The order imposing the ban, which was introduced in 1971, was renewed each year up to 1994. In January 1994, during the first peace process in Northern Ireland, the ban was finally lifted and the statutory provision was repealed in 2001.

***Murphy v. Ireland***

195. Series A, No. 133, judgment of 24 May 1988, p. 21, para. 32.
196. Series A, No. 298, judgment of 23 Sept. 1994.
197. Complaints in *Purcell* based on Art. 3 of Protocol No. 1 regarding free elections and under Art. 13 regarding effective remedies were also rejected as manifestly ill-founded.

*187.* The case of *Murphy v. Ireland*[198] concerned a ban on religious advertising on radio and television. The applicant, Pastor Roy Murphy, had submitted an advertisement to a local, commercial radio station in early 1995. The advertisement was for the showing of a video on the Resurrection of Christ in the Irish Faith Centre in Dublin. However, the then commercial broadcasting regulator, the IRTC, stopped the broadcast pursuant to section 10(3) of the Radio and Television Act 1988. When the High Court and Supreme Court upheld the decision of the IRTC, an application was lodged first with the European Commission of Human Rights and then transmitted to the Court in November 1998.

*188.* As is often the case, the ECtHR's deliberations centred around the 'necessity' test, as the restriction was found to be both prescribed by law and in furtherance of legitimate aims (§§62–64). The Court reiterated its long-held position that a narrow margin of appreciation applies in relation to political speech but that 'a wider margin of appreciation is generally available to the Contracting States when regulating freedom of expression in relation to matters liable to offend intimate personal convictions within the sphere of morals or, especially, religion'. This, it explained, was because 'in the field of morals, and perhaps to an even greater degree, there is no uniform European conception of the requirements of "the protection of the rights of others" in relation to attacks on their religious convictions'. (at §67). Accordingly, State authorities were 'in principle in a better position than the international judge to give an opinion on the exact content of these requirements with regard to the rights of others as well as on the 'necessity' of a 'restriction' intended to protect from such material those whose deepest feelings and convictions would be seriously offended' (§67). The Court, in addressing the issues of 'pressing social need' and 'proportionality', took account of the fact that the prohibition concerned only the audiovisual media and related only to paid-for advertising as opposed to programming; the applicant's religious expression was not otherwise restricted (§74). Other factors included that a blanket ban could be justified given that it would be difficult to distinguish between religions in applying a ban, and that it was likely that even a limited freedom to advertise would benefit a dominant religion more than those religions with significantly fewer adherents and resources (§§77–78). The Court decided, therefore, that, given the margin of appreciation accorded to the State in such matters, the State had demonstrated that there were 'relevant and sufficient' reasons justifying the interference and there had been no violation of the Convention (§82).

***Independent News and Media v. Ireland***

*189. Independent News and Media v. Ireland* originated as a defamation case taken by a prominent politician, Proinnsias de Rossa against the *Sunday Independent*, which was the largest circulation Sunday newspaper in Ireland, selling some 250,000 copies each week.[199] At the time, in 1992, Mr de Rossa, who was a member of the Oireachtas (parliament) and leader of a political party (Democratic Left), was engaged in post-election negotiations about his party's possible participation in government. The offending article was written by a well-known journalist, who commented on a recently discovered letter dating from 1986 that had been sent to the Central Committee of the Communist Party of the Soviet Union and bore what appeared to be the signature

198. Application no. 44179/98, judgment of 10 Jul. 2003.
199. Application No. 55120/00, judgment of 16 Jun. 2005.

of Mr de Rossa, although this was denied by Mr de Rossa during the court hearings and claimed to be a forgery. The letter referred to 'special activities' that had served to fund the Workers' Party, a political party of which Mr de Rossa had previously been leader. The article stated that the 'special activities' referred to were criminal, that among the crimes committed were armed robberies and forgery of currency. After two aborted trials of the defamation action, a High Court jury in 1997 found that Mr de Rossa had been defamed and awarded him IEP 300,000 (the equivalent of approximately EUR 380,000), as well as his legal costs. This amount of damages was three times more than the highest libel award (IEP 90,000) previously approved by the Supreme Court. The newspaper therefore appealed to that court on the basis inter alia that the damages awarded were excessive and disproportionate to the harm done. However, the Supreme Court, having considered the relevant provisions of the Constitution and the relevant Irish and English case law, as well as making reference to the case law of the ECtHR, found in favour of Mr de Rossa. The Chief Justice stated:

> Bearing in mind that a fundamental principle of the law of compensatory damages is that the award must always be reasonable and fair and bear a due correspondence with the injury suffered and not be disproportionate thereto, I am not satisfied that the award made by the jury in this case went beyond what a reasonable jury applying the law to all the relevant considerations could reasonably have awarded and is not disproportionate to the injury suffered by the Respondent.[200]

*190.* The newspaper then lodged a complaint with the ECtHR in Strasbourg, claiming that the domestic safeguards against disproportionately high jury awards in libel cases were inadequate, an argument they had also raised in the Irish Supreme Court. Although there were clear differences between the two, the Court took the view that the *Tolstoy Miloslavsky v. United Kingdom*[201] judgment should be its point of departure in examining this case and quoted extensively from it. It accepted as a matter of principle that unpredictably large damages' awards in libel cases were capable of having a chilling effect on freedom of expression and therefore required the most careful scrutiny (§114). Moreover, it held that 'a general finding that an award of damages is "unusual" is sufficient to prompt its review of the adequacy and effectiveness of the domestic safeguards against disproportionate awards'. However, the ECtHR gave credence to the 'requirement in Irish domestic law that jury awards in libel cases be proportionate' as it was 'the absence of this proportionality requirement in English law which meant that the libel award in the Tolstoy Miloslavsky case was considered to be 'particularly open to question'' (at §128, referring to §49 of the *Tolstoy* judgment). Consequently, the ECtHR concluded (at §132, Judge Barreto dissenting) that there was no violation of Article 10, as, 'having regard to the particular circumstances of the present case, notably the measure of appellate control, and the margin of appreciation accorded to a State in this context, the Court does not find that it has been demonstrated

200. *De Rossa v. Independent Newspapers* [1999] IESC 63, at §145. Denham, J. delivered a dissenting judgment in which she found that the award of damages was excessive.

201. Series A No. 323, judgment of 13 Jul. 1995. Regarding the differences between the two cases, *see* , for example, the ECtHR's own acknowledgment of some of the differences at §118 and §123.

that there were ineffective or inadequate safeguards against a disproportionate award of the jury in the present case'.

***Independent Newspapers v. Ireland***

*191.* In June 2017, the ECtHR gave judgment in the case in which Independent Newspapers had challenged a defamation award of EUR 1.25 million to Monica Leech, who claimed that a number of articles published by them intimated that she had obtained public contracts as a PR consultant because she was having an extra-marital affair with the then Government Environment Minister. She had originally been awarded EUR 1.872 million by a High Court jury but the Supreme Court, which would normally order a re-trial in such a case rather than substitute its own amount, reduced the award on the basis that the amount of damages was 'so disproportionate to the injury suffered and wrong done that no reasonable jury would have made such an award'. The ECtHR found unanimously, however, that even the lower award violated the right to freedom of expression, under Article 10 ECHR. Even the lower amount was higher than any award ever made by a jury or appellate court and the Supreme Court had not explained how it had arrived at that figure.[202]Besides, the Supreme Court had indicated that it did not consider the defamation to be one of the gravest or most serious. As 'unpredictably high damages in libel cases are considered capable of having a chilling effect' on freedom of expression, the ECtHR stated, 'they therefore require the most careful scrutiny and very strong justification'. (Paragraph 104 of the judgment)

***Keena and Kennedy v. Ireland***

*192.* The case of *Keena and Kennedy v. Ireland* was declared inadmissible by the Fifth section of the ECtHR in 2014.[203] The case concerned an unusual situation of legal costs being awarded against the applicants, a journalist and a former editor of *The Irish Times* newspaper, in their *successful* appeal to the Supreme Court. They appealed against an order of the High Court requiring them to appear before the Mahon Tribunal to answer questions regarding their source of information, contained in a copy of a letter, about the financial dealings of a former Taoiseach (Prime Minister). The case in the domestic courts, therefore, revolved around the issue of protection of journalists' sources. Although, the right of journalists to protect their sources was upheld by the Supreme Court, the fact that the journalists had destroyed the relevant document, led the Court to, in effect, 'punish' the journalists by requiring them to pay the costs of the hearing. Normally, legal costs are awarded to successful litigants. However, the ECtHR found that the role of the judiciary had been undermined and that as a general principle, costs were a matter for the discretion of the domestic courts. Furthermore, the order for costs in the circumstances of this case could have no impact on public interest journalists who vehemently protect their sources yet recognize and respect the rule of law.

---

202. *Independent Newspapers (Ireland) Limited v. Ireland*, Application no. 28199/15, judgment of 15 Jun. 2017 (Fifth Division). For further analysis, *see* T. McGonagle, Case-note, *Independent Newspapers (Ireland) v Ireland, European Human Rights Cases* 2017-12, no. 213, available at: https://www.ivir.nl/publicaties/download/Annotatie_EHRC_2017_12.pdf.

203. Application No. 29804/10. Decision of 30 September 2014 available at: http://hudoc.echr.coe.int/eng?i=001-147707.

# Part I. Freedom of Speech

## §1. Constitutional Framework

*193.* Article 40.6.1 of the Irish Constitution guarantees freedom of expression. The language used to do so is rather tentative and cautious but a positive right is nonetheless guaranteed, albeit within a framework of restrictions. The right is essentially a right to express one's opinions and convictions, subject to considerations of public order and morality. The right of the media to freedom of expression is specifically recognized and is justified by reference to the role of the media as organs of public opinion; their freedom of expression is, however, firmly circumscribed. The text reads as follows:

> The State guarantees liberty for the exercise of the following rights, subject to public order and morality:–
>
> (1) The right of the citizens to express freely their convictions and opinions.
>
> The education of public opinion being, however, a matter of such grave import to the common good, the State shall endeavour to ensure that organs of public opinion, such as the radio, the press, the cinema, while preserving their rightful liberty of expression, including criticism of Government policy, shall not be used to undermine public order or morality or the authority of the State.
>
> The publication or utterance of blasphemous, seditious, or indecent matter is an offence which shall be punishable in accordance with law.

*194.* A close analysis of the wording shows up some inconsistencies. The right of the citizens is said to be to express 'freely' their convictions and opinions, but that freedom is subject to public order and morality, as is stated at the beginning of the Article. Also, although there is considerable emphasis on public order and morality, which are referred to twice, they are not the only competing interests expressly mentioned. The media clause also refers to the requirement not to 'undermine the authority of the State'. The final sentence adds to the list of restrictions by singling out the publication or utterance of blasphemous, seditious, or indecent matter as offences. It is peculiar to find such a provision in a Constitution but it reflects abiding concerns in 1937 when the Constitution was drafted. Ireland was a predominantly Roman Catholic country (hence blasphemy and indecency) and an independent one only since 1922, still vulnerable following a civil war in the early 1920s and its aftermath (hence sedition).

*195.* Despite these weaknesses in the formulation, there is a positive, though limited, right at the core of Article 40.6.1.i, which all citizens have, to express 'freely' their thoughts, beliefs and views. As this amounts to a freedom to comment, some doubt existed for a time as to whether it included the freedom to express facts or to impart factual information. However, the Supreme Court held in *Roy Murphy v. IRTC,*[204] citing Barrington J. in *Irish Times Ltd v. Ireland,*[205] that Article 40.6.1.i included the right to communicate facts. Barrington J. on behalf of the Court stated that Article 40.6.1 is concerned with the public activities of the citizen in a democratic society. The right is a right not only to communicate opinions but also to communicate the facts on which those opinions are based. The Court also held *obiter* that Article 40.6.1 extends to commercial speech. The Court doubted if the guarantee in Article 40.6.1 was confined to those who wished to influence public opinion. Thus an advertisement, though apparently directed at an individual consumer, may be included, whether intended to influence consumers generally or not.

*196.* The right protected is thus a right to freedom of expression, including comment and fact, commercial and artistic speech as well as political speech. It is a qualified right, subject to a number of restrictions and considerations in practice, and not an absolute right. Furthermore, freedom of expression is subject to other restrictions referred to elsewhere in the Constitution and not just those specifically included in Article 40.6.1. These other restrictions include those justified by reference to the right to one's good name, which is a personal right under Article 40.3.1, and the right to a fair trial, in Article 38.

*197.* In addition, the Constitution houses a number of so-called unspecified or unenumerated rights, which may impinge on or interact with freedom of expression. Such rights are unspoken; they are left to the courts to identify, by reference to Article 40.3.1 and the words 'in particular' in Article 40.3.2, which signal that other personal rights are intended to be protected. The text of Article 40.3.1 and 2 is as follows:

(1) The State guarantees in its laws to respect, and, as far as practicable, by its laws to defend and vindicate the personal rights of the citizen.
(2) The State shall, in particular, by its laws protect as best it may from unjust attack and, in the case of injustice done, vindicate the life, person, good name, and property rights of every citizen.

*198.* Among the unspecified rights identified by the courts to date under this provision are the right to travel, to communicate, to earn a livelihood, to marital privacy and to privacy in one's telephone conversations. A further such right, as discussed below, is the right of the public to be informed. From the point of view of the media, the key rights in the Constitution are the right to freedom of expression and to communicate, but also the countervailing rights to good name and to privacy.

---

204. *Murphy v. Independent Radio and Television Commission* [1997] IEHC 71 (High Court); [1999] 1 I.R. 12; [1998] 2 ILRM 360.
205. *Irish Times Ltd. v. Ireland* [1997] IEHC 30 (High Court); [1998] 1 I.R. 359; [1998] 2 ILRM 161 (available at: www.bailii.org/.

## I. The Right to Communicate

*199.* As communication is vital to our existence as social beings, the right to communicate has been recognized by the courts since the 1980s as one of the unspecified personal rights guaranteed protection by the Constitution in Article 40.3. It was first enunciated by Costello J. in the High Court case of *AG v. Paperlink*[206]and reaffirmed by him in *Kearney v. Ireland.*[207]In *Paperlink*, a case which concerned the state monopoly on postal communications under the Post Office Act 1908, Costello J. held that:

> … the act of communication is the exercise of such a basic human faculty that the right to communicate must inhere in the citizen by virtue of his human personality and must be guaranteed by the Constitution. … The exercise of the right to communicate can take many forms … I conclude that the very general and basic right to communicate which I am considering must be one of those personal unspecified rights of the citizen protected by Article 40.3.1.[208]

Such a right, however, is not absolute:

> But the right to communicate is obviously not an absolute one. Laws may restrict the nature of the matter communicated (for example, by prohibiting the communication of confidential information or treasonable, blasphemous, obscene or defamatory matter) and laws may also restrict the mode of communication (for example, by prohibiting communication by advertisement contrary to the planning code or by radio contrary to wireless telegraphy regulations). It follows, therefore, that it is not correct, and indeed, can be misleading, to suggest that the defendants enjoy a right to communicate 'freely'. Along with other citizens they enjoy a right to communicate.[209]

*200.* The nature of the right to communicate was further considered by Barrington J. in the Supreme Court in the case of *Irish Times Ltd v. Ireland.*[210]He concluded that it must include not only the right to communicate facts but also convictions, opinions and even feelings. In some respects, therefore, the rights to communicate and to freedom of expression may overlap and may be complementary. Barrington, J. took the view that the overlap could perhaps be attributed to the different philosophical systems from which the two rights derive.[211] In other words he made a distinction between the *private* nature of Article 40.3.1 and 40.3.2, from which the right to communicate stems, and the *public* nature of Article 40.6.1, which is the basis for freedom of expression. Article 40.3.1 and 40.3.2 concern personal – essentially private – rights of the citizen, whereas Article 40.6.1 is concerned with the public activities of the citizen in a democratic

206. [1984] ILRM 373.
207. [1986] I. R. 116.
208. [1984] ILRM 373, at 381–382.
209. *Ibid.*, at 382.
210. [1997] IEHC 30 (High Court), available at www.bailii.org/.
211. *Ibid.*

society. A person could be entitled to invoke both. Both are personal rights and can, in certain circumstances, be limited in the interests of the common good.

## II. A Right to Be Informed

*201.* As the courts, therefore, have recognized that the constitutional right to communicate includes information and ideas, and as communication is a two-way process, it follows that there must be a concomitant right to *receive* the information and ideas that communication comprises. Likewise, the constitutional guarantee of freedom of expression, which concerns the public activities of the citizen in a democratic society, must carry a corollary right of the public to be informed. Given the widely acknowledged role of the media in a democratic society in informing the citizenry, the media not only have the task of informing the public but the public also have a right to be informed through the media.

*202.* In this regard, Denham J. in the defamation case of *de Rossa v. Independent Newspapers*[212]spoke of a 'right to information' as one of the 'relevant unspecified rights' protected by Article 40.3.1 of the Constitution. While she did not define the right, she did go on to state that the rights protected by Article 10 of the ECHR are similar to the rights of freedom of expression and 'freedom to be informed' under the Irish Constitution. Hamilton C.J., in *Irish Times Ltd v. Ireland*[213] referred to the public's right to know and be informed by the media but without designating it as an unspecified right in the Constitution in the way that Denham J. did in *de Rossa*. Also in that case, O'Flaherty, J recognized such a right of the public in relation to information concerning the courts. Keane J., likewise, recognized such a right in relation to the courts but he derived it from Article 34 of the Constitution, which enshrines the principle of 'open justice', rather than from Articles 40.3.1 or 40.6.1.[214] In dealing with the specific issues before her in the *de Rossa* case, Denham J. went on to say (at §477) that information does not fetter discretion, and that specific information would aid decision-making.

## §2. Scope

*203.* The media, therefore, have a right to freedom of expression, which is expressly stated to include the right to criticize government policy. They also have the right to communicate information and ideas. There are, however, restrictions on media rights, some of which are imposed in the interests of the public at large, while others are imposed in the interests of the individual. Thus, the right to freedom of expression, including the right to criticize government policy, may be exercised only to the extent that it does not undermine public order, morality, or the authority of the State. Moreover, the publication or utterance of blasphemous, seditious or indecent matter is an offence punishable by law, according to the Constitution (Article 40.6.1.i) and applies to the

212. [1999] 4 I.R. 432, at §§153 and 154.
213. *Irish Times Ltd. v. Ireland* [1997] IEHC 30 (High Court); available at www.bailii.org/.
214. *Ibid.*

media as to all citizens. The elements of such offences are found in statute law and/ or common law.

*204.* Other restrictions on media rights arise from the constitutional protection of other rights besides those specifically mentioned in Article 40.6.1. These include the right of individuals and 'legal persons', i.e., incorporated bodies such as companies, to their good name or reputation (Article 40.3.1), to privacy (an unspecified right included in Article 40.3.1) and the rights associated with due process or fair trial (Article 38). Thus, good name and privacy must be respected and anything broadcast, printed or posted online that would tend to harm a person's good name or reputation, could lead to those responsible being sued in the courts for defamation. Likewise, any media report or commentary, whether broadcast, printed or posted online that interferes with the constitutional right to fair procedures and a fair trial can lead to a criminal prosecution for contempt of court.

*205.* The guarantees of freedom of speech and of the media enshrined in the Constitution are given effect mainly through legislation and common law. As noted above, all legislation passed by the Oireachtas must comply with the Constitution. Restrictions on freedom of speech are also for the most part set out in legislation but in some instances also in common law. For example, if a person's privacy is invaded by a broadcaster, it could amount to a breach of the privacy provisions of the Broadcasting Authority Acts. Invasions of privacy may form the subject of complaints to the Compliance Committee of the Broadcasting Authority or may result in a constitutional challenge in the courts, i.e., asserting that one's constitutional right to privacy has been breached, as happened in *Kennedy and Arnold v. Ireland* (tapping of journalists' telephones – above paragraph 150). Increasingly, however, as a result of the incorporation at sub-constitutional level of the ECHR (ECHR Act 2003), breach of privacy cases are argued on the basis of ECtHR decisions and principles. In the case of media reports or commentary being challenged on the basis that they may interfere with the right of an individual to a fair trial, the common law rules of contempt of court will normally be applied, although the ECtHR jurisprudence on Article 6 may also be raised if relevant. It may be noted also in this regard that the courts have often stated, as Denham, J. did in the *de Rossa* case referred to above, that the rights protected by Article 10 of the ECHR are similar to the rights of freedom of expression under the Irish Constitution.

## §3. No A Priori Censorship

*206.* There is no express or specific ban on censorship in the Constitution. Although the right to freedom of expression in Article 40.6.1i is preceded by reference to public order and morality (*see* text above at paragraph 15), there is no suggestion that *a priori* censorship is contemplated. With respect to the media, the State is enjoined to 'endeavour to ensure' that their rightful freedom of expression is preserved but that it shall not be used to undermine public order or morality or the authority of the State. It is not clear whether at the time the Constitution was enacted *a priori (ex ante)* or *a posteriori (ex post facto)* restrictions were contemplated. The publication or utterance of blasphemous, seditious, or indecent matter, on the other hand, appears to fall outside the scope of freedom of expression and is deemed to constitute an offence which shall be punishable in accordance with law. Thus, it is left to the legislature or the courts (common law) to set the boundaries and scope of the restrictions.

*207.* Prior to the coming into force of the 1937 Constitution, *a priori* censorship in the form of prior restraint on films and publications, was commonplace and, as explained above, it was several decades before the practice of banning publications, and films, eased before more or less ceasing in recent years. Indeed, the Censorship Acts in force at the time the Constitution came into force in 1937 were relatively recent (Censorship of Films Act 1923 and Censorship of Publications Act 1929) and continued to be vigorously implemented, as amended, until the last few decades of the twentieth century. From then onwards, the courts in interpreting the constitutional, legislative and common law provisions have recognized the seriousness of imposing prior restraints on freedom of expression and freedom of the media. As a result, there has been a strong presumption against prior restraint.

*208.* In defamation cases, the courts are very circumspect and will rarely grant injunctions prohibiting publication.[215] Under section 33 of the Defamation Act 2009, an order prohibiting publication will only be made if the statement is defamatory and the defendant has no defence to the action that is reasonably likely to succeed. Proposed privacy legislation (Privacy Bill 2006), if passed, would have authorized a court to make an order prohibiting 'any act that it considers would violate the privacy of the plaintiff' and to 'order the defendant to deliver to the plaintiff any documents, articles, photographs', and other materials (section 8).[216] The hearing could also be held in private (section 13). However, it was also proposed that there be a defence for an 'act of newsgathering', subject to requirements of good faith, public interest, public benefit, and fairness and reasonableness in all the circumstances (section 5(1)(e)). These were narrowly drawn and the Bill was much criticized on a number of freedom of expression grounds, including its potential for use *a priori* as a means to prevent publication, to 'gag' the media. As Eoin O'Dell put it: '[T]he Bill proposes that court action in respect of invasions of privacy could be held in private; and this would include hearings seeking temporary injunctions to restrain publication pending full trial of the action. This has raised the spectre of the defamation gagging writ of old simply being replaced by a shiny new privacy gagging writ.'[217] In other words, the Bill could have allowed individuals to halt publication on the grounds that the proposed publication 'would violate' their privacy. The Bill was not enacted.[218]

---

215. *See* further above paragraphs 155–161.
216. Bill Number 44 of 2006, available at: http://www.oireachtas.ie/documents/bills28/bills/2006/4406/b4406s.pdf.
217. O'Dell, 'Why McDowell needs to look again at this privacy bill', *Irish Independent*, 25 Sept. 2006, available at http://www.independent.ie/opinion/analysis/why-mcdowell-needs-to-look-again-at-this-privacy-bill-26366432.html. *See also* M. McGonagle, 'Reforming Media Law in Ireland: the new defamation and privacy Bills', 11(6) *Communications Law-Journal of Computer, Media and Telecommunications Law*, 195–200 (2006).
218. The Bill remains on the Government's programme of government. The Government's intention is to allow the Press Council and the courts to handle breach of privacy issues and only to impose specific privacy legislation if the Press Council fails to be effective in relation to the print media. However, unsuccessful attempts were made by a number of Senators in 2012 (Privacy Bill 2012) to bring in a Bill based on the 2006 one.

*209.* In relation to the reporting of court cases, the 'open justice' principle in Article 34 of the Constitution has been strictly interpreted by the courts, with the result that media reporting of court cases cannot be subject to prior restraint except where there is a 'real' risk that the trial will be unfair as a result of reporting and the risk cannot be overcome by less intrusive measures, such as warnings and directions to the jury, where there is a jury present.[219] The courts must be open to the public and media 'except in such special and limited cases as may be prescribed by law' and the media when present are entitled to report on behalf of the public in their role as the representatives of the public. Among the 'special and limited cases' prescribed by law, which provide for the media to be excluded from court, are family law cases, under the so-called in camera rule. This rule, however, has been relaxed to some extent under the Courts and Civil Law (Miscellaneous Provisions) Act 2013, section 5. The new provision enables bona fide representatives of the Press to attend family law proceedings. However, they can be excluded or their attendance restricted where, in proceedings under a relevant enactment, a court is satisfied that it is necessary to exclude the media:

(1) in order to preserve the anonymity of a party to the proceedings or any child to whom the proceedings relate,
(2) by reason of the nature or circumstances of the case, or
(3) as it is otherwise necessary in the interests of justice.

*210.* Likewise the reporting of evidence may be restricted or conditions imposed on it on those grounds. Factors that the court 'shall' take into account in making such decisions include the desirability of promoting public confidence in the administration of justice and various matters pertaining to the parties and the 'best interests' of a child to whom the proceedings relate. The list of matters that the court 'shall' take into account is long and wide-ranging, so it is questionable to what extent family courts will actually be open to media reporting in practice.[220] So far, however, the provision is having the effect of opening up family law proceedings and seems to be working reasonably well in practice.

## §4. Spectrum of a Posteriori Restrictive Measures

*211.* It is clear from the wording of both Article 40.3.2 and Article 40.6.1 of the Constitution that the rights to communicate and to freedom of expression can be subject to *a posteriori* restrictions. First and foremost, considerations of public order and morality can give rise to restrictions. This is so in the case of both the individual citizen and the media. The latter, as organs of public opinion, are subject to the additional restriction of not undermining the authority of the State. The exact meaning to the phrase 'the authority of the State' is unclear but appears to be wider than merely the security of the State. Laws providing for sanctions in respect of the utterance or publication of blasphemous, seditious or indecent matter are also mandated.

---

219. *See Irish Times v. Ireland* [1997] IEHC 30 (High Court); available at www.bailii.org/.
220. Act Number 32 of 2013, 24 Jul. 2013, available at www.irishstatutebook.ie.

*212.* Apart from these areas of restriction referred to in Article 40.6.1 itself, there are other grounds of *a posteriori* restriction contained elsewhere in the Constitution. Thus, freedom of expression may have to be balanced with the right to good name (Article 40.3.2); likewise with the right to privacy (Article 40.3.1–2) and the right to a fair trial (Article 38). The balancing is effected for the most part through legislation and in some instances common law. The Defamation Act 2009 is the current legislation protecting good name or reputation. There is no specific Privacy Act but the right to privacy is protected by a range of legislative provisions, common law and equity. The Broadcasting Act, for example, requires broadcasters not to unreasonably encroach on the privacy of the individual; the Data Protection Acts 1988–2003 set out the requirements for the handling of personal and sensitive personal data; the Freedom of Information Acts 1997–2014 contain an exception for privacy, while the Communications (Retention of Data) Act 2011 authorizes the retention of telephonic and e-mail data and enables the Garda Síochána (police), defence forces and revenues commissioners to access to retained data, subject to certain safeguards. The Copyright and Related Rights Acts 2000–2007 can be used indirectly in some circumstances to protect privacy. Common law torts such as nuisance and trespass also offer protection for privacy in certain circumstances, as does the breach of confidence derived from equity. In relation to the right to a fair trial, various provisions of legislation apply, as does the common law offence of contempt of court. The main areas of restriction are set out below:

- protection of reputation (Defamation Act 2009);
- protection of the rights of others (e.g., Broadcasting Act 2009, restrictions on political and religious advertising);
- protection against hate speech (Prohibition of Incitement to Hatred Act 1989);
- protection of public decency (various Criminal and Criminal Justice Acts, e.g., Criminal Justice (Public Order) Act 1994, as amended; Censorship of Films Acts 1923–1992; Video Recordings Acts 1989–1992 and Civil Law (Miscellaneous Provisions) Act 2008; Censorship of Publications Acts 1929–1972);
- protection of military secrets and public security (e.g., Offences against the State Acts 1939–1972; Official Secrets Act 1963; Freedom of Information Acts 1997–2014);
- protection of privacy (e.g., Broadcasting Act 2009); Data Protection Acts 1998–2003; common law torts and equity, including actions for breach of confidence);
- protection in relation to court reporting (various Criminal Law and Criminal Justice Acts; various Family Law Acts, e.g., Family Law (Divorce) Act 1996; various Child Law Acts, e.g., Child Care Act 1991 (as amended), Children Acts 2001–2007; Courts and Civil Law (Miscellaneous Provisions) Act 2013; Tribunals of Inquiry Acts 1921–1979; common law offences of contempt of court);
- protection of minors (e.g., Broadcasting Acts and Codes; Prohibition on Child Trafficking and Pornography Act 1998);
- protection of public health (e.g., Public Health (Tobacco) Act 2002–2004, prohibition of advertising for tobacco products; Regulation of Information (Services Outside the State for Termination of Pregnancies) Act 1995, advertising of abortion services);

- protection of consumers (e.g., advertising rules in Broadcasting Acts and Codes; ASAI Code);
- protection of commercial interests (e.g., Companies Acts 1963–1990; Freedom of Information Acts 1997–2014; Copyright and Related Rights Acts 2000–2007).

## §5. No Prior Authorization for Publishing

*213.* There is no prior registration requirement for the publication of newspapers in Ireland, other than the general regulations that apply to the establishment of companies. There is also a general requirement applicable to all printed matter intended for the public, contained in the Offences against the State Act 1939 (section 14), that the printer's name and address be on all such documents. There is, however, an exception to this requirement in the case of newspapers printed on their own premises. There are no prior registration requirements for publishing on the Internet, apart from the regulation of domain names.[221]

*214.* A licence is required for broadcasting, however, and the conditions of the licence must be adhered to, but otherwise there is no prior authorization required for what is broadcast. Post-broadcast monitoring of programme content and advertising is carried out in accordance with the provisions of the Broadcasting Acts. Pre-vetting of broadcast advertisements is carried out by RTÉ, the national public service broadcaster. Prior to going to air, all radio and television advertisements must first be cleared for broadcast by RTÉ's internal Copy Clearance Committee, who consider both the verbal and visual content of the commercial, along with its suitability for broadcast, and its compliance with all existing legal and industry codes for advertising, as well as RTÉ's own internal guidelines.[222] Provisions in the Broadcasting Act impose certain obligations on broadcasters and include sanctions for breach of these provisions or of BAI codes. The BAI codes include requirements of fairness and impartiality in news and current affairs reporting, and not unreasonably encroaching on the privacy of individuals.

*215.* The Central Copy Clearance Ireland (CCCI) since 2003 pre-vets all alcohol advertisements against the BAI regulations and the ASAI self-regulatory code. No alcohol advertisements can appear on the Irish media before pre-vetting and obtaining a certificate from CCCI. Continuous monitoring of media advertisements generally has been conducted by ASAI since 2007, and the compliance rate has been as high as 99%.[223] Clearance from the UK-based Cinema Advertising Association (CAA) is required in order to show a commercial at cinemas in Republic of Ireland and Northern Ireland. No commercial may be exhibited in a cinema unless it has been cleared. The

---

221. *See* Electronic Commerce Act 2000 and S.I. 68 of 2003, European Communities (Directive 2000/31/EC) Regulations 2003, implementing EC Directive 2000/31/EC of the European Parliament and of the Council of 8 Jun. 2000 on certain legal aspects of information society services, in particular electronic commerce, in the Internal Market (Directive on electronic commerce), *OJ L 178,* 17 Jul. 2000, 1.
222. http://www.rte.ie/mediasales/television/traffic-copy-clearance.html.
223. *See* ASAI Annual Report 2010.

purpose of pre-vetting all cinema commercials is to ensure conformity with relevant advertising codes.[224]

224. http://www.cinemaadvertisingassociation.co.uk/about.php.

# Part II. Regulation of Print Media

## Chapter 1. The Journalists' Profession

### §1. Notion of Journalist

*216.* There are no legal requirements for prior registration or notification in order to work as a journalist in Ireland. Entry to journalism is open to all, and no specific academic or vocational qualifications are necessary, although most journalists now come through journalism courses offered by the Universities and various private colleges. There is no legislation concerning access to the practice of journalism. In specific legislation that contains provisions entitling the press to attend court cases not open to the general public, for example, access is permitted to those in possession of a 'press card', indicating that they are bona fide representatives of identified media organizations. The Courts and Civil Law (Miscellaneous Provisions) Act 2013, for instance, envisages 'bona fide representatives of the Press' being permitted to attend hearings that previously would have been held *in camera* and would therefore have excluded the press. However, there is no definition of 'bona fide representatives' in this Act or in any of the preceding legislation, such as the Bail Act 1997 or the Children Act 2001, which makes reference to 'bona fide representatives of the press'. This lack of definition has been criticized by the Ombudsman for Children.[225]

*217.* As stated above, the National Union of Journalists (NUJ) represents journalists working all over the island of Ireland. There are over 3,500 members in the Republic and 800 in Northern Ireland. Members include journalists, photographers and creative artists working editorially in newspapers, magazines, books, broadcasting, public relations and information, online/interactive and also advertising and fashion photographers, advertising copywriters and editorial computer systems workers. The vast majority of journalists in Ireland are members of the NUJ, a trade union which is organized at the national level in Ireland as the Irish branch of the National Union of Journalists in the UK. The activities of the union in Ireland are overseen by the Irish Executive Council facilitated by a full-time staff based in Dublin. At its head is the Assistant Secretary (Ireland) or 'Irish Secretary'. His/her responsibility includes the management of all union activities in Ireland, industrial matters relating to broadcasting

225. Advice of the Ombudsman for Children on the Courts Bill 2013, June 2013, available at http://www.oco.ie/assets/files/publications/Advice%20of%20the%20Ombudsman%20for%20Children%20on%20the%20Courts%20Bill%202013.pdf.

on the island of Ireland (except the BBC), freelance, newspapers, press and public relations in Northern Ireland. S/he is also responsible for industrial relations policy in the island of Ireland and governmental policy in the Republic. At the local level the NUJ operates in the form of 'chapels'. The chapel is the NUJ's workplace-based organization and is established wherever there are three or more members in an office or organization or where student members are attending a course of study. The chapel is responsible for maintaining and extending union organization in such office or organization; ensuring that union agreements are observed; seeking to ensure that its members uphold the code of conduct and that management recognizes and respects the code of conduct; and for safeguarding members' interests generally. The union seeks to defend and promote the professional and financial interests and welfare of its members, to promote the principles and practice of journalism, to defend and promote freedom of the media, speech and information and trade union principles and organization.

## I. NUJ Code of Conduct and Guidelines

*218.* The NUJ's Code of Conduct (*see* paragraph 171) has set out the main principles of British and Irish journalism since 1936. The code is part of the rules and all journalists joining the union must sign that they will strive to adhere to it.[226]The union has published, or supports, a range of guidelines on reporting issues such as terrorism, race, asylum and immigration, HIV, age and disability. In addition, there are NUJ, IFJ and suicide prevention groups' guidelines on reporting suicide and guidelines on reporting refugees in Ireland.

## II. Press Council of Ireland

*219.* Membership of the Press Council of Ireland is open to all print media organizations. The National Union of Journalists is represented on the Council, whose members are national and regional newspapers and magazines, published in Ireland. This includes Irish editions of British newspapers that circulate in Ireland. Otherwise, British newspapers are subject to the equivalent press complaints body (formerly the Press Complaints Commission, now the Independent Press Standards body (IPSO)) in London. Both print and online versions of member newspapers and magazines are subject to the Press Council's code of practice. Applications for membership have been received from online news sites and bloggers. Other publications, such as student publications, voluntarily commit to the PCI code of practice.

## III. Court Pronouncements on Journalists

*220.* Just as the Press Council grapples with the decision whether to widen the scope of its membership to new forms of media, the Irish courts have also addressed

226. The text of the Code is available at paragraph 171 above and at http://ethicnet.uta.fi/ireland/code_of_conduct.

the issue. In *Cornec v. Morrice*[227] a question arose as to whether a blogger could claim journalistic privilege in order to protect the identity of his sources. The court observed that a blogger 'is not a journalist in the strict sense of the term' but that 'the traditional distinction between journalists and laypeople has broken down in recent decades, not least with the rise of social media' (at §65). The judge held that 'A person who blogs on an internet site can just as readily constitute an 'organ of public opinion' (as per Article 40.6.1 of the Irish Constitution) as those which were more familiar in 1937 and which are mentioned (but only as examples) in Article 40.6.1, namely, the radio, the press and the cinema' (at §66). Therefore, the blogger had 'a similar interest' to that of a journalist 'in ensuring that his sources are likewise protected'. (at §67).

*221.* The Irish courts were slow to recognize the freedom of expression of the media and tended to focus instead on the often competing rights, such as the right to good name, enshrined in the Constitution. Strong pronouncements on the importance of the role of journalists began to emerge from the Supreme Court in particular, in the 1990s, and from that time onwards, the courts have taken a more considered account of the rights of journalists in weighing competing rights. The judgments of the Supreme Court judges in *Irish Times v. Ireland,*[228]a case which concerned court reporting, for instance, referred to the media as 'the eyes and ears of the public' and strongly recognized their important role in a democracy in informing the public. There is no doubt that the ECHR has exerted influence on the domestic courts in that regard.

## §2. Subsidies to the Press

*222.* Generally speaking, the printed press in Ireland are not subsidized. The only subsidies to the press are those allocated to Irish-language publications.[229] The weekly newspaper *Gaelscéal* was allocated EUR 1.6 million for a four-year period 2010–2014. Metro Éireann, a multicultural newspaper with sales of 10,000 copies and a strong subscription base, was founded in 2000 but was still not profitable when it became a weekly in 2006 and needed to attract more advertising.[230] Funding, where available, comes from various community and other government schemes and agencies.

*223.* Another form of subsidy for the printed press is the reduced level of VAT that applies to newspapers and periodicals. VAT on newspaper sales is levied at 13.5%, and, while that is a reduced rate in an Irish context, where the standard rate is 23% and the lowest rate 9%, it is still high in comparison with other European countries. Discounted postal rates also apply to newspapers and periodicals, which must pre-register and pay a small annual registration fee in order to avail of them.[231]

227. 2012 IEHC 376; judgment of Hogan J., High Court, 18 Sept. 2012; available at www.bailii.org.
228. *Irish Times v. Ireland* [1997] IEHC 30 (High Court); available at www.bailii.org/.
229. Irish-language weekly newspapers received more than €300,000 per annum in subsidies from the State, with total funding for Irish-language publications (8 print and one online) in 2010 amounting to EUR 567,694. *See* Foras na Gaeilge, *Media Report*, p. 16, quoting Máiread Ní Chinnéide, 13 Nov. 2010, and also the table at p. 52.
230. BBC News available at http://news.bbc.co.uk/2/hi/uk_news/northern_ireland/7144216.stm.
231. *See* http://www.anpost.ie.

# Chapter 2. Journalists' Rights

## §1. Role of Journalists as Watchdogs of Society

*224.* Under the common law, journalists did not have any greater rights than ordinary citizens and there was no recognition of the journalist/source relationship such as would give rise to a privilege against disclosure of the identity of a source. This was despite the fact that other relationships, such as priest/penitent, lawyer/client, did give rise to such a privilege.

*225.* Under the Constitution, journalists have the same rights to freedom of expression as all other citizens. The Constitution does, however, specifically mention the media and their role as 'organs of public opinion'. The freedom of expression clause pertaining to the media points to the importance of the 'education of public opinion' to the 'common good' but, while prompting the State to preserve the media's 'rightful liberty of expression', puts an onus on the State to ensure that the media are not used to undermine public order or morality or the authority of the State. Indeed, for many decades the freedom of expression guaranteed in the Constitution was regarded as too weak to support claims for enhanced protections for journalists. Lawyers rarely raised arguments based on it in defamation cases, which were fought largely according to the common law tradition. Judges, too, who were trained in that tradition, were reluctant to engage with freedom of expression arguments in defamation cases, since the right to good name was clearly protected as one of the personal rights of the citizen in Article 40.3.1.

*226.* Also, journalists were often held to be in contempt of court either as a result of refusing to reveal their sources to a court or for publishing reports or articles found to 'scandalize' the court, i.e., to bring the court into disrepute or to interfere with the administration of justice; or for publishing material 'calculated' to prejudice the right to a fair trial. The situation began to change gradually in that regard with pronouncements such as that of the Supreme Court in the case of *Cullen v. Tóibín* in 1984. The Court referred to the matter of the freedom of the press and of communication which is guaranteed by the Constitution and which cannot be 'lightly curtailed'. It should only be curtailed or restricted, the Court said, where it was 'necessary' to do so for the administration of justice.[232] In 1988, the Supreme Court adopted a test of proportionality, recognizing that:

> the law … must reflect a due balancing of the constitutional right to freedom of expression and the constitutional protection of every citizen's good name.[233]

---

232. [1984] ILRM 577, at 581.
233. *Hynes-O'Sullivan.v. O'Driscoll* [1988] IR 436 at p. 450, [1989] ILRM 349 at 361 – a non-media case.

*227.* In later cases, the higher courts began to refer more often to the centrality of freedom of expression, and freedom of the media, to democracy.[234] The unanimous decision of the Supreme Court in *Irish Times v. Ireland* in 1998 was a watershed. Indeed, the watchdog role of the media, as such, was not expounded in depth by the courts until the Supreme Court judgments in that case.[235] The case concerned the open justice principle and the right of the media to report contemporaneously on court cases. The five judges located the right of the media firmly in the Constitutional context, relying on the media role in the 'education of public opinion' and as 'organs of public opinion'. Rather than a right of the media, as such, the judges focused on the right of the public to be informed by the media. Hamilton, C.J., for example, propounded the view that 'the right of the wider public to be informed by the media …', in this case about the operation of the courts, was a matter 'of the greatest importance' (at §383). Denham, J. (dissenting) in a subsequent defamation case, *de Rossa v. Independent Newspapers,* spoke of 'the right to information' as one of the 'relevant unspecified rights protected by Article 40.3.1 0 of the Constitution'.[236]

*228.* The main catalyst for change was undoubtedly the jurisprudence of the ECtHR. Long before Ireland incorporated the Convention in 2003, it had ratified it and was guided by the jurisprudence of the ECtHR in relevant cases.[237] In fact, the Constitution Review Group in 1996 recommended that Article 40.6.1 of the Constitution be re-modelled in line with the wording of Article 10 ECHR.[238] In the years immediately prior to 2003, the courts frequently referred to Article 10 and the jurisprudence of the ECtHR in freedom of expression and media cases. The High Court in *Jonathan v. Ireland* in 2002, echoing the words of the ECtHR, referred to the ' *"chilling effect"* of the legislation which could have had the effect of restricting the media'.[239]

*229.* Since the incorporation of the ECHR Act in 2003, although at sub-constitutional level, ECHR principles are argued before the High Court and Supreme Court and the judges of those courts refer extensively to Article 10 ECHR in cases concerning journalists and freedom of expression. By 2007 a High Court judge was to refer to the 'cardinal importance' of press freedom and to state that any restriction on it had to be proportionate and no more than was necessary to promote the legitimate

234. Denham, J. in *Irish Times v. Ireland* in 1998, at 399, for example, spoke of freedom of expression as being central to democratic government to enable democracy to function. *See also* Barrington, J. in *Murphy v. IRTC* [1999] 1 I.R. 12 at p. 24.
235. *Irish Times v. Ireland* [1997] IEHC 30 (High Court); available at www.bailii.org/.
236. [1999] IESC 63, at §153); [1999] 4 IR 432 (30 Jul. 1999).
237. Up until 2003, when the ECHR Act was passed, Ireland was a dualist state in the sense that the ECHR was not part of Irish law and therefore did not have to be considered by Irish courts. Nonetheless, there are significant examples of cases involving the role of journalists in which the court did take account of Art. 10. *See* generally, Marie McGonagle, *Media Law,* 2003.
238. *Report of the Constitution Review Group,* Pn 2632, Government Publications, Dublin, 1996.
239. [2002] IEHC 59 (31 May 2002). The case concerned restrictions on media reporting in s. 19 of the Refugee Act 1996.

object of the restriction.[240] In the same year, a divisional (three-member) High Court in *Mahon Tribunal v. Keena & anor*, having reviewed the relevant case law of the ECtHR, spoke of 'the critical importance of a free press as an essential organ in a democratic society'. By 2009, in an appeal from the High Court in the same case, the Supreme Court, relying heavily on *Goodwin v. UK* and other relevant Article 10 case law of the ECtHR, had firmly copper-fastened the tentative protection for journalists' sources that had been gradually emerging in Ireland.[241]

## I. The Role of Journalists as Watchdogs

*230.* The role of the media is recognized in the Constitution, which refers to their 'rightful liberty of expression, including criticism of Government policy'. As seen above, the courts, as interpreters of the Constitution, have recognized the right of journalists to report on court cases, and their right to protect the identity of their sources. They have also recognized the important role they play in informing the public.

*231.* While there is no Press Law as such in Ireland, some legislation contains provisions which apply specifically to journalists and media, or are more general and are intended to safeguard freedom of expression, including that of the media. The Defamation Act 2009, for instance, introduced a new defence of fair and reasonable publication on a matter of public interest, which, as noted above, is a type of *Reynolds* defence, somewhat similar to that introduced by the House of Lords in the UK. The defence is intended to benefit journalists reporting on a public interest story, who, despite taking reasonable steps to check out their story, end up being pursued for defamation. In essence it is a defence of responsible journalism but in practice it is likely to be difficult to plead successfully, given the requirements of both fairness and reasonableness and a list of factors that the court must take into account, where relevant, in deciding whether the defendants have established it.[242] In a 'carrot and stick' approach, the legislation also provides for the track record of print media in adhering to the Press Council's code of practice to be taken into account if relying on certain other defences (*see* paragraph 307 below).

*232.* The Freedom of Information Acts do not make any special arrangements for or grant any special privileges to journalists, as such, although there is a provision that should avail journalists in some circumstances, namely, if 'some or all of the information contained in the record concerned would be of particular assistance to the understanding of an issue of national importance', fees can be reduced or waived (section 27(6)). The Data Protection Acts contain an exemption for journalists in cases

240. *Mahon v. Post Publications* [2005] IEHC 307, Kelly, J.; upheld by the Supreme Court: [2007] IESC 15, where Fennelly, J observed: 'The courts do not pass judgment on whether any particular exercise of the right of freedom of expression is in the public interest. The media are not required to justify publication by reference to any public interest other than that of freedom of expression itself. They are free to publish material which is not in the public interest.' (at §42).

241. High Court 23 Oct. 2007; Supreme Court [2009] IESC 64.

242. How the defence will work in practice is not yet clear. *See:Meegan v. Times Newspapers Limited t/a The Sunday Times*[2016] IECA 327, available at www.baillii.org.

where personal data are processed only for journalistic, artistic or literary purposes (section 21, *see* above paragraph 129).

*233.* The Code of Conduct of the NUJ (paragraphs 171–172 above) requires journalists to uphold and defend the principle of media freedom, the right of freedom of expression and the right of the public to be informed. The Preamble to the Code of Practice of the Press Council states:

> The freedom to publish is vital to the right of the people to be informed. This freedom includes the right of a newspaper to publish what it considers to be news, without fear or favour, and the right to comment upon it.

It goes on to acknowledge, however, that:

> Freedom of the press carries responsibilities. Members of the press have a duty to maintain the highest professional and ethical standards.

While setting out the standards that journalists and print media must adhere to, the Code clearly states that newspapers and magazines are entitled to advocate strongly their own views on topics (2.1) and that readers are entitled to expect that the content of a publication reflects the best judgment of editors and writers and has not been inappropriately influenced by undisclosed interests (2.3). As in the NUJ code, there is recognition of the importance of protection of sources to journalists and a statement that journalists shall protect confidential sources of information (6).

## §2. Journalists' Independence

### I. Written Press

*234.* As discussed above, the 'rightful liberty of expression' of the media is provided for in the Constitution and the courts have recognized the role of the media in a democratic society, including the need for journalists to be independent. There is no Press or Media Act as such in Ireland or any written law that expressly provides for journalistic or editorial independence in the print media. The Defamation Act 2009 does provide, however, that the Press Council shall be independent in the performance of its functions and that the seven directors of the Board shall be independent public interest directors, selected by an independent panel.

*235.* Editorial independence is addressed in the codes of both the NUJ and the Press Council. Principle 8 of the Code of Conduct of the NUJ states that a journalist:

> Resists threats or any other inducements to influence, distort or suppress information and takes no unfair personal advantage of information gained in the course of her/his duties before the information is public knowledge.

Principle 2.3 of the Press Council Code of Practice states that:

> Readers are entitled to expect that the content of a publication reflects the best judgment of editors and writers and has not been inappropriately influenced by undisclosed interests. Wherever relevant, any significant financial interest of an organization should be disclosed. Writers should disclose significant potential conflicts of interest to their editors.

## II. Audiovisual Media

*236.* In contrast to the print media, there are laws pertaining specifically to broadcast media. The current laws are the Broadcasting Act 2009 and various codes which it mandates; some secondary legislation in the form of Statutory Instruments (S.I.s), e.g., S.I. 258 of 2010, which along with the Broadcasting Act 2009, completed the transposition of AVMSD for linear, and to some extent, non-linear, services. There is also a Code of Conduct for ODAS.

*237.* The Broadcasting Act 2009 sets out *inter alia* broadcast journalists' duties and obligations. With regard to independence, the Broadcasting Act 2009 provides that the broadcasting regulator, BAI, and each of its statutory committees, shall be independent in the performance of their functions (section 24) and that its duties shall include providing a regulatory environment that will sustain independent and impartial journalism (section 25(2)(d)). In drafting codes, BAI is required to take account *inter alia* of the desirability of maintaining the independence of editorial control over programme content (section 42(3)(f)). As might be expected, the public service broadcasters are required to be independent in the pursuance of their objects (section 97) and in addition, all board members of the PSB corporations must safeguard the independence of the corporation, as regards the conception, content and production of programmes, the editing and presentation of news and current affairs programmes and the definition of programme schedules from State, political and commercial influence (section 87(d)). One of the functions of the Director General of a corporation (public service broadcaster) is to act as editor-in-chief in respect of content published by the corporation in pursuance of its objects under this Act (section 89(2)(b)).

*238.* Editorial independence is generally well protected and respected in Ireland but from time to time there are some concerns. For instance, the dominant player in the media market is now Denis O'Brien, who has a major involvement in radio broadcasting and has a 29.9% share in Independent News and Media (INM), the largest print media group in the State. Over the years Mr O'Brien has sued or threatened to sue a number of journalists for criticisms they have made of him on air or in print. One of those journalists, Sam Smyth, an experienced and widely respected investigative journalist, was removed from a radio programme he presented on Today FM, a station owned by Mr O'Brien[243] and claimed his removal was as a result of his criticism of Mr O'Brien in the context of the Moriarty Tribunal, although a different reason was given by Today FM. A fellow journalist who presented a programme on Newstalk FM,

243. *See* , for example, two articles published in the *Irish Examiner* on 22 Aug. 2012; available at: http://www.irishexaminer.com/archives/2012/0822/world/smyth-writes-back-in-row-over-departure-204908.html; and http://www.irishexaminer.com/archives/2012/0822/opinion/media-control-dominance-not-good-for-democracy-204887.html.

another radio station owned by Mr O'Brien, who supported Mr Smyth, was told he would have to take a 50% pay cut. He resigned.[244]

*239.* In February 2013 it was reported that an editorial charter for its journalists was produced by INM.[245] If it had been proceeded with, the charter would have required journalists *inter alia* to obtain the written approval of the company's managing editor before they would write any 'sustained or repeated adversarial material concerning individuals or organisations'. The charter was to apply to all those who are involved in INM's newspapers, periodicals, and online and digital platforms in Ireland. However, in 2015, a revised 'INM Editorial Code of Practice', without the above-mentioned provisions, was issued, with the Press Council code appended. More recently, in September 2017, all Irish Times journalists were banned by Newstalk and Today FM from appearing on their radio programmes as a result of criticism levelled at Newstalk by Irish Times columnist, Fintan O'Toole, following a controversy about opinions on rape expressed on air by a Newstalk presenter.[246] As the two stations are licensed by BAI, it is reported to be considering the situation.

## §3. Protection of Journalistic Sources

*240.* The common law did not recognize a privilege for journalists to protect their sources. Indeed, the law of contempt of court treated journalists like all other citizens, requiring them to answer questions in court even if it meant having to identify their sources. The penalty for not doing so was an immediate fine and/or imprisonment. Journalists adhering to their code of conduct (NUJ Code), which required them to protect their sources, often faced the threat of jail sentences. A broadcast journalist was sentenced to three months imprisonment in 1973 but on appeal his sentence was converted to a fine.[247] Another journalist who broke a major story in a Granada television programme in the UK about irregularities in the beef processing industry in Ireland was brought before the District Court in Ireland to face a criminal prosecution. The trial, however, failed on a technicality.[248]

*241.* The turning point was the decision of the ECtHR in *Goodwin v. UK* in 1996, which stressed that '[P]rotection of journalistic sources is one of the basic

244. *See* http://www.freedomhouse.org/report/freedom-press/2012/ireland; *see also* an opinion piece published in *The Irish Times* by another journalist, Vincent Browne, who was also sued by O'Brien: http://www.irishtimes.com/debate/o-brien-s-control-of-inm-should-be-stopped-1.542869?page=2.

245. *See* Roy Greenslade of the *Guardian* newspaper in the UK, 28 Feb. 2013: http://www.guardian.co.uk/media/greenslade+denis-o-brien; https://www.theguardian.com/media/greenslade/2013/feb/28/press-freedom-ireland; Colum Kenny, *Sunday Independent*, 24 Feb. 2013: http://www.independent.ie/opinion/analysis/proposed-charter-for-inm-reporters-is-bad-for-irish-journalism-29090602.html and Ciaran Hancock, *The Irish Times* 21 Feb. 2013: http://www.irishtimes.com/business/sectors/media-and-marketing/new-inm-charter-restricts-adversarial-material-1.1313574.

246. *See* https://www.irishtimes.com/business/media-and-marketing/bai-*see* ks-clarification-on-communicorp-s-irish-times-journalists-ban-1.3247326.

247. *In re Kevin O'Kelly* (1974) ILTR 97.

248. *DPP v. O'Keeffe* (1995); reported in *The Irish Times* 28 Jan. 1995.

conditions for press freedom.'[249] The judgment was first considered in Ireland in a Circuit Court case, where a journalist was in danger of being held to be in contempt of court for refusing to identify his source.[250] As a result, the journalist was not found to be in contempt of court. Although that decision was made only in a lower court, since then the Supreme Court has formally recognized the right of journalists to protect their sources.

*242.* This occurred in the case of *Mahon Tribunal v. Keena and Kennedy.*[251] Colm Keena was a journalist with the *Irish Times* and Geraldine Kennedy was the then editor of that newspaper. They had been called before a Tribunal of Inquiry and asked to identify the source of information they had published in relation to evidence pending before the Tribunal.[252] They were also asked to produce the documents, principally a copy of a private and confidential letter from the Tribunal to a businessman, on which the information was based. However, in order to protect their source, they destroyed the letter, despite orders from the Tribunal to produce the documents. As a result of that action, which it described as 'an astounding and flagrant disregard of the rule of law' the divisional High Court, consisting of three judges, concluded that:

> the defendants' privilege against disclosure of sources, is overwhelmingly outweighed by the pressing social need to preserve public confidence in the Tribunal and as there is no other means, by which this can be done other than the enquiry undertaken by the Tribunal, we are of opinion that the test "necessary in a democratic society" is satisfied.

*243.* Nonetheless, it is clear throughout the judgment that the Court accepted without question the right of journalists to protect their sources. It considered a number of decisions of the ECtHR, including *Goodwin* and in the course of its judgment stated:

> The starting point in this balancing exercise is the realisation that in a democratic society the right to freedom of expression is of the highest order of importance. Thus the non-disclosure of journalistic sources enjoys unquestioned acceptance in our jurisprudence and interference in this area can only happen where the requirements of Article 10(2) as set out above are clearly met.

*244.* However, the Supreme Court in the appeal taken by the journalists against this decision, held that the 'great weight' which the High Court attached to 'the reprehensible conduct of the appellants in destroying documents led it to adopt an erroneous approach to the balancing exercise' (at §68). In *Goodwin,* an order compelling

249. (1996) 22 EHRR 123.

250. *ReBarry O'Kelly*, 1996; reported in *The Irish Times* 27, 28 Nov. 1996, 20 Dec. 1996, 14 Jan. 1997.

251. [2009] IESC 78; *Keena and Kennedy v. Ireland* 29804/10, communicated 1 Oct. 2012, available at: http://www.echr.coe.int/NR/rdonlyres/D0F3B23E-DEB8-4D1F-9FAC-54AC91D3C36C/0/PCP_Ireland_en.pdf.

252. A Tribunal of Inquiry is a statutory body established by Government under the Tribunals of Inquiry Acts to inquire into a specific issue or issues and is not a court of law. It does not have power to try anyone and its findings cannot be used in a court of law.

the appellants to answer questions for the purpose of identifying their source could only be *'justified by an overriding requirement in the public interest'*, whereas it was 'very difficult to discern any sufficiently clear benefit to the Tribunal from any answers to the questions they wish to pose to justify the making of the order' (at §69). Thus, the Supreme Court found in favour of the journalists' right to protect their sources.

*245.* However, there was a sting in the tail because, even though they were successful, the Supreme Court still ordered the journalists to pay legal costs estimated at EUR 600,000.[253] The decision to make the journalists pay costs, even though they won their case, appears from the judgment to be in response to the Court's disapproval of the fact that they had destroyed the documents that they had been ordered to produce to the Tribunal. The journalists therefore lodged a complaint with the ECtHR on the issue of costs. However, the case was deemed inadmissible in 2014 (paragraph 192 above).

253. http://www.lexology.com/library/detail.aspx?g=e573c313-17ff-44ad-bc61-afa89a0cbc81.

# Chapter 3. Journalists' Liability

## §1. Cascade Liability

*246.* There is no specific concept of the 'responsible editor' in Irish law, so that a journalist, editor and publisher/broadcaster could all be sued in the civil courts. At common law and under statute law until 2010, all those involved in the publication process could be held liable for defamation, for example. That means, in the case of the print media, everyone from author to editor, publisher, printer and distributor could technically be liable and any or all could be sued at the choice of the plaintiff. There was, however, a common law defence for distributors who did not know and had no reason to believe that the publication they were distributing contained defamatory material, and whose lack of knowledge was not due to negligence on their part. Now, under the Defamation Act 2009, there is a similar defence of innocent publication also for printers and others who are not the author, editor or publisher and therefore have no control over content. The defence is available to those involved merely in the processing, copying, distributing or selling of films or electronic mediums, or in the provision of any electronic equipment that would enable copying, etc. (section 27). They must show, however, that they exercised reasonable care. There is no reference in the section 27 defence to live broadcasting or to 'breaking news' or other instantaneous postings on the Internet and thus those responsible for such content cannot rely on the defence. The Defamation Act 2009 allows for journalists (and others), however, to be indemnified against having to pay damages (financial compensation to the person(s) defamed). Thus, a media organization, such as a newspaper publisher or broadcast station, may undertake to pay any damages awarded against a journalist (section 40).

*247.* In the case of contempt of court (discussed further below), both the journalist(s) who wrote the offending article or broadcast material, and the editor could be fined or theoretically jailed, although the latter rarely, if ever, occurs in practice nowadays. More often, the offending newspaper or other publication is required to pay the costs of the trial and in more egregious cases may also be fined. For instance, the *Sun* newspaper was fined EUR 100,000 for its coverage of a trial, in which it referred to the accused persons as 'brutes'. The judge concluded that the newspaper had made a deliberate and conscious effort to prejudice the trial's outcome.[254] In another case, the *Irish Independent* and *Sunday World* were fined EUR 20,000 each and the editors EUR 2,500 each, as a result of articles published after the accused person had pleaded guilty but before the judge had handed down sentence.[255] As in the case of defamation, the common law of contempt of court applies to all journalists, print, broadcast and Internet.

---

254. *See: The Irish Times* 10 Feb. 2005.
255. *See: The Irish Times* 29 Jul. 2005.

## §2. Defamation

*248.* The right to one's good name is a specified right in the Irish Constitution (Article 40.3.2) and therefore journalists must be careful not to defame individuals or legal persons, i.e., companies and other incorporated entities. In Ireland, defamation is almost always a civil matter, a tort, heard in the civil courts. Other common law offences of criminal defamation, which had not been used for a very long time, were abolished by the Defamation Act 2009 and it is only blasphemous publication (Defamation Act 2009, section 36) that remains a criminal matter to be tried in the criminal courts.[256] The blasphemy provision is discussed below.

*249.* The common law tort of defamation is now defined in the 2009 Act section 6 (2) as follows:

> The tort of defamation consists of the publication, by any means, of a defamatory statement concerning a person to one or more than one person (other than the first-mentioned person) and 'defamation' shall be construed accordingly.

A 'defamatory statement' is defined in section 2 as

> a statement that tends to injure a person's reputation in the eyes of reasonable members of society and 'defamatory' shall be construed accordingly.

And a 'statement' is further defined as:

> a statement made orally or in writing; visual images, sounds, gestures and any other method of signifying meaning; a statement broadcast on radio or television, or published on the Internet; and an electronic communication.[257]

*250.* All journalists, therefore, whether print, broadcast or electronic, can be sued in the civil courts for the tort of defamation. Usually when they are sued, they are sued along with the publisher. In some instances only the publisher is sued, in that it is the publisher who is more likely to be able to pay damages if awarded against them. Both natural and legal persons (companies and other incorporated bodies) can sue. Legal persons typically make up about 7.5% of all litigants (plaintiffs) suing for defamation, so defamation actions against journalists are primarily taken by individuals. There is no provision for defamation of non-incorporated groups. If allegations are made about such a group, the group as such will not be able to sue, although individual members may be able to claim that they are personally identifiable and due in their

256. For a history of defamation law in Ireland, *see* McGonagle, *Media Law,* 2nd ed., 2003; Marie McGonagle and Annabel Brody, 'The Irish Defamation Act 2009 – too little, too late?' (2010) 15(2) *Communications Law*, 43–50*;* Law Reform Commission, *Consultation Paper* and *Report on the Civil Law of Defamation* in 1991; Newspaper Commission 1996; Legal Advisory Group on Defamation, 2003.

257. The term 'electronic communication' is also defined as including a 'communication or information in the form of data, text, images or sound (or any combination of these) by means of guided or unguided electromagnetic energy, or both'.

own personal capacity if the group is small.[258] The test, as set out in the Defamation Act 2009 section 10 is whether the statement could reasonably be understood to refer, in particular, to the member concerned.A person does not need to be named in order to sue for defamation; it is sufficient if some identifying details, such as location, attributes, even a nick-name, are given so that the person can claim that others who know him/her will think the reference is to them. The test is whether the person is reasonably identifiable. Journalists can be liable, therefore, even if they do not name a person.

*251.* Irish law does not recognize defamation of the dead. The Defamation Act 2009, however, makes provision for actions to continue for the benefit of a person's estate if s/he dies after the action has commenced or the cause of action has accrued. Likewise, if the defendant dies, the action will continue against his/her estate. In the case of journalists being sued along with their publisher, the action would continue against the publisher. However, in these situations general, punitive or aggravated damages will not be available (section 39); therefore, only nominal damages, a correction order (section 30), prohibition order (section 33) or alternatively, a declaratory order (section 28) would be available.

*252.* Prior to the Defamation Act 2009, journalists were sued frequently for defamation. Indeed, defamation was the single biggest legal issue for journalists and media on a day-to-day basis. There is no distinction made in Irish law between public and private persons suing for defamation, and many of those suing the media were prominent public persons. The largest category of plaintiffs suing the media was businessmen and members of the professions, many of them well known in the public sphere, followed by politicians and public servants. The plaintiffs almost always won in cases against the media.[259] Court procedures were often protracted and large sums of damages were routinely awarded, particularly in the High Court by juries.[260] The anomalies of jury awards can be seen in O'Brien v. Mirror Group Newspapers, in which a prominent businessman, who owns a major mobile phone company and a number of radio stations, was awarded over EUR 300,000 by a jury. On appeal, the Supreme Court was satisfied that 'the award in this case was disproportionately high and should be set aside'.[261] A re-trial was ordered, again before a jury. In the re-trial,

---

258. For example, *Cusack v. RTÉ,* reported in *The Irish Times* 15–16 Nov. 1989, where one of three revenue sheriffs, although not named, sued successfully; *Ahern v. O'Brien* (*The Irish Times* 11 Jul. 2001), where a reference to 'a senior Fianna Fáil politician' was sufficient.
259. For data and examples of cases, *see* McGonagle, *Media Law,* 2003; McGonagle, ed, *Law and the Media,* 1997; Kevin Boyle and Marie McGonagle, *A Report on Press Freedom and Libel* (NNI, Dublin, 1988).A rare example of a politician who lost a defamation action against the media was *Cooper-Flynn v. RTÉ* [2000] 3 I.R. 344, who was faced with costs of €2 million.
260. In the High Court there is always a jury of twelve persons drawn at random from the electoral register, but in the lower Circuit Court, the judge sits alone. For data on the frequency of defamation actions against journalists and the amount of damages awarded, *see* McGonagle, *Media Law*, 2003. The plaintiff politician in *de Rossa v. Independent News and Media* was awarded approx. €375,000 by a jury and the size of the award was upheld by the ECtHR [1999] 4 I.R. 432 (Sup. Ct); *Independent News & Media v. Ireland,* Application No. 55120/00, judgment of 16 Jun. 2005. This was the first defamation case from Ireland that was taken to the Strasbourg court.
261. [2000] IESC 70 (25 Oct. 2000).

a different jury, unaware of the amount of the earlier award, because under the law they could not be told, awarded Mr O'Brien EUR 750,000, more than double the original amount.[262] In *Leech v. Independent News and Media* in 2009, a High Court jury awarded a PR consultant EUR 1.872 million.[263] This award was appealed to the Supreme Court and reduced to EUR 1.25 million.[264]In 2017, in *McDonagh v. Sunday Newspapers Limited*, a long-running defamation case, the then Chief Justice, while agreeing with the majority of the Court that the original damages award of EUR 900,000 plus costs was disproportionate, and acknowledging that neither route was wholly satisfactory, took the view that it was better in the circumstances to order a re-trial than for the court to substitute its own assessment of damages.[265]

*253.* The Defamation Act 2009 has attempted to address these and other problems inter alia by requiring guidance for juries in relation to the size of damages, providing alternative remedies to jury trial, such as correction orders and declaratory orders with fast-track procedures. It has also eased the burden for journalists (and others) by reducing the limitation period within which actions can be commenced to one year from date of publication, where previously it was six years. All of these procedural improvements should benefit journalists.

*254.* Apart from the new defence of fair and reasonable publication on a matter of public interest referred to above, the defence of honest opinion (formerly 'fair comment') offers journalists some protection for the expression of opinions on matters of public interest, while the defence of qualified privilege offers some protection for fair and accurate reports of a wide range of public matters. The 2009 Act (section 17) affords absolute privilege to fair and accurate reports of a wide range of court proceedings, as well as statements made, and reports of statements made, in the Oireachtas, including its committees, and European Parliament. This parliamentary privilege, which stems from Article 15 of the Irish Constitution, means that elected representatives cannot be sued for defamation arising out of statements they make in either House of the Oireachtas. A challenge to that position was strongly rejected by the High Court in 2017.[266] The 2009 Act also contains an 'offer to make amends', which allows defendants to make in writing and publish a suitable correction and a sufficient apology and pay damages (if any) and costs to be agreed by the parties, or in the case of dispute, referred to the High Court. This revised procedure (there was an 'offer of amends' procedure in the previous Act) was tested in the High Court in 2016 in *Christie v. TV3* and an

262. *See* 'Record damages in O'Brien libel case', https://www.rte.ie/news/2006/1123/82889-obriend/.
263. *See* http://www.rte.ie/news/2009/0624/118798-leechm/ She claimed the newspaper made false allegations that she got public contracts as a PR consultant because she was having an extra-marital affair with the then Government Environment Minister. *Note*: In jury trials there are no written judgments and therefore no official law reports of the cases, unless they are appealed to the Court of Appeal (previously to the Supreme Court).
264. Supreme Court 19 Dec. 2014. *See* above paragraph 191 for discussion of the case at the ECtHR.
265. [2017] IESC 59 (27 July 2017).
266. The case was taken by Denis O'Brien against the Dáil and one of its committees following disclosure of aspects of his banking arrangements by two elected representatives after Mr O'Brien had got court injunctions restraining RTÉ from publishing the information. High Court decision 31 May 2017. In October 2017 Mr O'Brien was granted leave to appeal to the Supreme Court: *see* https://www.irishtimes.com/news/crime-and-law/courts/supreme-court/denis-o-brien-appeal-over-d%C3%A1il-comments-case-to-be-heard-in-supreme-court-1.3251280.

award of EUR 140,000 was made by the judge to the plaintiff, notwithstanding the correction and apology. On appeal to the Court of Appeal, the amount of damages was reduced to EUR 36,000.[267]

## I. Presumption of Falsity

*255.* At common law the litigant (plaintiff) was not required to prove that the allegations he contended were defamatory of him were in fact false. Instead, there was a presumption of falsity, which meant that once a person took a defamation action, the court *presumed* the allegations were false and would not inquire into the issue of falsity unless the defendant pleaded the defence of truth (then called 'justification', as a publication was 'justified' and not considered to amount to defamation if it was true). This practice meant that the onus was on the journalist to prove that what s/he had published was in fact true. The issue was addressed to some extent in the Defamation Act 2009 by the requirement on the part of each side, if relying on facts to establish their position, to swear an affidavit setting out all the facts on which they were relying. The Act also made it an offence attracting substantial penalties to make a false or misleading statement in an affidavit (section 8(7)).

## II. Defamatory Effect

*256.* Another hurdle for journalists is that there is no requirement for the plaintiff to prove actual harm arising from the allegations. The test is whether the allegations would 'tend' to make other reasonable persons think less of the plaintiff. The actual meaning of the words or other form of expression used is a matter for the judge or the jury if there is one. Allegations can be defamatory in their everyday meaning or by way of an innuendo, that is, a secondary meaning found by 'reading between the lines' or by reference to external information with which the audience or readership is familiar. Vulgar abuse, especially if spoken rather than written or if uttered in the heat of the moment, is not regarded as defamatory, although what constitutes vulgar abuse in particular circumstances is a matter for the judge or a jury if there is one.

## III. Internet and Social Media

*257.* Until the 1990s, the vast majority of defamation cases were taken against the Irish print media and, to a lesser extent, broadcasters. Since the beginning of the twenty-first century, however, defamation actions have been taken also in respect of Internet postings, website content, blogs, social network sites, e-mails, etc. So far, most have resulted in settlements outside court, with the result that not much in the

267. *Christie v. TV3 Television Networks Limited* [2017] IECA 128, 4 May 2017.

way of principle has been established.[268] However, more recently there have been some awards of damages and more indication of how the courts will deal with the issues arising. In *Muwema v. Facebook Ireland Ltd,*[269] the High Court initially granted an order for disclosure of the identity and location of the person who posted three allegedly 'highly offensive and defamatory publications' about the plaintiff on Facebook under a pseudonym. However, the judge refused the injunctions sought by the plaintiff under section 33 of the Defamation Act 2009 directing Facebook to take down the material already posted and to prevent the further publication of the material. The judge refused the injunctions – a form of prior restraint – on the basis that Facebook could avail of the statutory defence of innocent publication provided for under section 27(2)(c) of the Defamation Act 2009, as Facebook was not the author, editor or publisher of the impugned statements. Moreover, he held that Regulations 15–18 of the E-Commerce Directive 200/31/EC, as transposed into Irish law by European Communities (Directive 2000/31/EC) Regulations (S.I. No 68 of 2003), also provided Facebook with 'another line of defence'. Despite the judge's misgivings about anonymous persons posting defamatory remarks, no damages or injunctive relief could be granted. However, following new evidence from Facebook prior to the court order taking effect, it emerged that the person concerned was a political activist in Uganda and revealing his or her identity could lead to human rights abuses against him or her. The judge stated that 'it must be correct to say that a person's right to his good name must take second place to the right to life and bodily integrity of another where the threat to bodily integrity is sufficiently serious ...'.[270]

*258.* The Defamation Act 2009 is essentially technology neutral and does not expressly refer to the Internet except in the definitions of 'periodical' and 'statement' in section 2, and in relation to the period of limitation in section 38. Otherwise, all the provisions of the Act apply to the Internet, where appropriate. The defence of innocent publication (section 27), which is available for those who are not authors, editors or publishers, seems applicable to Internet Service Providers and others involved only in the technological, as opposed to the content, side of the Internet. Another provision that may prove valuable in the Internet and digital archives context is that contained

268. Examples include *Maguire v. Gill* in which a barrister sued in respect of a website that rated lawyers' performances (reported in *The Irish Times* 14 Sept.–24 Nov. 2006); *Casey v. Elwood and Lusby* a case in which a lecturer sued colleagues as a result of e-mails they circulated concerning him in 2005 (H.Ct. settlement 14 May 2010); *Traynor v. Bebo,* a case taken against the then popular social network site, Bebo, and which resulted in a settlement, Dublin H.Ct., reported in *The Irish Times* 17 Jul. 2010; *Barnes and Ó Donnchú v. Ardmayle*, in which a settlement of €100,000 was reported (*The Sunday Times* 31 Jan. 2010) to have been reached by a little-known blogger with an American book dealer and a civil servant in relation to remarks he had made in his blog in relation to the sale of James Joyce manuscripts to the National Library.

269. [2016] IEHC 519, available at www.bailii.org/.

270. However, following new evidence from Facebook prior to the court order taking effect, it emerged that the person concerned was a political activist in Uganda and revealing his or her identity could lead to human rights abuses against him or her. The judge stated that 'it must be correct to say that a person's right to his good name must take second place to the right to life and bodily integrity of another where the threat to bodily integrity is sufficiently serious ...'. *See Muwema v. Facebook* (No. 2) [2017] IEHC 69.

in section 10 which establishes a single publication rule. Thus, unlike the situation prior to the 2009 Act, only one action could be taken against a newspaper that published the same defamatory remarks in its print edition, online edition, website, twitter account and archives.

## IV. Criminal Defamation

*259.* Prior to the 2009 Act, various common law offences of criminal libel (including obscene libel, seditious libel and blasphemous libel), which had been used against journalists and publishers in earlier centuries, were still extant but very seldom used. All forms of criminal libel were abolished by the 2009 Act, except for one controversial provision regarding blasphemy (section 36). As the publication or utterance of blasphemous matter is specified as 'an offence' which is 'punishable in accordance with law' under the Constitution (*see* paragraph 15 above), the legislature decided that some form of offence had to be retained in legislation to give effect to the constitutional provision, which can only be changed by referendum of the people. In the case of obscene and seditious libels, it was deemed that there was sufficient other legislation already in place to deal with them, but not so in the case of blasphemous libel, as there was no legislation in place providing for an offence of blasphemous libel; rather, the Defamation Act 1961 merely provided penalties for such an offence. The measure which was introduced was stated to be a temporary one, pending a referendum to change the Constitution in this regard, which has not yet taken place but is scheduled for 2018.[271] Nonetheless, the inclusion of the provision in the 2009 Act provoked a public outcry and was condemned by journalists' organizations, Non-Governmental Organisations (NGOs) and others on freedom of expression grounds.[272]

*260.* The new offence introduced in the Defamation Act 2009 is one of publishing or uttering blasphemous matter – the terms used in the Constitution – that is 'grossly abusive or insulting in relation to matters held sacred by any religion, thereby causing outrage among a substantial number of the adherents of that religion'. An intention to cause such outrage is required and it is a defence to prove that 'a reasonable person would find genuine literary, artistic, political, scientific, or academic value in the matter to which the offence relates'. For the purposes of the section, 'religion' does not include 'an organisation or cult:

(a) the principal object of which is the making of profit, or
(b) that employs oppressive psychological manipulation:

271. In September 2017, the Government set October 2018 as an indicative timeframe for the referendum: *see* https://merrionstreet.ie/en/News-Room/News/Government_Sets_Indicative_Timetable_For_Referendums.htm.

272. *See* , for example, Art. 19 statement of 18 Jun. 2009, available at: https://www.article19.org/data/files/pdfs/press/ireland-blasphemy-amendment-contrary-to-free-speech.pdf For further analysis, *see* T. McGonagle, 'A draft obituary for the offence of blasphemy in Ireland', in András Koltay & Jeroen Temperman, Eds., *Blasphemy and Freedom of Expression. Comparative, Theoretical and Historical Reflections after the Charlie Hebdo Massacre* (Cambridge, Cambridge University Press, 2017), pages 456-479.

(1) of its followers, or
(2) for the purpose of gaining new followers'.

The offence carries a penalty of a fine not exceeding EUR 25,000 upon conviction on indictment. Following conviction a court warrant may be granted to the Garda Síochána (police) for search and seizure of any offending material (section 37). At the time of writing the provision has not been invoked except in the form of a complaint to the Gardaíin 2015 by a member of the public that references to God made by British comedian and actor, Stephen Fry, on an RTÉ programme, constituted blasphemy under the Act. In 2017 it was reported that the investigation by the Gardaí had been dropped, as they had failed to find a 'substantial number' of outraged people, as required by the Act.[273]

## §3. Privacy

*261.* Privacy in Ireland is governed by common law and numerous statutory provisions. While there is specific legislation covering particular aspects of privacy, such as the Data Protection Acts 1988–2003 and the Communications (Retention of Data) Act 2011, there is no Privacy Act as such. However, privacy, and various aspects of it, are protected under the Constitution; in specific legislative provisions; in an array of common law measures; and in the law of Equity.

### I. Constitution

*262.* While there is no right to privacy expressly provided for in the Constitution, the courts have recognized a right to privacy as an unspecified, personal right under Article 40.3.1. Thus, it is possible to take a court action claiming that one's constitutional right to privacy has been infringed and seeking a declaration to that effect and damages.[274]

*263.* The protection afforded to privacy by the Constitution is further buttressed by the ECHR Act 2003, which means that the Article 8 jurisprudence of the ECtHR can now be argued directly in Irish courts. While the Convention was incorporated at sub-constitutional level, it has already informed many of the decisions of the Irish courts in relation to privacy (*see* cases referred to below).

### II. Legislation

*264.* With regard to legislation, of particular interest is the section of the Broadcasting Act 2009, which places an obligation on broadcasters not to unreasonably encroach on the privacy of any individual either in programmes broadcast or in the

273. https://www.independent.ie/irish-news/news/garda-launch-blasphemy-probe-into-stephen-fry-comments-on-the-meaning-of-life-35684262.html;https://www.irishtimes.com/news/crime-and-law/stephen-fry-will-not-be-prosecuted-for-blasphemy-1.3075938.
274. As in *Kennedy and Arnold v. Ireland* [1987] I.R. 587, [1988] ILRM 472.

means employed to make such programmes (section 39(1)(e)). A similar provision contained in earlier broadcasting legislation was considered in the case of *Cogley & Aherne v. RTÉ.*[275] A court injunction was sought on privacy grounds to prevent the broadcasting of an RTÉ current affairs programme about poor standards in a nursing home for elderly people. The owners of the home complained about the methods used to get the information, namely the use of a secret camera, and claimed that the privacy of the patients had been breached. However, the court found that the privacy of the patients was to be protected in the broadcast by the use of pixilation and/or by obtaining the consent of the patients' families. On the matter of the owners' privacy, the court took the view that the low standards in the conduct of their business were a matter of public interest, which outweighed their privacy. On the matter of the use of the secret camera, the court found that although it was prima facie in breach of the owners' right to privacy, the issues raised in the programme were of the highest public interest and, therefore, a very significant weight had to be attached to them in deciding whether to grant an injunction to prevent the broadcasting of the programme. The injunction was refused.

*265.* The Broadcasting Act 2009 also requires the BAI to draft codes on programme standards, incorporating broadcasters' statutory obligations, including observance of the right to privacy in section 39. Under the Act, the Compliance Committee of BAI deals with complaints from the public about breaches of the codes and all decisions of the Committee are published at regular intervals on the BAI website.[276] The number of complaints of invasion of privacy remains very low.

*266.* Other legislation, including the Copyright and Related Rights Act 2000, can offer an indirect remedy when photographs of a private nature are published, for example, although protection of privacy is only incidental to the main purposes of the Act. The Data Protection Acts 1998–2003, which are concerned with informational privacy, specifically personal data and sensitive personal data, contain an exemption for journalists from some of the obligations imposed on data processors. The exemption is confined to data that is processed purely for journalistic, artistic or literary purposes. The process must be undertaken solely for the purpose of publication and the Data Controller must reasonably believe that, 'having regard in particular to the special importance of the public interest in freedom of expression, such publication would be in the public interest' (2003 Act, section 22A). Despite the exemption, data protection issues are raised increasingly often in privacy cases, including those taken against the media.

*267.* Some concerns with surveillance are addressed in Acts such as the Postal and Telecommunications Services Act 1983 and Interception of Postal Packets and Telecommunications Messages (Regulation) Act 1993. *See*, for example, the *Herrity* case discussed below. However, a Law Reform Commission paper and report on the topic of surveillance and invasion of privacy in 1998 recommended the introduction of legislation providing for a specific tort of privacy and for new criminal offences relating to installing surveillance devices and trespassing for the purpose of surveillance. This led to the introduction of a Privacy Bill in 2006, which has not been enacted (*see* further below).

275. [2005] IEHC 180.

276. http://www.bai.ie/en/latest-broadcasting-complaints-decisions-published.

## III. Common Law

*268.* In *Cogley & Aherne v. RTÉ* (above) it was also contended that the secret filming on the premises amounted to trespass. Common law torts such as trespass, whether trespass to land, goods or person, can provide a cause of action and remedies for breach of privacy. The tort of nuisance also, which involves interference with the use or enjoyment of one's property, can provide an avenue for redress. These torts could be used in relation to surveillance or harassment, for example, including by journalists. However, they are limited in scope and are mainly fall-back options now that the constitutional right to privacy has been established and Article 8 ECHR jurisprudence can be raised in argument.

## IV. Equity

*269.* An action for breach of confidence was developed in Equity to meet a gap in the common law and, while used much more in the UK than in Ireland to protect privacy, it has been used to some extent in Ireland also. It has been used to prevent publication of the proceedings of disciplinary inquiries, such as those of the Bar Council and Medical Council, where the courts found that there were serious and intimate privacy issues to protect.[277] In contrast, the public interest in the prevention of wrongdoing was found to outweigh the confidentiality between a bank and its customers.[278]

**Examples of Recent Privacy Cases**

*270.* In *Herrity v. Associated Newspapers (Ireland) Ltd*[279] the judge said that privacy would rarely outweigh freedom of expression. However, the circumstances of the case, which involved the tapping of the telephone of a woman in an effort by her husband to get information about her affair with a Catholic priest, were such as to amount to a deliberate, conscious and unjustified invasion of her privacy. The woman's right to privacy therefore prevailed over the right to freedom of expression in publishing the information obtained. Although the ECHR Act 2003 was not in force at the time the publication occurred, arguments based on the ECHR were advanced and considered in the judgment.

*271.* In contrast to *Herrity,* the court found no breach of privacy in *Hickey v. Sunday Newspapers,*[280]where the circumstances included the fact that the plaintiff was in a public place, was carrying out a public function (registering the birth of her baby), had previously courted publicity and had chosen to bring the baby with her.

---

277. *See* , for example, the Supreme Court in *Barry v. Medical Council* [1998] 3 I.R. 368.

278. *NIB v. RTÉ* [1998] 2 I.R. 465; [1998] 2 ILRM 196. *See also Haughey and others v. Moriarty and others* [1999] 3 IR 1.

279. [2008] IEHC 249; [2009] 1 I.R. 316. The principles relied on in *Herrity* were subsequently relied on in *K. [a minor] v. Independent Star Ltd & Ors* [2010] IEHC 500-85.

280. [2010] IEHC 349. Contrast *Sinnott v. Carlow Nationalist,* reported in *The Irish Times* 27 Jan. 2007, 17 Feb. 2007, where the incident (photograph published of a sportsperson on the pitch at a moment his shorts fell down and his private parts were exposed) was also in a public place but publication was not in the public interest and was regarded by the judge as a 'negligent' intrusion on privacy.

*272.* There is no specific recognition of image rights, as such, in Irish law. Issues arising would be likely, therefore, to be considered under defamation or privacy law, or depending on the circumstances, other legislative or common law provisions. There is a common law tort of malicious falsehood, for example, which encompasses 'slander of title' and 'slander of goods', which is included in the Defamation Act 2009, section 42. The publication must have been untrue, published maliciously and must have referred to the plaintiff, his or her property or his or her office, profession, calling, trade or business. In order to succeed in an action the plaintiff must prove 'special damage' or 'that the publication of the statement was calculated to cause and was likely to cause financial loss to the plaintiff in respect of his or her property or his or her office, profession, calling, trade or business.

*273.* The privacy right of convicted prisoners has emerged as an issue for the media in Ireland in recent years. In *Murray v. Newsgroup Newspapers Ltd,*[281] for example, a convicted sexual offender, who had served his prison sentence, was the subject of numerous newspaper articles referring to him variously as a 'rapist' and 'monster'. He took a court action claiming that the adverse media coverage had led to him being hounded out of his home and having to quit his job. An injunction against the media was refused, however, on the basis *inter alia* that the plaintiff had reoffended and there was no documentary or independent supportive evidence as to his rehabilitation. Given the privacy, freedom of expression and important public interest issues involved, the judge took the view that the case should go to a full hearing. The issue of a convicted offender having some residual right to privacy, however, was not ruled out. Indeed, in the area of defamation law, the courts have already recognized a residual right to reputation in another case involving a convicted offender, *Watters v. the Star on Sunday.*[282]

## V. Co-regulation

*274.* Concerns about intrusion by media on individuals' privacy led for several decades to sporadic calls from politicians and others for the setting up of a Press Council in Ireland. British newspapers, which had always circulated in Ireland, began to target the Irish market in the 1990s, establishing editorial offices in Ireland and publishing Irish editions. These newspapers, particularly the tabloids, were much more vigorous in pursuing private details of people's lives than Irish papers had been, and, as a result, the incidence of intrusion on privacy by the Irish media, which began to compete with them, increased. In response, successive governments threatened to introduce privacy legislation.[283] As part of a quid pro quo with government, the print media, which had been seeking defamation law reform since the mid-1980s, agreed

281. [2010] IEHC 248.
282. [2010] IECC 1; *see* Carol Coulter, 'Defamation win by man jailed for child pornography', The Irish Times 4 Nov. 2010, available at: https://www.irishtimes.com/.../defamation-win-by-man-jailed-for-child-pornography-....
283. The Working Group on Privacy was established by the then Minister for Justice in 2005 and reported in 2006. Report available at http://justice.ie/en/JELR/WkgGrpPrivacy.pdf/Files/WkgGrpPrivacy.pdf.

to establish a press council and press ombudsman scheme on an independent footing in 2007. The Press Council and Press Ombudsman were subsequently given statutory recognition in the Defamation Act 2009, which brought in defamation law reform. Publishers and journalists must now abide by the Code of Practice implemented by the Press Council and Press Ombudsman. Principle 5 of the Code is as follows:

> 5.1 Privacy is a human right, protected as a personal right in the Irish Constitution and the European Convention on Human Rights, which is incorporated into Irish law. The private and family life, home and correspondence of everyone must be respected.
>
> 5.2 Readers are entitled to have news and comment presented with respect for the privacy and sensibilities of individuals. However, the right to privacy should not prevent publication of matters of public record or in the public interest.
>
> 5.3 Sympathy and discretion must be shown at all times in seeking information in situations of personal grief or shock. In publishing such information, the feelings of grieving families should be taken into account. This should not be interpreted as restricting the right to report judicial proceedings.
>
> 5.4 Public persons are entitled to privacy. However, where a person holds public office, deals with public affairs, follows a public career, or has sought or obtained publicity for his activities, publication of relevant details of his private life and circumstances may be justifiable where the information revealed relates to the validity of the person's conduct, the credibility of his public statements, the value of his publicly expressed views or is otherwise in the public interest.
>
> 5.5 Taking photographs of individuals in private places without their consent is not acceptable, unless justified by the public interest.

In response to the setting-up of the Press Council, the Government decided to put a stay on the Privacy Bill 2006 (*see* paragraph 208) to see how effective the Council would prove in handling complaints of invasion of privacy. The Press Council's annual reports give statistics on all complaints, including privacy-related complaints, which in 2014 accounted for 8.4% of all complaints and in 2015, 13.7%.[284] Attempts by individual members of Parliament to resurrect the Bill have so far failed.

---

284. Statistics for 2014 and 2015 available at: http://www.presscouncil.ie/_fileupload/Statistics%20 2015.pdf.

## §4. Contempt of Court

*275.* Journalists also have obligations imposed by the common law of contempt of court. Contempt of court is judge-made law, originally designed to enable judges to maintain discipline in court, but developing later to prevent criticism of the courts by media and others, and finally to protect the right to a fair trial. To that extent it corresponds to a large degree to the principle of 'maintaining the authority and impartiality of the judiciary' in Article 10.2 of the ECHR. Its compatibility with Article 10 was first examined by the ECtHR in the English case of *Sunday Times v. UK*,[285] where certain aspects of the law of contempt as it operated in the UK at that time were found not to be compatible with the Convention.

*276.* Historically, there were two kinds of contempt: civil contempt, which related to refusal to obey court orders and rarely applied to the media; and criminal contempt, which could take a number of different guises. It is the area of criminal contempt that mainly affects the media. One form of criminal contempt, namely contempt in the face of the court, can affect protection of journalists' sources. Another form of criminal contempt, which is rarely invoked against the media nowadays, is contempt by scandalizing the court, i.e., criticism going beyond acceptable boundaries and accusing courts of partiality or corruption. Here the concern was to maintain public confidence in the courts and the administration of justice.

*277.* A third form of criminal contempt is contempt by interfering with the right of an accused person to a fair trial. In this regard, the media are subject to the so-called *sub judice* rule (literally 'under the judge', i.e., pending in court). Under this rule, the media must be careful once a case is pending or ongoing not to publish anything that could prejudice the right of the accused person(s) to a fair trial, or the right of civil litigants to a fair hearing. A civil case is deemed to be pending once the required documents are lodged in court with a view to commence proceedings. In a criminal case, the rule applies from the time that a person or persons are charged with an offence, the case being from that point onwards in the hands of the judge.

*278.* Anything that is reported while the *sub judice* rule is in operation that would undermine or interfere with the presumption of innocence, or anything that is reported that lawyers for the accused person(s) feel may prejudice their case, can lead to the media concerned being called into court to face charges of contempt of court. For instance, inaccuracies or sensational media coverage of a trial can give rise to contempt charges.[286] The test developed by the courts is whether there is a 'real risk' of an unfair trial. In less serious incidents, where publication of the offending material is the result of human error, the trial judge may accept journalists' and editors' apologies. When the media are deemed to have created a 'real risk' of an unfair trial, however, they are often fined and/or required to pay the costs of the trial where the jury has to be sent away and the case put back for re-hearing at a later date.[287] Whether a trial

285. Application no. 6538/74, available at: http://hudoc.echr.coe.int/eng?i=001-57584.

286. An interesting comparison may be made between the Irish courts' handling of the risk to a fair trial in *DPP v. Nevin* (2000),*DPP v.Nevin* [2003] 3 I.R. 321 and *News Verlags GmbH v. Austria*, Application No. 31611/96, judgment of 21 Mar. 2002.

287. *See* , for example, *Irish Independent* and *Sunday World*, reported in *The Irish Times* 29 Jul. 2005.

needs to be aborted or put back for a later hearing before a different jury depends on the application of the 'real risk' test accompanied by a consideration as to whether the 'real risk', if there is found to be one, could be averted by some less drastic measure, such as judicial instructions to the jury. The 'real risk' test applies also in relation to the effect of pre-trial publicity.

*279.* As jury trial is the norm in criminal cases except in the lowest courts, i.e., the District courts, which deal with the least serious cases, most concern is to ensure that the jury, made up of twelve citizens drawn at random from the electoral register, will not be prejudiced by media reporting or comment. It is widely, though not universally, accepted that judges, on the other hand, because of their legal training, will not be influenced by what they see, hear or read in the media.

*280.* The *sub judice* rule ceases to apply when the administration of justice in the given case is complete. A Supreme Court decision in 1984 indicated that, where an appeal was pending involving only judges dealing with points of law, the *sub judice* rule would no longer apply.[288] However, the opinion of a later Supreme Court that the rule would continue until the administration of justice in the case is completed suggests that the media need to be careful and treat the rule as applying even at the appeal stage.[289] The Supreme Court in that latter case took the view that if an accused person is found guilty by a jury but the judge adjourns sentencing (until s/he has heard a victim impact report, for example), the *sub judice* rule may continue to apply, even though it is perhaps less likely that media coverage will affect the sentencing judge than it would the lay members of a jury.[290]

*281.* In 2016, the Law Reform Commission began work on a project concerning contempt of court and other offences and torts involving the administration of justice. The Commission will take account of recent developments in this area since the publication of its 1994 Report on Contempt of Court (LRC 47-1994), which recommended that the common law rules on criminal contempt and civil contempt should be replaced with statutory provisions.[291]

---

288. *Cullen v. Tóibín* [1984] ILRM 577.
289. *Kelly v. O'Neill and Brady* [1999] IESC 81, available at: http://www.bailii.org/ie/cases/IESC/1999/81.html.
290. *Ibid.*
291. Law Reform Commission, 4th Programme of Law Reform, Project 4, 2016. *See* http://www.lawreform.ie/welcome/1-legal-system-and-public-law.378.html.

# Chapter 4. Right to Reply

*282.* There is no long-standing tradition of a statutory or voluntary right of reply in the print media in Ireland, although individual newspapers did from time to time offer an 'opportunity for reply' and all newspapers had, and continue to have, sections dedicated to 'letters to the editor'. Almost all have websites now that enable input from readers on debate topics, chats, polls, etc., on news items or comment pieces. There is no provision for a right of reply in the Defamation Act 2009, other than in the context of the defence of qualified privilege. The defence arises where the media have published a fair and accurate report of a public event or meeting, of a type listed in the Act, and a person referred to in the report contends he has been defamed by what was said at the event or meeting. That person may request the media that published the allegedly defamatory remarks to 'publish in the same medium of communication in which he or she published the statement concerned, a reasonable statement by way of explanation or a contradiction' (section 18(4)). There is, however, a right of reply contained in the Broadcasting Act 2009 (*see* paragraphs 401–405, which may be used in a defamation action as a means of mitigating damage (section 49(14)).

*283.* Many of the complaints to the Press Ombudsman and Press Council are resolved through a process of conciliation and in some instances the issue is resolved by the newspaper or magazine concerned offering and publishing a right of reply. An example given on the Council's website is of a complaint about an article published in *The Sunday Times* about a beneficial owner of a share in a property trust and her husband. The complaint was resolved when the newspaper published a right of reply from her. Another example is one in which a man complained about an article regarding an EU Commission Report that he considered was unfair and inaccurate. The newspaper offered to give the complainant a right of reply by publishing a letter to the editor. While the complainant did not take up the offer, the complaint was resolved when a letter from him, setting out his views on the article under complaint, was sent to the newspaper's editor for consideration in the context of any future coverage of the matters in question.[292]

292. *See* http://www.presscouncil.ie/cases-appeals/resolved-through-concilliation.300.html.

# Chapter 5. Access to Public Information

*284.* A culture of secrecy pervaded the public service throughout most of the twentieth century in Ireland and all public service workers were subject to the Official Secrets Act 1963. The Act covered a very wide range of information and carried a range of criminal sanctions. As a result, although it was not often enforced, it hung as a threat over staff. Media organizations which published confidential information were prosecuted under the Act on occasion.[293] By the 1980s, some measure of openness was gained by the passing of the Ombudsman Act (1980) and the National Archives Act (1986). A major breakthrough occurred when the Freedom of Information Act was passed in 1997. The Act carried a presumption that all information in the possession of public bodies would be open to the public to the greatest extent possible consistent with the public interest and the right to privacy.

## §1. Public Documents

*285.* The Freedom of Information Acts from 1997 onwards gradually opened up the public service to public scrutiny. For journalists, the 1997 Act presented an additional tool with which to elicit information on behalf of the public. Journalists initially comprised between 14% and 20% of those making requests for information and uncovered numerous stories, including serious news stories, which would not otherwise have come to light. Under the 1997 Act, there was no fee for making requests, other than the costs associated with search and retrieval, and photocopying. However, in 2003, an amending Act, the Freedom of Information (Amendment) Act 2003, introduced fees for non-personal information. The stated intention of Government in introducing fees was to discourage 'trawling expeditions', in which large amounts of information were requested by a small number of people using the Act. The introduction of sizeable fees acted as a deterrent to journalists and others, with the result that the number of requests for information fell in the following years.[294] The figure for journalists using the Act fell to just 7% in 2004 and 6.5% in 2005. The quite substantial fees charged and the timeline involved for responding to requests and if necessary appealing decisions, acted as deterrents to journalists, particularly those who worked for less well-resourced organizations and to tight deadlines. However, the Act was used extensively by print journalists, particularly those working on Sunday and weekly newspapers where time was less of an issue than on dailies.[295]

293. *See* McGonagle, *Media Law,* 2003, Ch. 10.

294. *See* the annual reports of the Information Commissioner, available at: http://www.oic.gov.ie/en/Publications/Annual-Reports/. The fees set by Government were €15 for an initial request; €75 for an internal review and €150 for an appeal to the Information Commissioner. Total net fees in 2011, for example, were €87,439 (OIC annual report 2011).

295. *See* the annual reports of the Information Commissioner for details of usage of the Act by journalists; available at http://www.oic.gov.ie/en/Publications/Annual-Reports/.

*286.* Interesting High Court decisions under the 1997 Act, as amended in 2003, include *RTÉ v. Information Commissioner*[296] in which the national public service broadcaster successfully challenged the decision of the Commissioner that it should release certain data. The data was to be used for programme content purposes, which involved the making of editorial decisions in accordance with the relevant broadcasting legislation.[297] One of the few cases to proceed to the Supreme Court on a point of law from the High Court was *Sheedy v. Information Commissioner,*[298]which arose from a request from *The Irish Times* newspaper for information concerning school inspectors' reports. The Department of Education refused to grant the request but the Information Commissioner decided that the information should be released. The main concern expressed about the release of the information was that it would be used to compile league tables of schools' performance. The Education Act of 1998 section 53 gave the Minister for Education discretion to refuse information if it 'would enable the compilation of information (i.e., not otherwise available to the general public) in relation to the comparative performance of schools in respect of the academic achievement of students enrolled therein... '. The Supreme Court upheld the appeal from the High Court and overturned the Commissioner's decision for the release of the reports on this ground, even though any personal information contained in the reports had been redacted.

**Freedom of Information Act 2014**

*287.* One of the weaknesses in the 1997 Act, which continued in the 2003 amending Act, was that certain bodies, such as the Garda Síochána (Police), were not brought within the scope of the Act. However, the Freedom of Information Act 2014 has expanded the coverage of the Act to ensure that all statutory bodies and all bodies significantly funded from the public purse are covered in whole or in part.[299]

*288.* In relation to access to records held by public bodies and all those covered by the Act, section 11(3) makes the overall goals clear:

> An FOI body, in performing any function under this Act, shall have regard to–
>
> (a) the need to achieve greater openness in the activities of FOI bodies and to promote adherence by them to the principle of transparency in government and public affairs,
> (b) the need to strengthen the accountability and improve the quality of decision-making of FOI bodies, and
> (c) the need to inform scrutiny, discussion, comment and review by the public of the activities of FOI bodies and facilitate more effective participation by the public

296. [2004] IEHC 113 (11 Jun. 2004), available at: http://www.bailii.org/ie/cases/IEHC/2004/113.htm l.
297. The Broadcasting Authority Act 1960, s. 18, as amended. The section set out RTÉ's obligations, including an obligation to observe impartiality in news and current affairs programming.
298. [2005] IESC 35.
299. The Garda Síochána (police) are included but certain types of records held by them are not (s. 42(b)); likewise certain records held by the Criminal Assets Bureau, the Defence Forces and others specified in s. 42. The Act is available at: http://www.oireachtas.ie/documents/bills28/acts/2014/a3014.pdf.

in consultations relating to the role, responsibilities and performance of FOI bodies.

*289.* A public body for the purposes of the Act is stated in section 6(1) to be the following:

> (a) a Department of State; (b) an entity established by or under any enactment (other than the Companies Acts); (c) any other entity established (other than under the Companies Acts) or appointed by the Government or a Minister of the Government, including an entity established (other than under the Companies Acts) by a Minister of the Government under any scheme; (d) a company (within the meaning of the Companies Acts) a majority of the shares in which are held by or on behalf of a Minister of the Government; (e) a subsidiary (within the meaning of the Companies Acts) of a company to which paragraph (d) relates; (f) an entity (other than a subsidiary to which paragraph (e) relates) that is directly or indirectly controlled by an entity to which paragraph (b), (c), (d) or (e) relates; (g) a higher education institution in receipt of public funding; (h) notwithstanding the repeal of the Act of 1997 by section 5, and subject to this Act, any entity that was a public body (including bodies or elements of bodies prescribed as such) within the meaning of the Act of 1997 on the enactment of this Act.

The public bodies covered in whole and in part, the details of the process, the time-frame for each stage, the powers and role of the Commissioner, the review and appeal processes are set out in the Act.

*290.* Access is to 'any record' and the term 'record' is defined very broadly in the Act:

> 'record' includes– (a) a book or other written or printed material in any form (including in any electronic device or in machine readable form), (b) a map, plan or drawing, (c) a disc, tape or other mechanical or electronic device in which data other than visual images are embodied so as to be capable, with or without the aid of some other mechanical or electronic equipment, of being reproduced from the disc, tape or other device, (d) a film, disc, tape or other mechanical or electronic device in which visual images are embodied so as to be capable, with or without the aid of some other mechanical or electronic equipment, of being reproduced from the film, disc, tape or other device, and (e) a copy or part of any thing which falls within paragraph (a), (b), (c) or (d), and a copy, in any form, of a record shall be deemed, for the purposes of this Act, to have been created at the same time as the record.

*291.* There are a number of exempt records, however, some of them mandatory (such as records which contain information that was obtained or prepared for the purpose of intelligence in respect of the security or defence of the State (section 33(3)) and others discretionary (such as records that contain matter relating to the deliberative processes of an FOI body, including opinions, advice, recommendations, and the results of consultations, considered by the body, the head of the body, or a member of the body or of the staff of the body for the purpose of those processes (section 29)).[300] The Act amends, but does not repeal, the Official Secrets Act 1963.[301]

*292.* Overall, the Act has addressed the perceived drawbacks inherent in the original Act, such as the bodies that were excluded from the remit of the Act, and the retrograde measures introduced in the 2003 amending Act, such as the imposition of substantial fees. Since the abolition of fees, other than search and retrieval fees,[302] usage by journalists has increased, so that in 2015 20% of the requests for access came from journalists and the total number of requests received increased significantly compared to previous years.[303]

## §2. Court Hearings and Documents

*293.* There is a principle of open justice contained in the Irish Constitution (Article 34.1). Accordingly, all court hearings must be open to the public 'save in such special and limited cases as may be prescribed by law'. The media are entitled, therefore, to attend and report on court proceedings, subject to certain limitations in specific cases that are provided for in law. For instance, under the Criminal Law (Rape) Acts 1981–1990 section 7–8, the media are permitted to attend and report on rape, sexual assault and incest cases but are not permitted to publish anything that would be likely to identify the accused person unless or until convicted and even then not if it would be likely to identify the victim.[304] If a victim waives the right to anonymity, the identity of the perpetrator will normally be revealed.

*294.* The significance of the open justice principle was addressed by the Supreme Court in the case of *Irish Times Ltd v. Ireland* in 1998.[305] The case concerned the trial of a number of non-nationals for importing a large consignment of drugs. The trial judge, who was concerned at a number of previous inaccuracies in media reporting and conscious of the serious nature of the case, permitted reporters to remain in court but banned them from reporting until the trial would end. In a unanimous decision, the Supreme Court found that the ban on contemporaneous reporting was contrary to the constitutional principle of open justice. Emphasizing the need for justice not only to be done but to be seen to be done, the judges focused on the public nature of justice and the right of the public to be informed by the media on how justice is being administered in the courts in their name. The media are the 'eyes and ears of the public

300. *See* further, Part 4, ss 28–37.
301. Section 51.
302. *See* s. 27. In some instances the media should be able to rely on s. 27(6) which enables search and retrieval fees to be waived if 'some or all of the information contained in the record concerned would be of particular assistance to the understanding of an issue of national importance'.
303. Annual Report of the Commissioner 2015, available at: http://www.oic.gov.ie/en/publications/annual-reports/2015-annual-report/online/index.html.
304. *See* , for example, discussion of the sections of the Act in the context of a claim for damages for breach of the provisions in *K. [a minor] v. Independent Star Ltd & Ors* [2010] IEHC 500-85.
305. [1998] 1 I.R. 359.

and any curtailment of the press must be viewed as a curtailment of the access of the people to the administration of justice'.[306]

*295.* Exceptions to the open justice principle, which exclude the media from attending and reporting, include family law hearings, in the interest of the privacy of the parties, and particularly children. Section 45(1) of the Courts (Supplemental Provisions) Act 1961 makes provision for justice to be administered 'otherwise than in public' in the case of applications of an urgent nature for relief by way of habeas corpus, bail, prohibition or injunction; matrimonial causes and matters; lunacy and minor (children) matters; and proceedings involving the disclosure of a secret manufacturing process. Proceedings in matrimonial causes and matters, therefore, may be held otherwise than in public. Many family law statutes provide accordingly, although the terminology used sometimes differs. Some provide, for instance, for family law matters to be held '*in camera*', meaning literally in the judge's chambers, and giving rise to the so-called in camera rule. When a hearing is conducted 'in camera', the media are not entitled to attend. Publication of any material from the hearing is not automatically banned, but can be restrained by injunction or may be punished as contempt of court. In *M. v. Drury* (1994),[307]for instance, only publication of material from the *in camera* judicial separation proceedings was restrained, while other matter relating to the wife's alleged affair with a Catholic priest was not restrained from publication in a newspaper; however, the identities of the wife and children were to be protected. It may be noted in this regard that when judgments in family law cases are published in official law reports only the initials of the parties are given, so as not to identify them.

*296.* The Civil Liability and Courts Act 2004, section 40, which came into operation in 2005, contained a provision that relaxed the overall effects of the *in camera* rule to a limited extent. Its effect was to allow a barrister, solicitor or other person designated in regulations by the Minister to report on family law proceedings, subject to safeguarding the identities of the parties and any child to whom the proceedings relate.[308] Section 40(3) was subsequently amended by section 31 of the Civil law (Miscellaneous Provisions) Act 2008 to give access to relevant court documents to any persons designated under the Regulations to attend and report.

*297.* For a long time the question of reporters having access to court documents was somewhat uncertain. The situation improved with the establishment of the Courts' Service[309] in 1999, following enactment of the Courts Service Act 1998. The Service incorporates a Media Relations Service with a designated media relations adviser, who is a journalist. A particular issue arose in 2002 in relation to the practice of court documents not being read out in court but nonetheless being formally entered into the court record. The President of the High Court, acknowledging the 'watchdog' role of

306. *Per* Denham, J at 398.

307. [1995] ILRM 108.

308. The relevant regulations are the Civil Liability and Courts Act 2004 (s. 40(3)) Regulations 2005 S.I. No. 337/2005), which specify that certain persons, including family mediators, as well as persons engaged in family law research, approved by the Minister, may attend and report. Also, persons engaged by the Court Service may attend to prepare court reports of proceedings under relevant enactments.

309. *See* www.courts.ie.

the media in court, said that affidavits read in such a way should be treated as read in open court and 'may in such circumstances be made available to the press'.[310] Since then, the issue of the *in camera* rule has been addressed again by the legislature. The Courts and Civil Law (Miscellaneous Provisions) Act 2013, section 5, makes provision for bona fide representatives of the press to attend and report on in camera proceedings subject to a number of listed considerations (as discussed in paragraphs 209–210).

*298.* The Freedom of Information Act 2014, also has provisions which make clear that it does not generally apply to court documents. Section 41 states:

> 42. This Act does not apply to– (a) a record held by– (i) the courts, or (ii) a service tribunal within the meaning of section 161 of the Defence Act 1954, and relating to, or to proceedings in, a court or such a tribunal, other than– (I) a record that relates to proceedings in a court or such a tribunal held in public but was not created by the court or tribunal and whose disclosure to the general public is not prohibited by the court or the tribunal, or (II) a record relating to the general administration of the courts or the offices of the courts or such a tribunal or any offices of such a tribunal.

Also section 31 states in this regard:

> (1) A head shall refuse to grant an FOI request if the record concerned– (a) would be exempt from production in proceedings in a court on the ground of legal professional privilege, (b) is such that the head knows or ought reasonably to have known that its disclosure would constitute contempt of court.

310. Reported in *The Irish Times* 17 Sept. 2002.

# Chapter 6. Press Council

*299.* Until 2007, Ireland did not have a press council as such. The National Union of Journalists' Code and a variety of in-house standards, guidelines and protocols on various aspects of law and ethics, supplemented the general laws of defamation, contempt of court, privacy, official secrets and so forth that affected the day-to-day operations of the media and media content. As a result, the only option available to a person aggrieved as a result of media content was to seek a remedy through court action if they had a cause of action. Court actions, however, are costly, stressful and can take a long time to be heard. The principal concern of newspapers and media generally was with the defamation laws, which were invoked very frequently against them and resulted in costly settlements or even more costly awards of damages (financial compensation) as well as high legal fees in the courts.

*300.* Following research commissioned by the NNI in 1986,[311] a campaign began for defamation law reform. The research showed, however, that in addition to much-needed law reform, newspaper publishers could, and needed to, do much to help themselves, by improving in-house processes and relations with their readers. One result was that readers' representatives or ombudsmen were appointed in-house in all the national newspapers in 1989.[312] However, despite the report of the Law Reform Commission on defamation in 1991[313] and draft and Private Members' Bills which followed, reform of defamation law was a very slow process. One response of the government was to establish a Commission on the Future of the Newspaper Industry in 1995 to address various legal and market issues facing newspapers, including the financial drain resulting from defamation law. The Commission recommended that defamation law be reformed as a matter of urgency and that a press ombudsman system, rather than a press council,[314] be established by the industry to deal with issues such as intrusions on privacy and to respond to readers' complaints.

*301.* As time progressed, however, successive governments became more concerned about protection of privacy, which had become a more pressing issue since British newspapers, particularly the British tabloids, had begun to establish Irish editions. In fact, when a new defamation bill was drafted in 2005, so too was a privacy bill but the latter was so problematic in terms of its drafting and scope that it was not enacted, although it remains dormant and could be revisited at any time. The establishment of a press council or similar body duly became the quid pro quo for defamation law reform and for staving off government threats to introduce privacy laws and a statutory press council. The print media decided that an independent press council of its own

311. The research was commissioned on an independent basis from Professor Kevin Boyle and Marie McGonagle: *A Report on Press Freedom and Libel* (NNI, 1988).
312. Kevin Boyle and Marie McGonagle, *Media Accountability: The Readers' Representative in Irish Newspapers*, Dublin, National Newspapers of Ireland, 1995.
313. The Boyle & McGonagle report was referred by the Attorney General to the Law Reform Commission in January 1989 with a view to proposals for reform.
314. As intrusion on privacy was not a major issue at the time although there had been a few incidents that had generated a lot of coverage and public debate. Most complaints at the time were about accuracy, typographical errors and such like.

making was a price worth paying and the government proceeded with the new defamation bill. Included in the bill was provision for recognition of a press council and setting out some of the parameters for it. The privacy bill was 'parked' to see how effective the press council would be in addressing privacy issues.

*302.* The Press Council and Press Ombudsman scheme was set up, therefore, in 2007 and has been operational since January 2008. Initially established by the NNI, along with the Regional Newspapers Association, the Periodical Publishers Association, the National Union of Journalists and the British titles with Irish editions, on an independent footing, it applied for and was granted recognition as the Press Council of Ireland under the Defamation Act 2009.[315] That Act, which came into operation in January 2010, provided for recognition as the Press Council of Ireland of a body, and only one body, that met the requirements set out in the Act. The Act provides that the legal status of the Press Council shall be that of a company limited by guarantee and that it shall be independent in the performance of its functions.

*303.* Two important aspects of that independence that are stipulated in the Act are in relation to its composition and the appointment of members. First of all, the majority of the members of the Press Council must be lay people: of the thirteen 'directors', seven must represent the public interest ('independent public interest directors'), five represent the interests of owners and publishers of periodicals (as defined in the Act) and one represents the interests of journalists. The chairperson is appointed from among the independent public interest directors. Second, the independent public interest directors must be appointed through an open independent appointments' process. Once appointed, the Press Council then appoints the Press Ombudsman, again through an open public recruitment process.

*304.* The Press Council is not, therefore, merely a self-regulatory body, although it is funded by the industry; nor is it a statutory body in the normal sense, although its existence is recognized in statute and some of its essential features are set out in statute. It is best described as a co-regulatory body in that it is not government-appointed but the legislature has determined its composition in broad terms and the Minister retains certain powers in relation to it. For instance, the selection of directors of the Press Council must be by a panel of persons who, in the opinion of the Minister, are independent of the interests of owners, publishers and journalists; and the selection process must be advertised to members of the public 'in a manner that the Minister considers to be sufficient'. Also, if the Press Council, so appointed, fails to meet the minimum requirements set out in the Act, the Minister may, after first allowing the incumbent body to make representations to him/her and having laid the draft order before the Houses of the Oireachtas (Parliament), revoke the order recognizing the incumbent body as the Press Council but only if the Oireachtas has passed a resolution approving the draft order.

*305.* In addition to the framework outlined above, the Act laid down the principal objects of the Press Council, namely that it is to ensure the protection of freedom of expression of the press, protect the public interest by ensuring ethical, accurate and truthful reporting by the press, maintain certain minimum ethical and professional standards among the press, and ensure that the privacy and dignity of the individual is protected. The statute also requires the Council to adopt a code of standards which

315. Section 44 and the Second Schedule of the Act deal specifically with the Press Council.

shall specify the standards to be adhered to, and the rules and practices to be complied with, by the members of the Press Council. These include ethical standards and practices, rules and standards intended to ensure the accuracy of reporting where a person's reputation is likely to be affected, and rules and standards intended to ensure that intimidation and harassment of persons does not occur and that the privacy, integrity and dignity of the person is respected.

*306.* As the Press Council and Press Ombudsman scheme is essentially one of handling complaints, the Act makes provision for the Press Ombudsman to investigate, hear and determine complaints with a view to reaching an expeditious and informal resolution of the matter where appropriate. If that is not possible after all reasonable efforts have been made, the Ombudsman must make a determination and decide on appropriate remedial action by the newspaper or periodical concerned, which may range from publication of the decision in whatever form and manner s/he directs, to the publication of a correction with due prominence, or of a retraction or 'such other action as the Ombudsman may, in the circumstances, deem appropriate'. The last-mentioned provision leaves considerable discretion to the Ombudsman. Appeals from decisions of the Ombudsman go to the Press Council itself.

*307.* It is of interest that the Defamation Act also encompasses certain protections for the Council and Ombudsman, and incentives for print media organizations to become and remain members of the Press Council. For instance, the protection of the defence of qualified privilege in a defamation action is available for any determination and related statement of the Press Council or any report of the Press Council relating to the past performance of its functions; likewise, it applies to the determinations and related statements of the Press Ombudsman, and statements made in the course of investigations and appeals. An incentive for the print media is that, in relation to determining if a print media defendant in a defamation action can rely on the defence of fair and reasonable publication on a matter of public interest, a court must take into account 'the extent to which the person adhered to the code of standards of the Press Council and abided by determinations of the Press Ombudsman and determinations of the Press Council' (section 26(2(f)).

*308.* To date, the Press Council system is operating smoothly and the Press Ombudsman has reported a high degree of compliance by the print media. One criticism levelled at the system itself is the fact that the Ombudsman and Council can only handle complaints submitted to them by those affected or their representatives. However, if it were to be otherwise, there is a possibility that the system could be swamped by complaints from interested or outraged onlookers with no real or specific interest in the issue. It is also the case that the Ombudsman and Council do not have power to instigate complaints themselves, although the Defamation Act does state that one of its principal objects is to 'protect the public interest by ensuring ethical, accurate and truthful reporting by the press', while another is to 'maintain certain minimum ethical and professional standards among the press' and yet another to 'ensure that the privacy and dignity of the individual is protected'. It is at least arguable that these 'principal objects' give the Ombudsman and Council some scope for being pro-active or for making statements in response to issues raising questions of accuracy or truthfulness or press standards even where no complaints are received, although a later section of the Act (section 8 (1) of the Second Schedule) gives the Council authority to 'receive, hear and determine complaints concerning the conduct of its members', without mention of initiating complaints themselves.

*309.* The success of the Press Council to date resulted in the Press Ombudsman being asked to address the Leveson Inquiry into press standards in the UK in July 2012 about the operation of the Irish model.[316] Indeed, the Leveson report drew heavily on the Irish model and experience.

316. *See* http://www.levesoninquiry.org.uk/wp-content/uploads/2012/07/Submission-by-Professor-John-Horgan-Irish-Press-Ombudsman.pdf.

# Part III. Regulation of Audiovisual Media (Broadcasting)

*310.* The EU Audiovisual Media Services Directive (hereinafter: AVMS Directive/ AVMSD), adopted at the end of 2007, was transposed into Irish law as required on 19 December 2009. The Broadcasting Act 2009, passed in July 2009, had already incorporated most of the requirements of the AVMS Directive. It had made provision for necessary changes particularly in relation to traditional television broadcasting, identified in the Directive as 'linear' services. The Directive adopts a two-tier or graduated regulatory approach, distinguishing between linear services, which, as fixed menu services, are deemed to require a higher level of regulation, and non-linear services, which as individual choice services, are deemed to require a lower level of regulatory intervention.

*311.* While linear services are provided for in primary legislation, namely the Broadcasting Act 2009, non-linear services are provided for in secondary legislation, namely the European Communities (Audiovisual Media Services) Regulations 2010 (Statutory Instrument S.I. 258 of 2010). These Regulations were made by the Minister for Communications 'for the purpose of giving *further* effect to Council Directive 89/552/EEC of 3 October 1989 as amended by Directive 2007/65/EC of the European Parliament and of the Council of 11 December 2007'.[317]

*312.* A voluntary code also applies to ODAS. The code was developed in furtherance of section 13(1) of the EC Regulations 2010 (Statutory Instrument 258 of 2010). This code of conduct for providers of on-demand audiovisual services (hereafter: ODAS Code) was jointly launched on 4 May 2011 by the ODAS group within the AF of the IBEC and TIF, the BAI and the Advertising Standards Authority for Ireland (ASAI). The code sets out the minimum standards required of service providers, provides a complaints mechanism for consumers and complies with European directives.[318]

*313.* The code covers all ODAS made available under the jurisdiction of the Republic of Ireland. Complaints are handled by the ASAI. The Compliance Committee of the BAI accepts appeals against the resolution offered by the service provider with regard to breaches of subsections 1 & 2 of PART 2 (incitement to hatred and protection of minors) of the Code and makes determinations on complaints. These links to the well-established schemes operated by ASAI and BAI are intended to ensure an effective complaints and enforcement system for on-demand services.

317. Available at www.irishstatutebook.ie/eli/2010/si/258/made/en/print.
318. Available at: http://www.ibec.ie/IBEC/Press/PressPublicationsdoclib3.nsf/vPages/Newsroom~industry-launches-code-of-conduct-for-on-demand-services-04-05-2011/$file/On+Demand+Audiovisual+Media+Services+Code+Final.pdf and at: http://www.bai.ie/en/news-and-information/publications/.

# Chapter 1. Public Service Broadcasting

## §1. The Concept and Mission of Public Service Broadcasting

*314.* Broadcasting in Ireland from its inception was envisaged as, and took the form of, PSB. Commercial broadcasting did not become a reality until the end of the 1980s. PSB is currently governed by the Broadcasting Act 2009. Part 7 of that Act is headed 'Public Service Broadcasting'. Sections 79–112 set out the 'Common Principles', which are followed by 'Provisions specific to RTÉ' (sections 113–116), 'Provisions specific to TG4' (sections 117–119), and provisions related to spectrum licensing, public funding of RTÉ and TG4, as well as provision for the introduction of two new channels, namely a parliamentary channel (Houses of the Oireachtas channel) and an Irish film channel (sections 120–128). Oireachtas television is available throughout Ireland on a number of channels.[319] The film channel has not yet been commenced.

*315.* The essence of PSB is that it is independent in its operation, available FTA on a universal basis, pursues an informational, cultural and educational role, and upholds democratic values. Programming must *inter alia* reflect cultural and linguistic diversity, including minority interests.

### I. History and Evolution

*316.* Raidió Teilifís Éireann (translated literally as 'Radio Television of Ireland'), which is generally referred to as RTÉ, is the national public service broadcaster. Previously, as Radio Éireann, it operated a radio station only but was established as a television broadcaster under the Broadcasting Authority Act 1960. From the beginning it was dual funded, relying on the television licence fee and revenue from advertising. It began with one channel and then for many years it operated two television channels, RTÉ1 and RTÉ2 (since 2004 re-named RTÉ One and RTÉ Two). The TnaG, now called TG4, was initially established in a temporary arrangement under the legislation pertaining to RTÉ as part of the RTÉ system but was later established on an independent footing under the Broadcasting Act 2001. It is also a public service broadcaster and, although a much smaller entity, its structure and statutory remit mirror those of RTÉ.

*317.* RTÉ now has a number of digital-only services also. Saorview is the DTT service owned and managed by RTÉ.[320] It carries both RTÉ and non-RTÉ channels and services. The television services include RTÉ One, RTÉ Two HD, TV3, TG4, RTÉ News Now, 3e, RTÉjr, RTÉ One + 1, RTÉ Digital Aertel (teletext) and Oireachtas TV. The radio services available on Saorview include: RTÉ Radio 1, RTÉ 2fm, RTÉ Lyric fm, RTÉ Raidió na Gaeltachta, RTÉ Pulse, RTÉ 2XM, RTÉ Gold and RTÉ Chill. The infrastructure required to transmit the Saorview service was constructed and is operated by RTÉNL (a wholly owned subsidiary of RTÉ) and was launched in May 2011.

319. *See* http://www.oireachtas.ie/parliament/watchlisten/watchoireachtastv/.
320. www.saorview.ie.

Ministerial consent is required for new services and variations in channels (2009 Act, section 103).

*318.* The switchover from analogue to digital, which took place on 24 October 2012, was co-ordinated with the switchover in Northern Ireland with the result that RTÉ and TG4 now have a place on the Northern Ireland multiplex. The MoU entered into in 2010 committed the two Governments to facilitating the widespread availability of RTÉ services in Northern Ireland on a FTA basis and BBC services in Ireland on a paid for basis. The provision of BBC throughout Ireland was a commercial decision for BBC as, unlike RTÉ, BBC does not have a mandate to provide its services throughout the Island of Ireland. The Memorandum also ensured the continuing widespread availability of TG4 in Northern Ireland following the digital switchover.[321]

*319.* In addition, RTÉ operates a website (www.rte.ie) and i-player. Indeed, section 114 of the Broadcasting Act 2009 includes in the objects of RTÉ the establishment, maintenance, and operation of one or more national multiplexes (section 114(1)(i)); maintenance of a website and teletext services, as well as archives and libraries related to its services, and orchestras, choirs and other cultural performing groups.

*320.* Today, RTÉ, which enjoyed a monopoly of sound and broadcasting services for several decades, competes with numerous commercial radio stations and one national commercial television station, TV3, as well as a number of regional and city-based television stations and a host of European and foreign stations available via cable, satellite and digital technology. TV3, although a commercial broadcaster, has many of the 'public service' obligations that RTÉ has under the Broadcasting Act 2009.

## II. Mission

*321.* The mission or 'objects' of RTÉ, the national public service broadcaster, are set out in section 114(1) of the Broadcasting Act 2009. They include section 114(1)(a) 'to establish, maintain and operate a national television and sound broadcasting service which shall have the character of a public service, be a FTA service and be made available, in so far as it is reasonably practicable, to the whole community on the island of Ireland'. A similar provision at section 114(1)(f) requires it 'to establish, maintain and operate a television broadcasting service and a sound broadcasting service which shall have the character of a public service, which services shall be made available, in so far as RTÉ considers reasonably practicable, to Irish communities outside the island of Ireland'. Under the Act, RTÉ is also required, as far as is reasonably practicable, to provide community, local and regional services, 'which shall have the character of a public service, and be available free-to-air' (section 114(1)(g)), as well as 'non-broadcast non-linear audio-visual media services, in so far as it is reasonably practicable, which shall have the character of a public broadcasting service' (section 114(1)(h)). Section 114 (2) states that:

In pursuit of the objects outlined in subsection (1), RTÉ shall–

321. *See* http://www.dcenr.gov.ie/Broadcasting/Digital+Television/.

(a) be responsive to the interests and concerns of the whole community, be mindful of the need for understanding and peace within the whole island of Ireland, ensure that the programmes reflect the varied elements which make up the culture of the people of the whole island of Ireland, and have special regard for the elements which distinguish that culture and in particular for the Irish language,
(b) uphold the democratic values enshrined in the Constitution, especially those relating to rightful liberty of expression, and
(c) have regard to the need for the formation of public awareness and understanding of the values and traditions of countries other than the State, including in particular those of other Member States.

*322.* Furthermore, section 114(3) provides that RTÉ shall ensure that the programme schedules of the broadcasting services referred to in section 114(1):

(a) provide a comprehensive range of programmes in the Irish and English languages that reflect the cultural diversity of the whole island of Ireland and include programmes that entertain, inform and educate, provide coverage of sporting, religious and cultural activities and cater for the expectations of the community generally as well as members of the community with special or minority interests and which, in every case, respect human dignity;
(b) provide programmes of news and current affairs in the Irish and English languages, including programmes that provide coverage of proceedings in the Houses of the Oireachtas (i.e., Parliament) and the European Parliament; and
(c) facilitate or assist contemporary cultural expression and encourage or promote innovation and experimentation in broadcasting.

*323.* Under section 101 of the Broadcasting Act 2009, RTÉ is required to publish a Public Service Statement every five years setting out the principles to be observed and activities to be undertaken by RTÉ in order to fulfil its public service objects. The first Statement was published in 2010 and the most recent was published in 2015.[322]

*324.* RTÉ states its vision, values and mission as follows:

Vision:

- RTÉ's Vision is to enrich Irish life; to inform, entertain and challenge; to connect with the lives of all the people

Values:

- Understand our audiences and put them at the heart of everything we do
- Be creative, innovative and resourceful
- Be responsible, respectful, honest and accountable to one another and to our audiences

322. The 2015 Statement is available at: https://static.rasset.ie/documents/about/rte-public-service-statement-english.pdf.

Mission:

- Deliver the most trusted, independent, Irish news service, accurate and impartial, for all the connected age
- Provide the broadest range of value for money, quality content and services for all ages, interests and communities
- Reflect Ireland's cultural and regional diversity and enable access to major events
- Support and nurture Irish production and Irish creative talent.[323]

## §2. THE ORGANIZATION OF PUBLIC SERVICE BROADCASTING

*325.* The organization of PSB is set out in broad terms in the Broadcasting Act 2009. Originally, Radio Éireann, the first and for several decades the only licensed broadcaster in the State, operated from 1926 onwards under the control of the Government's Department of Posts and Telegraphs. It became RTÉ, with the status of a semi-state body, in 1960 when its remit as a national public service radio broadcaster was extended to the provision also of a television service under the Broadcasting Authority Act 1960. Its governing authority was the RTÉ Authority, which was to be a body corporate with perpetual succession and power to sue and be sued in its corporate name and to acquire, hold and dispose of land (1960 Act, section 3). The Chairman and members of the Authority were to be appointed by the Government (section 4) and the Government retained the power to remove a member of the Authority from office (section 6).[324] The Authority itself had power to appoint a chief executive officer to be known as the Director General (section 11).

*326.* This organizational structure was changed in the Broadcasting Act 2009, which overhauled the structure of broadcasting in Ireland and made provision for the establishment of the BAI) BAI replaced the former BCI and was given a wider remit, including certain powers in relation to the public service broadcasters, RTÉ and TG4.[325] For instance, all of the codes which BAI is mandated to draft by the Act apply to all broadcasters, including public service broadcasters.

*327.* RTÉ remains a corporation, a body corporate (section 79), but is now headed by a Board, instead of the RTÉ Authority. The Board has a narrower remit than

---

323. *See* 'RTÉ today, tomorrow, together – a new RTÉ for the connected age', available at: http://www.rte.ie/documents/about/vmv-booklet-web.pdf; *see also* 'RTÉ Statement of Performance Commitments 2016', available at: https://static.rasset.ie 'documents' 'about'.

324. The Authority itself was removed from office in 1972 and the legislation was then amended to provide a number of safeguards to ensure its independence, e.g. henceforth a resolution of both Houses of the Oireachtas was to be required for the removal of the Authority.

325. Examples are s. 26(1)(l): to prepare and issue guidance to RTÉ and TG4 as to the fulfilment of their obligations under ss 109(11) and 112(2), regarding respectively cost accounting principles and methods; and a code of fair trading practice setting out the principles that it shall apply when agreeing terms for the commissioning of programming material from independent producers. BAI may also give a direction to RTÉ or a multiplex contractor requiring that RTÉ or the contractor include as part of a television multiplex an electronic programme guide prepared under an electronic programme guide contract referred to in *subs. (8)*, and RTÉ or the contractor shall comply with the direction (s. 74(9)).

the Authority had, given the overarching role of BAI. The appointment and membership of the members of the Board are set out in the Act, as are the criteria for membership, which require *inter alia* experience in any of a range of media, cultural, business or public service-related areas (section 82(1)). The Government appoints the Chairperson from among the membership of the Board (section 85(1)). Candidates for political office are excluded from membership of the Board (section 86); likewise employees of the corporation, except in the case of one member who is elected to the Board by the staff (section 83). When appointed, every member of the board of a corporation shall perform his or her functions in such a manner as to:

(a) represent the interests of viewers and listeners,
(b) ensure that the activities of the corporation in pursuance of its objectives as set out in section 114(1) or 118(1) are performed efficiently and effectively,
(c) ensure that the gathering and presentation by the corporation of news and current affairs is accurate and impartial, and
(d) safeguard the independence of the corporation, as regards, the conception, content and production of programmes, the editing and presentation of news and current affairs programmes and the definition of programme schedules from State, political and commercial influences.

The corporation itself is to be independent in the pursuance of its objects (section 98).

*328.* As was the case with the previous RTÉ Authority, the corporation appoints a person to be the chief executive officer of the corporation, to be known as the Director General (section 89). The Director General manages the administration of the corporation and acts as editor-in-chief in respect of content published by the corporation. The chairperson of the Board and the Director General are accountable to the Committees of the Oireachtas (Parliament) (section 92). The RTÉ Executive Board is responsible for the day-to-day running of RTÉ and is chaired by the Director General. The Board is made up of the Managing Directors of Television, Radio, News & Current Affairs, Digital, Corporate Development; the Chief Financial Officer, Group Commercial Director and Chief Technology Officer.

*329.* The Broadcasting Act 2009 section 93 provides that members of the board of a corporation must disclose any interests they may have in any body or in any concerns with which the corporation has made a contract or proposes to make a contract, or any interest they may have in any contract which the corporation has made or proposes to make and shall not be present at any deliberation or decision of the board of the corporation relating to the contract. Staff and contractors for services must also disclose certain interests (section 94). RTÉ and TG4 must also draw up and adopt a code of conduct in respect of controls on interests and ethical behaviour to apply to each member of the board, member of staff, adviser, member of an advisory committee and member of an audience council of the corporation or a subsidiary of the corporation, as well as contractors for services (section 95). It must then publish the code on its website.

*330.* The Broadcasting Act 2009 also requires the establishment of an audience council by each public service corporation (section 96), whose members are representative of the viewing and listening public and in particular of Gaeltacht (i.e., Irish-speaking) communities and persons with a sight or hearing disability. The principal function of an audience council is to represent to the board of its corporation the views and interests of the general public with regard to PSB by the corporation (section 96(10)). Among its powers, an audience council may require its corporation to conduct, or arrange to be conducted, as far as is reasonably practicable, a survey of children and young persons (section 96(11)), or of elderly persons (section 96(12)), for the purpose of ascertaining their views in respect of PSB by the corporation. An audience council is required to make an annual report to the Minister, the board of its corporation and the Authority (BAI), of its proceedings during the preceding financial year (section 96(16)). As well as the requirement to establish an audience council, a corporation *may* establish advisory committees to advise and assist it in the performance of its functions (section 97(1)). A corporation and its director general must have regard to the advice of any advisory committee but shall not be bound by it (section 97(4)).

*331.* Among its other duties, a corporation must provide a public service statement to the Minister. Following a public consultation, it must 'prepare, not later than 12 months after the passing of this Act, and every 5 years thereafter, or as required by the Minister, a public service statement setting out the principles to be observed, and activities to be undertaken by the corporation in order to fulfil its public service objects'. (section 101). It must also prepare an ASPC in accordance with its objects, strategy statement and public service statement (section 102). Specific issues to be addressed are set out in the Act (section 102(3)).

*332.* As RTÉ is in receipt of public funding by means of a universal licence fee, there are a number of requirements set out in the statute to delimit the public interest uses that can be made of that money and to monitor compliance. Public monies can only be used for the purpose of pursuing its public service objects (section 123(2)). In that regard, a corporation must furnish a statement to the Minister at the end of each financial year in which it distinguishes between monies spent on activities in pursuance of its public service objects, and activities in pursuance of its exploitation of commercial opportunities (section 109(9)).

*333.* Each year, the BAI is required (section 124) to carry out a review of both RTÉ and TG4 which examines:

- The extent to which a PSB has, during the previous financial year, fulfilled its commitments as set out in the broadcaster's ASPC.
- The adequacy, or otherwise, of public funding to allow the PSB meet its public service objectives.

*334.* The BAI's work in this area is guided by the requirements of the Broadcasting Act, as amended by the Communications Regulation (Postal Services) Act 2011,[326] and is underpinned by the 2009 European Commission Communication on PSB. The report is submitted to the Minister for Communications. The Minister's response, together with any report and recommendations of the Authority (BAI), is laid before

326. The Communications Regulation (Postal Services) Act 2011 amends ss 118(9) to include TG4; s. 123(1) regarding apportionment of licence fee receipts to RTÉ and TG4 and s. 123(2) regarding usage of amounts received by TG4 to be used solely for public service objects and paying levies; and s. 124(5) giving effect to the changes to s. 123.

the Houses of the Oireachtas. Once this process is complete, it is the Authority's policy to make available a public version of the report and any associated recommendations of the Authority.[327]

*335.* The Broadcasting Act 2009 (section 124) also requires that within three years of the passing of the Act, and every five years thereafter, the BAI must carry out a review of the adequacy of public funding in enabling PSBs to fulfil their public service objectives. The Act sets out a range of issues that the BAI must take account of in undertaking this five-year review. These include a review of the PSBs' strategic plans to determine their consistency with agreed remits and the extent to which they properly address audience, market and technology challenges; to assess the adequacy of funding available to deliver those plans, in the light of commercial income potential, cost expectations and any efficiency savings; advise on public funding levels for the period of the plan; agree performance goals and the broad remit against which performance can be assessed over the coming years; and establish the key accounting processes, and reporting measures, which PSBs must implement to demonstrate compliance with EC guidelines on transparency and over-compensation, as well as meeting domestic expectations on fair conduct in commercial markets. The first five-year review was held in 2012. The BAI Report and Recommendations were completed in April 2013 and submitted to the Minister for Communications in July 2013.[328]

**Complaints**

*336.* The formerly separate broadcasting complaints body, the Broadcasting Complaints Commission (BCC), originally established under the Broadcasting Authority (Amendment) Act 1976 to deal with complaints from the public against RTÉ, was further developed over the years to deal with complaints from commercial stations also. The Broadcasting Act 2009, however, dissolved the Broadcasting Complaints Commission and replaced it with the Compliance Committee of the BAI. The principal functions of the Compliance Committee under the Act (section 28) are to monitor compliance with, and enforce, the terms and conditions of the contracts awarded by BAI to broadcasters. With regard to the public service broadcasters, the Committee monitors and enforces their compliance with advertising times and limits. It also monitors and enforces compliance by all broadcasters, including PSB, with broadcasting codes and rules. Another important part of its functions is to investigate and decide upon complaints from the public (section 48) and to investigate and decide upon a request for a right of reply, under the right of reply scheme (section 49). In both those cases, the Committee's remit extends to all broadcasters, including PSB.

327. *See* BAI, Annual Report 2015, p. 33 'Annual Review of Public Funding', available at: http://www.bai.ie/en/news-and-information/publications/.

328. *See* 'Public Funding Review of Public Service Broadcasters' – a report for the Broadcasting Authority of Ireland by Oliver and Ohlbaum Associates Limited, July 2015, available at: http://www.dccae.gov.ie/communications/Lists/Publications%20Documents/Annual%20Reviews%20of%20Funding%20of%20PSB/Annual%20Review%20of%20Funding%202014%20-%20Redacted%20report.pdf. *See also* http://www.bai.ie/en/news-and-information/publications/?q=five%20year%20review%20of%20PSB&q=five%20year%20review%20of%20PSB; or for a summary of the recommendations, *see* http://www.bai.ie/blog/2013/07/18/bai-publishes-recommendations-on-future-funding-for-public-service-broadcasting/.

## §3. The Financing of Public Service Broadcasting

*337.* As indicated above, RTÉ, the public service broadcaster, is dual funded on a 50/50 basis, and has been funded in that way from the beginning. There really was no choice, as the weak economic situation that pertained in Ireland during the 1950s meant that Ireland could not afford to have its own television service if it were to be a drain on the exchequer. RTÉ is partly funded, therefore, by means of a licence fee levied on every household that has a television set. The fee is collected by An Post, the postal service. Over the years there have been a number of court cases involving challenges to the licence fee, particularly by Irish-language speakers who objected to paying it when there was relatively little Irish-language content provided by RTÉ. However, with the launch of a dedicated Irish-language television station in 1996 that issue was resolved.

*338.* RTÉ initially received the full amount of the licence fee, less the amount paid to An Post to collect it. RTÉ was required to provide a certain amount of programming to the Irish-language station TG4, equivalent to one hour per day.[329] The Minister for Communications, with the consent of the Minister for Finance, was authorized under the Act (section 51) to pay to TG4 such amount as s/he deemed reasonable to defray the expenses incurred by it in performing its functions. TG4 later became independent of RTÉ.[330]

*339.* The Irish-language broadcasting stations, Raidió na Gaeltachta (radio)and TG4 (television), are state-funded. TG4 has a total budget of about EUR 37 million.[331] In the Budget 2011, it was announced that EUR 10 million (5%) of the licence fee would be allocated from RTÉ to TG4. This replaced direct funding of TG4 from Government.[332] TG4 also secures funding on behalf of the independent production sector from the BAI Sound &Vision II Fund and the Northern Ireland Irish Language Broadcast Fund (ILBF).[333] This funding goes directly to independent producers and enables the production of programming projects; additional programmes/series are produced in conjunction with Bord Scannán na hÉireann/the Irish Film Board.[334] In 2017 TG4, Bord Scannán na hÉireann/The Irish Film Board (BSÉ) and the BAI joined in launching a Development Scheme, *Cine4*, a new joint-funding initiative to support the development and production of feature films in the Irish language. Any films

329. Broadcasting Act 2001, s. 47.
330. Broadcasting Act 2009.
331. TG4 Annual Report 2016. This was an increase from €35.5 million in 2016, *see* http://opac.oireachtas.ie/AWData/Library3/CCAEdoclaid13072017_125554.pdf. TG4's Annual Report, Codes and Statements are available at: http://www.tg4.ie/en/corporate/corporate-governance/. In its Statement of Performance Commitments for 2015, TG4 stated that it had undergone an 18% reduction in Grant-in-Aid over the past number of years; *see* http://s3.amazonaws.com/tg4-docs/tg4-redesign-2015/wp-content/uploads/2015/07/Statement-Public-Service-Committments.pdf.
332. http://www.saortv.info/2010/12/08/dso-also-tg4-funding/.
333. For information on the Irish Language Broadcast Fund, *see* http://northernirelandscreen.co.uk/categories/7/ilbf.aspx.
334. A breakdown of funding allocated under the Sound and Vision scheme in 2016 is available at: http://www.bai.ie/en/more-than-e5-8m-allocated-to-124-projects-under-sound-vision-scheme/.

produced under the *Cine4* Development Scheme will be given a full festival life and theatrical release prior to their broadcast premiere on TG4.[335]

*340.* BAI operates other funding support schemes. These include The Community Broadcasting Support Scheme (CBSS), a development fund which allows community radio and community television stations to carry out evaluation activities internally and externally. The Scheme also funds CRAOL (the Community Radio representative and training body) networking and training activities.[336]Community radio stations rely on public funding derived from grants from a number of government departments and various agencies. These grants make up one element in a wider mix of revenues, which include advertising and sponsorship.

*341.* With a view to supporting PSB into the future, a further portion of the licence fee was set aside in accordance with a scheme provided for in the Broadcasting (Funding) Act 2003. The scheme was to take 5% of the licence fee collected each year and place it in a fund, which was to be administered by the then BCI, and now the BAI. This 'Sound and Vision Scheme', which was approved in 2005 by the European Commission under State Aid and competition rules, enables all broadcasters in the State, both public service and private commercial, to apply for grants for the production of new high-quality television and radio programmes in English or Irish in the areas of Irish culture, heritage and experience and adult literacy. The scheme was extended under the Broadcasting Act 2009 to offer funding also for programmes dealing with the themes of media literacy and global affairs.[337] The Act also increased the percentage level of funding for the Scheme via the television licence fee to 7%.[338]

*342.* Under the scheme, grants are only available for programmes that will actually be broadcast; therefore, independent producers must confirm that they have a contract with a broadcaster to broadcast the programme if funding is granted, and broadcasters must confirm their commitment to broadcast the programme and to give it a prime time slot. To be eligible, television broadcasters must be FTA and have near universal coverage, as per section 153 of the Broadcasting Act 2009, while network providers must be as defined in section 77(1) of the Act or an MMD system as part of a community content provision contract under section 72. Radio broadcasters must be those operating under a contract with BAI or operated by RTÉ. Thus, although 7% is taken from the total licence fee, RTÉ still benefits from it to an extent via the Sound and Vision fund.[339]

---

335. *See* http://www.bai.ie/en/bai-supports-major-funding-initiative-new-irish-language-feature-film-production/.
336. Research funded by the Broadcasting Authority of Ireland's Media Research Funding Scheme, *Cross-National Comparative Analysis of Community Radio Funding Schemes,* is available at; http://www.bai.ie/en/research-report-published-analysis-of-community-radio-funding-schemes/.
337. BAI launched its new media literacy policy on 6 Dec. 2016. *See* http://www.bai.ie/en/bai-launches-media-literacy-policy/.
338. www.bai.ie. Details of the current scheme Sound and Vision 3 scheme are available at: http://www.bai.ie/en/news-and-information/publications/.
339. BAI also manages a small funding scheme, the Community Broadcasting Support Scheme, specifically for community radio and television stations to aid their development. Details of the 2015 scheme are available at: http://www.bai.ie/blog/2015/08/20/community-broadcasting-support-scheme-2015/.

*343.* BAI also developed a funding Scheme for the archiving of broadcast material, which was launched in 2012. Public service, commercial and community broadcasters can apply for funding. Programme Material eligible for funding includes: television content, radio content and advertising and similar material which was broadcast in whole or in part or was recorded for broadcast; as well as stills and photographs produced from such material or in the context of the recording of such material. Special consideration is given to the archiving of programme material which preserves a historical record of Irish culture, heritage and experience and assists in the development of an integrated approach to the archiving of programme material produced in the State. Examples are: programme material in the Irish language; programme material that relates to Irish culture and life; concerns Irish music, drama and entertainment; is news, current affairs or documentary.[340]

*344.* Until now, the licence fee has applied to ownership or possession of a television set. Under the Broadcasting Act 2009, only television sets require a licence, not computers, mobile phones or other means of receiving television programmes (section 142(3) of the Act and S.I. No 319 of 2009 Television Licence (Exemption of Classes of Television Set) Order 2009). The Order excludes non-portable television sets capable of exhibiting television broadcasting services distributed by means of the publicly available Internet, and portable television sets, which are defined as being designed to be carried around and capable of displaying an image of not more than 160 square centimetres. There has always been an element of evasion of the licence fee[341] and as viewers switch to the Internet and mobile phones to receive television services, the licence fee income is likely to drop further. The government announced plans, therefore, to transfer from the current system to a universal household charge, in the same way as electricity and other services are charged, and as is already the means of collection on some other countries. The proposed new charge, which was to be known as the 'public broadcasting charge' was to be levied on 'all households and applicable businesses, regardless of the device used to access content'. It was due to come into operation from 1 January 2015 but that did not happen. At the time of writing the plan is still on hold although but it, as well as the matter of extending the licence fee to devices other than television sets, has been raised again.[342]

---

340. Details of the Archiving Funding Scheme are available at: http://www.bai.ie/en/broadcasting/funding-development-3/#al-block-4.

341. Estimated at 15% or EUR 25 million per annum – *see* http://debates.oireachtas.ie/dail/2012/01/18/00019.asp (18 Jan. 2012, Deputy Pat Rabbitte, Minister for Communications).

342. *See* Laura Slattery, 'Online viewing licence loophole may be closed', *The Irish Times* 2 Dec. 2016, available at: http://www.irishtimes.com/business/media-and-marketing/online-viewing-licence-fee-loophole-may-be-closed-1.2889724; Kevin Doyle, 'Now laptop, iPad and PC users will have to buy a TV licence', Irish Independent 27 Mar. 2017, available at:https://www.independent.ie/business/now-laptop-ipad-and-pc-users-will-have-to-buy-a-tv-licence-35567457.html; also independent.ie News desk 10 Nov. 2017, available at: https://www.independent.ie/irish-news/major-new-report-proposes-increase-in-tv-licence-fee-and-a-charge-for-every-home-even-if-you-dont-own-a-tv-36306849.html. An Oireachtas Joint Committee Report on the Future Funding of Public Service Broadcasting, 28 Nov. 2017, recommends that the current model be replaced by a household-based charge to be collected by the Revenue Commissioners; *see* https://data.oireachtas.ie.

*345.* The other funding source for PSB is advertising revenue. From the beginning of television broadcasting, advertising time was limited by statute, initially section 20 of the Broadcasting Authority Act 1960, which required the RTÉ Authority to fix the total daily time and distribution, subject to the approval of the Minister. This was amended in the 1976 Broadcasting Authority (Amendment) Act to specify total daily times and maximum hourly times.[343] When commercial broadcasting became a reality at the end of the 1980s and the new stations were struggling financially to establish themselves, measures were introduced in the Broadcasting Act 1990 to cap the advertising revenue earned by RTÉ, so as to free up some advertising for the new stations. As RTÉ had had a monopoly for nearly three decades and had built up a strong advertising base, it was deemed necessary to limit the amount of advertising it could take in order to 'level the playing-pitch' for the new entrants. However, the measures adopted proved unworkable and were abolished by the Broadcasting Authority (Amendment) Act 1993.

*346.* In 2011, the Competition Authority conducted an investigation into the scheme operated by RTÉ for the sale of television advertising airtime, in particular the discounts granted by RTÉ to individual advertisers depending on, among other factors, the percentage (or share) of each advertiser's total television advertising budget committed to RTÉ. The issue was whether this could amount to a breach of section 5 of the Competition Act, 2002 and/or Article 102 of the Treaty on the Functioning of the European Union (TFEU). An agreement was reached on the basis of undertakings given by RTÉ that it would discontinue the share of budget element of the scheme and implement a new scheme by 1 July 2012.[344]

*347.* Section 43(1) of the Broadcasting Act 2009 requires the BAI to prepare, and from time to time as occasion requires, revise rules with respect to the total daily and hourly times permitted for advertising and teleshopping, but these do not apply to RTÉ. Instead, in RTÉ's case, limits on advertising per hour and per day for public service broadcasters are set by the Minister for Communications, Energy and Natural Resources. At present, the hourly maximum for RTÉ is six minutes.[345] No advertising is permitted on the RTÉjr or RTÉ News Now digital channels.

*348.* Prior to going to air, all radio and television advertisements must first be cleared for broadcast by RTÉ's internal Copy Clearance Committee. The Committee considers both the verbal and visual content of the commercial, along with its suitability for broadcast and its compliance with all existing legal and industry codes for advertising, as well as RTÉ's own internal guidelines.[346]

343. Later the Broadcasting Act 2001 required the RTÉ Authority to set daily and hourly time limits also for teleshopping. This followed the EC Television without Frontiers Directive of 1989, as amended in 1997.
344. Competition Act 2002, Decision of the Competition Authority (Case COM/10/02): RTÉ's conduct in the market for television advertising, 17 Jan. 2012; Enforcement Decision Series (E/12/001) available at http://www.tca.ie/EN/News--Publications/News-Releases/Successful-resolution-to-complaint-against-RT.aspx.
345. Broadcasting Act 2001, s. 31; the same applies in the case of TG4 (Broadcasting Act 2001, s. 49(1)).
346. For further details on copy clearance, *see* https://tvmediasales.rte.ie/copy-clearance-traffic/copy-clearance/airtime-information/.

# Chapter 2. Private Broadcasting

*349.* Private broadcasting began in Ireland in 1989, following the enactment of the Radio and Television Act 1988 and the Wireless Telegraphy Act of the same year. At the time, RTÉ was the only licensed broadcaster in the State but there were approximately ninety 'pirate' radio stations operating without licences, since no licences had been forthcoming from successive governments. The Wireless Telegraphy Act 1988 was designed to put the pirate stations off air but it provided encouragement to them to cease broadcasting by midnight on 31 December 1988 in order to be eligible to apply for licences to broadcast legally. The Radio and Television Act provided for the scheme of licensing for the new services. It also established the IRTC as contracts and content regulator. The IRTC was later replaced by the BCI in the Broadcasting Act 2001, which in turn became the BAI under the Broadcasting Act 2009.

## §1. Different Categories of Private Broadcasters

*350.* The main category of private broadcasters is that of independent commercial broadcasters. There are currently three national commercial television services (TV3 and TV3 + 1 and 3E, all part of the TV3 group, now owned by Virgin Media, as is UTV which was recently acquired by TV3). UTV was re-branded as be3 and TV3 is due to be re-branded as Virgin Media TV in 2018. There are currently ten content provision contracts, which include Setanta Sports Ireland (now owned by eir). Many more private commercial broadcasters, licensed in the UK, also broadcast into, or are available, in Ireland. The private commercial radio services (currently thirty-four in total) include one national service (Today FM); one quasi-national service (Newstalk); four youth radio services (Beat FM, Spin South West, iRadio NW and iRadio NE); one multicity service (4FM); and 25 local radio services;[347] one Dublin City and Commuter Belt service (Radio Nova) and one Local Youth Radio Service (Spin 103.8). New licences are issued by BAI from time to time.

*351.* An additional distinct category of broadcasting is Community broadcasting. It is defined as follows:

> A community radio station is characterised by its ownership and programming and the community it is authorised to serve. It is owned and controlled by a not-for-profit organisation whose structure provides for membership, management, operation and programming primarily by members of the community at large. Its programming should be based on community access and should reflect the special interests and needs of the listenership it is licensed to serve.[348]

---

347. The full list is available at: http://www.bai.ie/en/broadcasters/.

348. http://www.bci.ie/documents/comm_radio_policy.pdf The AMARC Community Radio Charter for Europe was adopted in 1994 as a statement of the objectives community stations should strive to achieve (*ibid.*).

Community stations are funded from a variety of sources, including fundraising and advertising, although no more than 50% of income can be obtained from commercial activity.

*352.* Section 43(1) of the Broadcasting Act, 2009 requires the BAI to prepare, and from time to time as occasion requires, revise rules with respect to the total daily and hourly times permitted for advertising and teleshopping, which apply to commercial and community broadcasters. The current rules provide that the maximum daily amount of advertising and teleshopping on commercial television stations must not exceed 18% of the total broadcasting day. The hourly time must not exceed twelve minutes in any clock hour, while in the case of children's programming it is ten minutes.[349] The minimum uninterrupted duration of teleshopping windows is fifteen minutes in any clock hour, with a daily maximum of eight windows, not exceeding 3 hours in total.[350] In the case of community stations, a maximum of six minutes per hour is permitted and the advertisements must relate to the specified area. The teleshopping limits for community television services is the same as for commercial television stations.

## §2. Licensing Requirements

*353.* Commercial broadcasting services were first licensed under the Radio and Television Act 1988. The stations were primarily sound broadcasting services, including temporary and institutional broadcasting services. Initially the licensing requirements, application processes and criteria were set out in the Radio and Television Act 1988 and later the Broadcasting Act 2001. A small number of unsuccessful court challenges to licensing decisions were taken. Cases such as *Spin Communications Ltd t/a Storm FM v. IRTC*[351]concerned the refusal of licences or refusal to renew broadcast licences. Provision was also made for a television programme service. The Broadcasting Act 2001 augmented the range of services by making provision for additional cable, satellite and MMD contracts. These new services included digital services (digital content contracts) (Part II of Act), local interest channels (local content contract), community channels (provision of community content contract), satellite content contracts, commercial cable and MMD system contracts (cable-MMD content contracts) (Part V of the Act).[352] The Broadcasting Act 2009 Part VI now deals with Broadcasting Contracts and Content Provision Contracts relating to Commercial and Community Broadcasters. In the first instance, licences have to be granted to the BAI by the

349. In 2010, BAI increased the maximum advertising per hour for commercial television stations from 10 minutes to 12 minutes.

350. This does not apply to self-promotion channels and channels exclusively devoted to teleshopping. The maximum for commercial radio is 15% and ten minutes per hour. Institutional and temporary radio broadcasters may not carry advertising. The BAI Advertising and Teleshopping Rules (2010) are available at: http://www.bai.ie/en/codes-standards/.

351. [2002] ILRM 98. Only one broadcasting licence has been terminated by the regulator to date for persistent breaches of contractual obligations. That was the case of *Radio Limerick One Ltd v. IRTC* [1997] 2 I.R. 291.

352. BAI has drafted guidelines on each of the different forms of contract; available at http://www.bai.ie/en/broadcasting/licensing-2/radio/ and http://www.bai.ie/en/broadcasting/licensing-2/television/.

ComReg.[353] BAI then allocates the licences to broadcasters and enters into contracts with them.

## I. Radio Broadcasters

*354.* RTÉ, as the public service broadcaster, which was in existence before the licensing of commercial and other broadcasting services began, is not required to obtain a licence to broadcast under the licensing system operated by BAI. It receives its licence directly from the Communications Regulator, ComReg (Broadcasting Act 2009, section 121). When it wishes to bring in new channels or services, it must seek the approval of the Minister for Communications.

*355.* The licensing system operated by BAI, in conjunction with ComReg, applies to all other broadcasters in the State. When licences have been granted to BAI by ComReg, BAI issues a sound broadcasting contract for a period, currently ten years. Every broadcasting contract must contain a condition requiring the broadcasting contractor to establish, maintain and operate the broadcasting transmitter concerned, in accordance with such terms and conditions as the Communications Regulator attaches to the broadcasting licence to which the contract relates, and, so long as the terms and conditions are complied with, the contract has the effect of conveying the benefits of the licence to the broadcasting contractor (section 59(3)). Conditions of a broadcasting licence can be varied for reasons set out in the Act, including in the interests of good frequency management or if it is in the public interest (section 60). Terms and conditions that BAI can insert in the sound broadcasting contract are set out in section 69 of the Broadcasting Act 2009 and include restrictions on assigning the contract or making material changes without the consent of BAI.

*356.* Certain restrictions on the granting of a sound content contract are specified in the Act. For instance, persons convicted of an offence, such as engaging in or facilitating illegal broadcasting (under the terms of the Broadcasting and Wireless Telegraphy Act 1988) within a year of the date s/he is to begin broadcasting shall not be recommended by the Contract Awards Committee to the BAI for the grant of a licence (2009 Act, section 62). When this happens for that or other reasons, such as the previous track-record in broadcasting of an applicant, the Contract Awards Committee must give reasons and the score given to the application (section 66).

*357.* In certain instances BAI is required by the Act to liaise with ComReg, for instance in relation to the preparation of a frequency allocation plan, so as to ensure the orderly development of broadcasting and to allow for the establishment of a diversity of services in an area, catering for a wide range of tastes, including those of minority interests (2009 Act, section 65). This plan forms the basis for the setting of the specific areas to which the sound broadcasting contracts will attach. Applications are then invited and assessed in accordance with the provisions of the Act (sections 65–66). The detailed criteria for consideration in determining the most suitable applicant, as set out in the Act (section 66), are important for the BAI in fulfilling its role not only

353. ComReg, which was established by the Communications Regulation Act 2002, is in essence the infrastructural regulator, with a remit that extends to telecoms, spectrum allocation and the postal service.

in granting licences but also in setting its policy on pluralism and diversity.[354] The principal considerations include the following: the character, expertise and experience of the applicant; the adequacy of the financial resources that will be available to each applicant and the extent to which the application accords with good business and economic principles; the quality, range and type of the programmes proposed, including programmes in the Irish language; the desirability of having pluralism of ownership and diversity of services; the need to serve local and minority interests.

*358.* There are also requirements in relation to recording and storage of broadcast material 'in order to avoid the loss of sound programme material inimical to the preservation of a historical record of Irish culture, heritage and experience and as an initial step towards the development of an integrated approach to the archiving of programme material produced in the State' (section 69(6)). As required by the Act (section 154(1)(e)), BAI developed a funding scheme in respect of archives, which was approved by the Minister in January 2012. The Scheme is being financed through a percentage of the annual Broadcasting Fund derived from the television licence fee.[355] Prior to the Ministerial approval for the scheme in 2012, when approval was sought from the European Commission in 2010, the wording of section 154(1)(e) was found to be incompatible with EU state aid rules, as it related only to material produced in Ireland. As a result, an amendment was made to section 154(1)(e) in the Communications Regulation (Postal Services) Act 2011.[356]

Finally, every broadcasting contract must be open to inspection by members of the public at the Authority's registered office (section 69(5)).

## II. Television Broadcasters

*359.* As in the case of radio, RTÉ, the public service broadcaster, is not required to obtain a licence to broadcast under the licensing system operated by BAI. Instead, a licence is issued directly to RTÉ by the Communications Regulator (ComReg); the same is the case with TG4 (Broadcasting Act 2009, section 121). However, in 2001 when RTÉ announced plans to have its radio and television channels carried on the SKY satellite platform, the BCI, the regulatory authority for broadcasting in the State at the time, pointed out that RTÉ required a satellite content contract under section 36 of the Broadcasting Act 2001 (section 36) in order to enter into the deal with SKY. A satellite retransmission contract was duly granted by BCI to RTÉ in accordance with the Act.[357]

354. Particularly criteria (g) – (j). The policy on pluralism and diversity devised by the BAI's predecessor is called the 'Ownership and Control' policy. The current version is the BAI Ownership and Control Policy 2012 is available at: http://www.bai.ie/en/news-and-information/publications/.

355. http://www.bai.ie/en/broadcasting/funding-development-3/.

356. *See* Damien McCallig, 'Ireland – Approval of Funding Scheme for Broadcast Archiving', IRIS 2012-4:1/29, available at http://merlin.obs.coe.int/.

357. *See* IRIS 2002-4:7/15 Ireland– Digital Television, available at http://merlin.obs.coe.int/iris/2002/4/article15.en.html.

*360.* With regard to licences for multiplexes, the 2009 Act states that the Communications Regulator, ComReg, at the request of RTÉ, shall issue to RTÉ a licence in respect of the establishment, maintenance and operation of television broadcasting multiplexes (section 132) and sound multiplexes (section 133). For the reasons explained above (paragraphs 25, 40), there are no commercially operated multiplexes in Ireland to date.

*361.* As in the case of radio, the licensing of all television services other than public service broadcasters is now operated by BAI in accordance with the Broadcasting Act 2009. The main provision is section 70, which deals with television programme service contracts, which involve 'the right and duty, subject to the terms of the contract, to establish, maintain and operate television broadcasting transmitters for the purpose of transmitting the television programme service as a free-to-air service'. (section 70(1)). BAI has to ensure that the service provided by a television programme service contractor under this section shall in its programming:

(a) be responsive to the interests and concerns of the whole community, be mindful of the need for understanding and peace within the whole island of Ireland, ensure that the programmes reflect the varied elements which make up the culture of the people of the whole island of Ireland, and have special regard for the elements which distinguish that culture and in particular for the Irish language;
(b) uphold the democratic values enshrined in the Constitution, especially those relating to rightful liberty of expression;
(c) have regard to the need for the formation of public awareness and understanding of the values and traditions of countries other than the State, including in particular those of other Member States; and
(d) include a reasonable proportion of news and current affairs programmes. (section 70(2))

In other words, along with the established public service television broadcasters, commercial television stations licensed by BAI are required to meet certain public service standards. Furthermore, BAI must ensure that a reasonable proportion of the television programme service is produced in the State or in another Member State, and is devoted to original programme material produced therein by persons other than the contractor, its subsidiary, its parent or existing broadcasting organizations (section 70(4)).

*362.* Provision is made also for television content provision contracts, where compilations of material are being made available as part of a multiplex (digital television), or being transmitted as a broadcasting service in the State, part of the State or elsewhere by means of an electronic communications network including a satellite network, an MMD system, a fixed or mobile terrestrial network, a cable television network, an IPTV network or any other form of electronic communications network (section 71(2)(b)).[358] Conditions attached to content provision contracts include requirements to comply with broadcasting codes and rules (BAI) and to comply with national law and the AVMS Directive in relation to incitement to hatred; if breached BAI 'may' terminate the contract and if a second breach has occurred within six months

358. RTÉ and other free-to-air services are specifically excluded.

of the first, BAI 'shall' terminate the contract (section 71(6)). Most recently, the Minister made an Order, entitled the 'Broadcasting Act 2009 (section 130(1)(a)(iv) Designation) Order 2016', dated 23 June 2016, designating the television service, to be provided by Teilifís Mhaigh Eo Teoranta in accordance with a content provision contract between it and the BAI under section 71 of the Broadcasting Act 2009, as having the character of a public service for the purposes of section 130(1)(a)(iv) of the Act.[359] Known as 'Irish TV', itis a local and international channel offering a mix of live and recorded programming relevant to Irish people at home and abroad.

*363.* In relation to community content contracts, two or more members of a local community or community of interest may supply a compilation of programme material for the purposes of its being transmitted as a broadcasting service under and in accordance with an MMD system transmission licence or by an appropriate network provider (section 72(1)). The conditions attached include that:

(a) those members are representative of, and accountable to, the community concerned; and
(b) the supply of programme material in pursuance of the contract will be effected with the sole objective of:

    (1) specifically addressing the interests of, and seeking to provide a social benefit to, the community concerned; and
    (2) achieving a monetary reward of no greater amount than is reasonably necessary to defray the expenses that will be incurred in effecting that supply.

*364.* Contracts are also required for the provision of electronic programme guides (section 74). Provision of content without a content provision contract (section 71(1)) or provision of an electronic programme guide without a contract (section 74(1)) can result in a fine of up to EUR 5,000 on summary conviction or EUR 100,000 on indictment (section 78).

359. Available at: http://www.dccae.gov.ie/communications/en-ie under 'Legislation'.

# Chapter 3. Programme Standards

**Introduction**

*365.* Under section 42 of the Broadcasting Act 2009, the BAI) – the independent statutory body with responsibility for regulating the broadcasting sector in Ireland– is mandated to prepare and revise codes governing standards and practices to be observed by broadcasters. In doing so, section 42(3) of the 2009 Act requires the BAI to have regard to the following matters:

(a) the degree of harm or offence likely to be caused by the inclusion of any particular sort of material in programmes generally, or in programmes of a particular description;
(b) the likely size and composition of the potential audience for programmes included in television and sound broadcasting services generally, or in television and sound broadcasting services of a particular description;
(c) the likely expectation of the audience as to the nature of a programme's content and the extent to which the nature of a programme's content can be brought to the attention of potential members of the audience;
(d) the likelihood of persons who are unaware of the nature of a programme's content being unintentionally exposed, by their own actions, to that content;
(e) the desirability of securing that the content of a broadcasting service identifies when there is a change affecting the nature of the service that is being watched or listened to and, in particular, a change that is relevant to the application of the codes set under this section; and
(f) the desirability of maintaining the independence of editorial control over programme content.

*366.* The 2009 Act also requires the BAI to engage in a process of consultation when developing a broadcasting code. The current Code of Programme Standards in operation in Ireland came into effect on 1 March 2015. It applies to all programme material broadcast by broadcasters within the jurisdiction of Ireland. It does not apply, however, to commercial communications, such as advertising, programme sponsorship or teleshopping or to complaints about fairness, objectivity and impartiality in news and current affairs content. That is so because there are separate codes to deal with commercial communications (General Commercial Communications Code and Children's Commercial Communications Code) and with fairness, objectivity and impartiality in news and current affairs content (Code of Fairness, Objectivity and Impartiality).[360]

## §1. Impartiality

*367.* According to section 25 of the Broadcasting Act 2009, among the stated objectives of the BAI is the provision of a regulatory environment capable of sustaining

360. The Codes are all available at: http://www.bai.ie/en/codes-standards/.

independent and impartial journalism. Further, section 39 of the 2009 Act places a number of duties on broadcasters (i.e., broadcasting companies rather than individuals, although that should not be taken to mean that individual presenters, or programme staff, are exempt):[361]

(1) Every broadcaster shall ensure that –

(a) all news broadcast by the broadcaster is reported and presented in an objective and impartial manner and without any expression of the broadcaster's own views,

(b) the broadcast treatment of current affairs, including matters which are either of public controversy or the subject of current public debate, is fair to all interests concerned and that the broadcast matter is presented in an objective and impartial manner and without any expression of his or her own views, except that should it prove impracticable in relation to a single broadcast to apply this paragraph, two or more related broadcasts may be considered as a whole, if the broadcasts are transmitted within a reasonable period of each other,

...

(5) A broadcaster shall ensure that the broadcast treatment of any proposal, being a proposal concerning policy as regards broadcasting, which is of public controversy or the subject of current public debate, which is being considered by the Government or the Minister, shall be reported and presented in an objective and impartial manner.[362]

*368.* In addition, section 42 of the 2009 Act requires the BAI to prepare and revise codes governing standards and practices to be observed by broadcasters, including those listed in section 39 in relation to impartiality. Thus, in February 2012, in order to assist broadcasters in meeting their statutory obligations under section 39 of the 2009 Act with respect to fairness and impartiality, the BAI launched a public consultation on a Draft Code of Fairness, Objectivity and Impartiality in News and Current Affairs.[363] In this first phase of the consultation process, the BAI invited views on the Draft Code from all interested parties – including broadcasters, journalists, political parties, voluntary and professional organizations and members of the public.[364] The resulting

361. The distinction is pointed out in the Guidance Notes that were issued with the Code of Fairness, Objectivity and Impartiality in News and Current Affairs, 2013.

362. Broadcasting Act 2009, s 39(1)(a) and (b), and s. 39(5). The 'Minister' means the Minister for Communications, Energy and Natural Resources (Broadcasting Act 2009, Part 1, s. 2), now the Minister for Communications, Climate Action and Environment.

363. Broadcasting Authority of Ireland (BAI), 'BAI Launches Consultation on Draft Code of Fairness, Objectivity and Impartiality in News and Current Affairs' (Press Release, 1 Feb. 2012).

364. *Ibid.*

code was also underpinned by a national survey and research on other jurisdictions.[365] The Code, which is accompanied by Guidance Notes to aid understanding, became effective from 1 July 2013.

*369.* The principles underpinning the Code are: (1) fairness, (2) objectivity and impartiality, (3) accuracy and responsiveness, and (4) transparency and accountability. The Code restates the statutory duties of broadcasters in respect of fairness and impartiality (as set out in section 39 of the 2009 Act) and contains a range of more specific rules under the following headings: (1) fairness rules, (2) objectivity and impartiality rules, (3) election and referendum coverage, (4) broadcasting policy matters, (5) legal requirements.

*370.* Objectivity and impartiality rules span issues such as accuracy, misrepresentation, acknowledgment and rectification of mistakes, the requirement that presenters do not express their own views and the handling of conflicts of interest of anyone involved in the editorial process. The Guidance Notes, issued with the Code, state in respect of impartiality that the 'principles of objectivity and impartiality are concerned with ensuring that news and current affairs content is compiled, produced and presented in a manner which is and can be seen as independent, unbiased, and without prejudgement'. They further stress that the rules set out in the Code with regard to objectivity and impartiality 'should not be taken to imply that a presenter or a reporter cannot convey critical views or pursue vigorous lines of questioning. Indeed, this is often required in order to achieve fairness, objectivity and impartiality. What is necessary, however, is that production, reporting and questioning on any news or current affairs item is credible, trustworthy and editorially independent'.

*371.* Election and referendum coverage are subject to separate codes and guidelines, discussed below. Complaints alleging breaches of the Codes, as is the case with complaints generally, are handled by the Compliance Committee of BAI. The public service broadcaster RTÉ issues its own journalistic guidelines for its staff in accordance with the statutory provisions of the 2009 Act and the BAI Codes.[366]

## §2. Cultural Diversity

### I. Access to Airtime for Cultural Groupings

*372.* Following an unprecedented wave of immigration into Ireland from the turn of the twenty-first century, the Irish media have responded to the resultant multicultural nature of Irish society both in their programming and by devising institutional policies. Broadcasters have moved 'from first-wave programmes – mainly aimed at representing migrant lives and experiences to a mainstream Irish audience

365. [357] M. McGonagle et al, *Fairness and Balance in News and Current Affairs – A Review of other Jurisdictions* (2011), Dublin, Broadcasting Authority of Ireland.

366. The RTÉ guidelines address impartiality: RTÉ, *Journalism Guidelines*, 2014, s. 8, available at: https://static.rasset.ie/documents/about/rte-journalism-guidelines-2014.pdf.

– to a still-evolving emphasis on integrating diversity into programming'.[367] For instance, multicultural radio programming on RTÉ began in 2000 and various programmes have been developed since, becoming increasingly integrated, with multicultural issues becoming part of mainstream programming.[368]

*373.* As noted above, the Broadcasting Act 2009 contains a number of provisions relating to cultural diversity. For example, section 25(1)(a) and 25(2)(h) require BAI *inter alia* to endeavour to ensure that the number and categories of broadcasting services made available best serve the needs of the people of the island of Ireland, bearing in mind their languages and traditions and their religious, ethical and cultural diversity.

*374.* Provision is made in the Act, as in previous Acts, for community, community of interest, temporary and institutional radio licensing, which enable small geographical areas; interest groups having a shared interest, association or bond; and institutions, such as hospitals, to have their own services (section 64). Local communities or communities of interest may get a content provision contract to supply a compilation of programme material for the purposes of its being transmitted as a broadcasting service under and in accordance with an MMD system transmission licence or by an appropriate network provider (section 72) and BAI may require the service or network provider to transmit it (section 76(4) and section 77(8)). Community television licences are also available.

*375.* With regard to airtime, there is no provision for set amounts of airtime to be dedicated to cultural groupings. In respect of party political broadcasts during election and referenda campaigns, free airtime is provided to registered political parties according to the number of their elected representatives; thus the large parties get longer airtime and the small parties considerably less. The allocation of such airtime is subject to requirements of fairness as set out above.

*376.* While not related directly to airtime, as such, but in order to promote the understanding and enjoyment of programmes by persons who are deaf or have a hearing impairment, persons who are blind or partially sighted and persons who have a hearing impairment and are partially sighted, BAI is mandated by the Broadcasting Act 2009 (sections 43(1)(c), 43(2), 43(3) and 43(6)) to draw up Access Rules. The Rules set the levels of subtitling, sign language and audio description that broadcasters licensed in Ireland are required to provide. Specific targets have been identified for each broadcast service and broadcasters must comply with the targets and timeframes applying to their service(s). All the targets set are based on a five-year timeframe. Broadcasters are required to indicate through the use of a standard symbol those programmes for which access provision (subtitling, sign language or audio description) is available. Insofar as possible, broadcasters must also ensure that any programme listings also indicate those programmes for which access provision is available.

---

367. However, Titley et al. found in their 2010 study that immigrants' engagement with Irish broadcasting was rare. *See* Titley et al., *Broadcasting in a New Ireland – Mapping and Envisioning Cultural Diversity,* Research Report for BAI, 2010. Community broadcasting has played an important role in facilitating migrant-produced programming – *ibid.*

368. Titley et al., *op. cit.,* 2010, p. 96. A Community Radio Forum report of 2003, cited by Titley et al., noted that many stations specifically cited ethnic minorities, asylum *see* kers and refugees as a social group targeted for specific forms of engagement, including training and programming.

## II. Content Obligations (Quota)

*377.* The Broadcasting Act 2009 contains provisions referring to cultural diversity in various contexts relating to content. In relation to programme content, section 70(2)(a) requires BAI to 'be responsive to the interests and concerns of the whole community, be mindful of the need for understanding and peace within the whole island of Ireland, ensure that the programmes reflect the varied elements which make up the culture of the people of the whole island of Ireland, and have special regard for the elements which distinguish that culture and in particular for the Irish language'.

*378.* RTÉ is also required to ensure that the programmes reflect the varied elements which make up the culture of the people of the whole island of Ireland, and have special regard for the elements which distinguish that culture and in particular for the Irish language' (section 114(2)(a)). It must provide a comprehensive range of programmes in the Irish and English languages that reflect the cultural diversity of the whole island of Ireland and include programmes that entertain, inform and educate, provide coverage of sporting, religious and cultural activities and cater for the expectations of the community generally as well as members of the community with special or minority interests and which, in every case, respect human dignity (section 114(3)(a)). In its annual statement of commitments also, RTÉ is required to address *inter alia* 'original children's programming, commissioned or produced by the corporation, relevant to the social and cultural needs and interests of children in Ireland and including animation and children's programming in the Irish language, to be broadcast by the corporation' (section 102(2)(a)).[369] TG4 has similar obligations, with particular regard for the Gaeltachtaí (Irish-speaking communities) (section 118(2)(a)).

*379.* In each of its 'RTÉ Annual Statement of Performance Commitments', RTÉ sets out in detail its achievements in fulfilling the commitments it had undertaken for the year in question in accordance with its objects, its Statement of Strategy and its Public Service Statement.[370]In its Annual Reports also, in detailing its activities over the particular year, RTÉ indicates how it addressed or furthered its public service commitments. In its Annual Report for 2015, for instance, it signalled how it had addressed its commitment to develop its digital media services to best meet the changing needs of audiences and how it had reached out to all Irish-language speakers at home and abroad in its provision of Irish-language programming and services. In its 2015 report it also highlighted *inter alia* the fact that it had broadcast 4,710 hours of home-produced programming in 2015, that RTÉ News Now was the number one news app that year with 1.5 million downloads and that the number of homes with Saorview had risen by 10%.[371]

*380.* RTÉ is required, under section 116 of the Broadcasting Act 2009, to maintain an 'Independent Programmes Account'. RTÉ is obliged under the same section to allocate a percentage of its income (EUR 40 million in 2009), to be paid into its

369. *See also* RTÉ's Public Service Charter: www.rte.ie/documents/about/public-service-broadcasting-charter.pdf.

370. The Annual Statement of Performance Commitments for 2015 is available at: https://static.rasset.ie/documents/about/18259-rte-statement-performancecommitment-v2.pdf.

371. RTÉ's Annual Report for 2015 is available at: http://www.rte.ie/annualreport/PDF/RTE_AnnualReport_2015.pdf.

independent programmes account for the commissioning the making of independent television or sound broadcasting programmes). The amount stipulated in the Act for 2009 was EUR 40 million. A minimum percentage of the moneys set aside must be allocated to independent sound broadcasting programmes. This amount began at 1.25% but it was specified that it would increase to 3% from 2013 onwards. The statutory amount RTÉ was required to spend in 2015 was EUR 39.5 million (2014: EUR 39.4 million). However, RTÉ actually exceeded the required spend, with total expenditure in 2015 being EUR 40.6 million.[372] The Minister may from time to time by order vary the appropriate amount to be allocated, having taken account of the factors set out in section 116(9). The term 'independent programme' is defined in section 116(12). This statutory requirement is in accordance with the 10% allocation under Article 17 AVMSD.

*381.* In relation to commercial radio broadcasting, the Broadcasting Act (section 39(1)(c)) provides that not less than 20% of the broadcasting time must be devoted to news and current affairs programming, and if the broadcasting service is provided for more than 12 hours in any one day, 2 hours of broadcasting time between 7am and 7pm must be news and current affairs. There is, however, provision for a derogation from this obligation. BAI may authorize a derogation from the requirement in question in whole or in part in the case of a sound broadcasting service but only if it is satisfied that the authorization of such a derogation would be beneficial to the listeners of the sound broadcasting service.

## III. Language Requirements

*382.* BAI is required to 'promote and stimulate the development of Irish language programming and broadcasting services' (Broadcasting Act 2009, section 25(2)(h)). In granting licences, BAI's Contract Awards Committee must have regard to 'the quantity, quality, range and type of programmes in the Irish language and the extent of programmes relating to Irish culture proposed to be provided' (section 66(2)(d)) and 'the extent to which the applicant will create within the proposed broadcasting service new opportunities for talent in music, drama and entertainment and in particular in respect of Irish culture' (section 66(2)(e)).

*383.* TG4, the Irish-language television station, is required 'to provide a comprehensive range of programmes, primarily in the Irish language, that reflect the cultural diversity of the whole island of Ireland and include programmes that entertain, inform and educate, provide coverage of sporting, religious and cultural activities and cater for the expectations of those of all age groups in the community whose preferred

372. *See* RTÉ, 'Independent Productions Annual Report 2015', available at: http://www.rte.ie/commissioning/documents/18679_RTE_IPU_AnnualReport_V7.pdf.

spoken language is Irish or who otherwise have an interest in Irish' (section 118(3)(a)).[373] Among its policies and guidelines, RTÉ also has an Irish-language policy.

*384.* Athena Media, reporting in 2010, found that there was little content available in languages other than English/Irish, and no local or community services offering specific choices to minorities, whether new communities such as the Polish, or established minorities, like the Irish Travellers.[374] However, since then some of the community stations do provide access for groups to broadcast in their own languages. These have included the Chinese community, Nigerian community and Serb community. Polish is now the most widely spoken language in Ireland after English and the Dublin community radio station, Near FM, for example, has broadcast a weekly programme in Polish for over eleven years.[375]

## IV. Representation of Minorities on the Screen

*385.* The Guidance Notes, which apply to the BAI Code of Programme Standards, contain a section (3.4) headed 'Persons and Groups in Society'. The rules under this section of the Code 'outline the standards required of broadcasters when it comes to the manner in which persons and groups in society are featured during programme material. Broadcasters should be mindful of the diverse and changing nature of their viewing and listening audiences and the range of social, political and religious cultures which exist in contemporary Irish society'. Briefly stated, the rules require that the manner in which persons and groups in society are represented is appropriate and justifiable; does not support or condone discrimination against any person or section of the community; and does not stereotype or stigmatize people with a disability, including in the language used. Broadcasters must not make an unwarranted correlation between a criminal act and the mental health of a perpetrator during programme material featuring criminal activities; and, although the critical scrutiny of religion is permissible, broadcasters must take measures to prevent undue offence in the treatment of religious views, beliefs or images during programme material.

*386.* Some explanation of each of these rules and examples of their application are also given in the guidelines. For instance, in relation to Rule 3.4.1, that broadcasters must 'ensure that the manner in which persons and groups in society, in particular, minorities, are treated in programme material is appropriate and justified', the guidance is that: 'Mild comments or humour about characteristics of persons and groups in society may in certain circumstances be acceptable' but not if they 'touch on the

373. *See* further analysis of the cultural diversity provisions of the 2009 Act in T. McGonagle, *Promoting cultural diversity in the Irish broadcasting sector: an assessment of international standards and best practices with a view to their operationalisation in an Irish context,* research report commissioned by BAI, 2010; available at: http://www.bai.ie/en/news-and-information/publications/?q=Promoting%20cultural%20diversity%20in%20the%20Irish%20broadcasting%20sector.

374. Athena Media, *Irish Broadcasting Landscape – Economic and Environmental Review* for BAI, 2010, p. 54.

375. *See* https://inclusiondes.eu/?p=168.

essential characteristic of a person or group such as their colour, ethnicity, culture, disability' and so forth.

*387.* On many such issues that arise in relation to programming, BAI commissions research so as to inform and guide its development of policy. For example, BCI, the forerunner of BAI, commissioned wide-ranging research on the representation of persons with disabilities in broadcasting, which BAI later updated.[376]

## §3. Protection of Minors

*388.* The statutory provisions referring to children (minors) are set out above. They range from the requirement that the BAI 'protect the interests of children taking into account the vulnerability of children and childhood to undue commercial exploitations' (Broadcasting Act 2009 section 25(2)), to the requirement that broadcasting codes shall provide that programming material in respect of the portrayal of violence and sexual conduct, shall be presented by a broadcaster 'with due regard to the impact of such programming on the physical, mental or moral development of children (section 42(2)(f)(ii)). Other provisions relate to children and commercial communications (section 42(2)(g)) and a children's commercial communications code is in operation. There is also provision in the Act for conducting a survey of children and young persons for the purpose of ascertaining their views and interests in respect of PSB (section 96(11)). As noted above also, RTÉ's statement of commitments must include original children's programming (section 102(2)(a)).

*389.* The main provisions in relation to programming, as opposed to commercial communications, are contained in the BAI Code of Programme Standards (referred to above), under the heading 'Protection for Children' (Principle 4). The Code expressly states that broadcasters share responsibility with parents and guardians when it comes to protecting children, who are defined as persons under 18 years of age, from exposure to inappropriate or harmful content. Broadcasters are required to 'have due regard to the protection of children when scheduling programme material'. More specifically, broadcasters are required to:

- ensure that programme material that might seriously impair the physical, mental or moral development of children is not broadcast when children are likely to be viewing, in particular, programmes that include pornography or gratuitous violence;
- take particular care when broadcasting programme material to children or at times when children may be watching or listening. This will include, in particular, programme material broadcast before the watershed;
- take particular care when scheduling programming material that is broadcast either side of programmes that are likely to be watched or listened to by children, such as after the watershed, during school runs, and during school holidays;

376. The research comprised: 'Public Attitudes to the Representation of People with Disabilities in Republic of Ireland Broadcast Media – National Survey'; 'Representation of People with Disabilities in Irish Broadcast Media – A review of other jurisdictions' and update report 2013 (M. McGonagle et al.); 'Representations of People with Disability in Irish Broadcast Media – Content and Discourse Analysis'. These research reports are available at http://www.bai.ie.

- take particular care to ensure that trailers and promotions for programming not reasonably regarded as suitable for children shall not be shown immediately before, during or after children's programming or before the watershed.

*390.* The term 'children's programming', for the purpose of the Code, is defined as 'programmes that are commonly referred to as such and/or have an audience profile of which over 50% are under 18 years of age'. This principle recognizes that children of different ages require different levels of protection and broadcasters provide a range of programming for children, some of which may deal with more mature themes, appropriate to the lived reality and experience of older children.

*391.* The BAI Children's Commercial Communications Code focuses on commercial communications in and around children's programmes. The current Code dates from 2013.[377] In relation to on-demand services, the Regulations (S.I. 258 of 2010) only refer to children in the context of commercial communications. The ASAI Code, section 7, which applies to broadcasting and all other advertising media, also deals with children's 'marketing communications'. Children in the context of commercial communications are discussed in Chapter 5 below.

## §4. Human Dignity (Prohibition of Hate Speech)

*392.* The Preamble to the Irish Constitution refers to one of the aims in adopting the Constitution as being that: '... the dignity and freedom of the individual may be assured... '.

Ireland has ratified the relevant international human rights instruments that contain provisions outlawing racism, such as the International Covenant on Civil and Political Rights, Article 20.2: 'Any advocacy of national, racial or religious hatred that constitutes incitement to discrimination, hostility or violence shall be prohibited by law.' Ireland ratified the International Convention on the Elimination of Racial Discrimination (ICERD) in January 2001, once the Equal Status Act 2000 had been put in place.

*393.* Legislation creating an offence of incitement to hatred on racial grounds was already in place prior to that. The Prohibition on Incitement to Hatred Act 1989 is not limited to racial hatred, however. The term '*hatred*' in the Act is stated to mean 'hatred against a group of persons in the State or elsewhere on account of their race, colour, nationality, religion, ethnic or national origins, membership of the travelling community or sexual orientation'. Hate speech or actions on any of these grounds are prohibited by the Act. The Act makes it an offence (section 2(1)):

(a) to publish or distribute written material; or
(b) to use words, behave or display written material – in any place other than inside a private residence, or inside a private residence so that the words, behaviour or material are heard or seen by persons outside the residence; or

377. Available at http://www.bai.ie/wordpress/wp-content/uploads/201308_CCCC_English_vFinal.pdf.

(c) to distribute, show or play a recording of visual images or sounds, if the written material, words, behaviour, visual images or sounds, as the case may be, are threatening, abusive or insulting and are intended or, having regard to all the circumstances, are likely to stir up hatred.

*394.* The offence, therefore, is limited to 'stirring up hatred' (incitement to hatred). It does not cover other forms of racist speech that fall short of incitement. The *mens rea* required for the offence is intention or, if not intention, the likelihood of stirring up hatred, the likelihood being adjudged on the basis of all the circumstances. First of all, the essence of the offence is that, whatever form it takes, the material must be 'threatening, abusive or insulting'. These elements when taken together with stirring up hatred, as well as intention or likelihood, mean that the threshold for establishing the offence is set at a high level. A number of defences provided for in the Act reflect these various elements. As a result, prosecutions are rare and tend to end in acquittals or successful appeals.[378] Specifically, in relation to broadcasts that are likely to stir up hatred, those guilty of an offence are: the person providing the broadcasting service concerned; any person by whom the item concerned is produced or directed; and any person whose words or behaviour in the item concerned are threatening, abusive or insulting (section 3). Again, a number of defences are available, including lack of knowledge that the material was to be broadcast.

*395.* While there has been public criticism of the high threshold and a review of the Act was announced by government ten years after its enactment, no reform of the Act has taken place. A major concern with any attempt to lower the threshold is that a lower threshold would threaten or act as a chilling factor on freedom of expression.

*396.* The earlier prosecutions mentioned above, which were taken under the Act, did not involve the media but rather a local politician in one instance, who had made derogatory remarks about the Travelling community (ethnic minority) at a public meeting, and a bus driver in another instance, who had made racist remarks to a Gambian man. In at least one instance which involved the media, the Director of Public Prosecutions (DPP) decided not to prosecute. This occurred in 1996 and concerned derogatory remarks about Traveller culture in an article published in a leading Sunday newspaper, the *Sunday Independent*.[379] The DPP is not obliged to give reasons for a decision not to prosecute but it was believed that the requirement to improve intention or likelihood of incitement contributed to it. A few years later, in 2000, the same journalist wrote a very disparaging article on the Paralympics for the same newspaper.[380] In this instance advertisers threatened to withdraw advertising from the paper and the paper subsequently apologized and the journalist resigned. Again, the high threshold for establishing an offence under the Act would likely have been a factor in deciding whether to bring a prosecution. In cases involving journalists, however, and potentially in both of these cases, another possible avenue of redress would be a disciplinary hearing under the NUJ code of conduct, which provides that a journalist, who is a member of the Union, and who must therefore abide by the principle:

378. *See* cases referred to in M. McGonagle, 2003, Ch. 8.
379. Decision of DPP reported in *The Irish Times* 3 Sept. 1996.
380. *Sunday Independent* 22 Oct. 2000.

10. Produces no material likely to lead to hatred or discrimination on the grounds of a person's age, gender, race, colour, creed, legal status, disability, marital status, or sexual orientation.

Only a very small percentage of journalists in Ireland at the time were not members of the NUJ but the journalist who wrote the offending articles about the Travellers and the Paralympics, was one of that small minority and therefore not subject to the NUJ code.[381]

*397.* The first prosecution under the Act arising from online material occurred in 2011. The charge under section 2 of the Act resulted from materials published on a social networking website, in this case, Facebook, and concerned the Travelling Community.[382] The District Court (lowest court) judge, however, held that there was a reasonable doubt that there was an intent to incite hatred towards members of the Traveller community and dismissed the case. The Judge referred to the fact that the man had set up the Facebook page on a 'once off' basis and had not added to or commented on the page after it was created, even though plenty of others had done so. There is no specific reference to the Internet in the Act, which is not surprising given that the Act dates from 1989, but terms such as 'distribute' and 'publish' are widely defined so as to encompass the Internet.

*398.* The term 'human dignity' as such is referred to in a media context in the Broadcasting Act 2009 in relation to RTÉ's programme schedules and programming, which must 'in every case respect human dignity' (section 114(3)(a)). As the Act transposed the AVMSD, it contains provisions giving effect to Article 22 and 3b. A content provision contract, for example, can be terminated if material supplied:

(a) contravenes Article 22 or 3b of the Council Directive or the Prohibition of Incitement to Hatred Act 1989, or
(b) constitutes an incitement to commit an offence. (section 71(6))

*399.* Human dignity is also referred to in the BAI Code of Programme Standards, Principle 5:

> The manner in which persons and groups in society are represented shall be appropriate and justifiable and shall not prejudice respect for human dignity. Robust debate is permissible as is the challenging of assumptions but programme material shall not stigmatise, support or condone discrimination or incite hatred against persons or groups in society in particular on the basis of age, gender, marital status, membership of the Traveller community, family status, sexual orientation, disability, race, nationality, ethnicity or religion.

The requirements of broadcasters in order to fulfil their obligations are then set out:

> In fulfilment of Principle 5, broadcasters shall:

381. *Ibid.*
382. *DPP v. Kissane*, Killarney District Court, October 2011. *See* http://www.pila.ie/bulletin/2011/october/5-october-2011/irish-district-court-dismisses-traveller-facebook-hate-speech-case/.

- Not broadcast material involving threatening, abusive or insulting visual images or sounds with the intent to stir up hatred or where it is likely that hatred will be stirred up as a result against persons or groups in society, including on the grounds of race, religion, sex, ethnicity, sexual orientation or nationality.
- Only emphasise age, colour, gender, national or ethnic origin, disability, race, religion or sexual orientation when such references are justified, having regard to the principles of this Code, in particular, the importance of context.
- Recognise that the use of terms, references and images that could be considered offensive to persons and groups in society and associated colloquial terms of abuse aimed at any group requires editorial justification for their inclusion in programming.
- Show due respect for religious views, images, practices and beliefs in programme material. This is not intended to prevent the critical scrutiny of religion by means of information, drama or other programming.

*400.* The General Commercial Communications Code, section 3.2 deals with human dignity offence and harm. The Children's Commercial Communications Code also contains a number of provisions that specifically refer to human dignity. The ODAS Code applicable to on-demand services contains an anti-discrimination provision (1(c)(ii)). The ASAI code refers to dignity and not causing offence. All of these codes, as they relate to human dignity in commercial communications are discussed below in Chapter 5.

## §5. Right of Reply

*401.* A statutory right of reply in broadcasting has existed since the Broadcasting Act 1990, prompted by the TWFD of 1989. Currently, a right of reply is provided for in section 49 of the Broadcasting Act 2009, which states that any person whose honour or reputation has been impugned by an assertion of incorrect facts or information in a broadcast shall have a right of reply. As it is confined to incorrect facts or information it is more in the nature of a right of correction than an open right of reply. Moreover, the remedy provided is not direct access to the airwaves for the requester, but rather the broadcasting of a scripted statement drafted and delivered by the broadcaster and approved by the requester.

*402.* Under section 26(1)(f) of the Act, the BAI was mandated to prepare a scheme for the exercise of a right of reply and the requirements of the scheme are set out in considerable detail in section 49(3) – (28). A right of reply must be broadcast within a reasonable time period subsequent to the request for a right of reply being made, and at a time and in a manner appropriate to the broadcast to which the request refers (section 49(5)). The granting of a request for a right of reply will not constitute an express or implied admission of liability by the defendant in any subsequent defamation action and will not be relevant to the determination of liability in the action (section 49(13)), although it may serve to mitigate damage on the part of the media defendant that s/he granted or offered it (section 49(14)). Neither is the granting of a right of reply admissible in any civil proceedings as evidence of liability on the part of the defendant (section 49(16)).

*403.* If a broadcaster refuses to grant a right of reply, the requester can have the decision reviewed by the Compliance Committee of BAI. If the Committee annuls the broadcaster's decision, the broadcaster will be required to broadcast the Committee's decision. Failure to broadcast the decision may lead to an application by BAI to the High Court (section 49(23–24)).

*404.* The current BAI right of reply scheme dates from 2011.[383] The scheme (section 2) sets out the procedure for making a right of reply request, the time limit within which such a request must be made to the relevant broadcaster, how the request is to be processed by the broadcaster and the potential outcomes of making such a request. Section 3 details the information that should be contained within a right of reply statement and the form such a statement should take, while section 4 sets out the process of review following the refusal of a right of reply request by a broadcaster. Section 5 details the reasons why the Compliance Committee of BAI, one of the functions of which is to investigate and decide upon a request made under section 49, might reject an application for review of a refusal of a right of reply request by a broadcaster.[384] Finally, section 6 of the Scheme sets out important information on the relationship between the right of reply and a potential action in defamation law, on the availability of information on the right of reply (on the website of the BAI and on broadcasters' websites) and on the maintenance by broadcasters of 'due and proper' records in relation to any requests for a right of reply.

*405.* The overall purpose of the Scheme, therefore, is to provide speedy redress, free of charge, for any person wishing to exercise his/her right to the correction of incorrect facts or information, with the potential of avoiding time consuming and costly legal proceedings normally involved in such a process. However, BAI has confirmed that no request for a right of reply has been received to date.[385]

383. Available at: http://www.bai.ie/en/codes-standards/.

384. *Ibid.* at s. 5.

385. Reply to author by e-mail received from BAI on 8 Oct. 2013. The Annual Report of 2014 did not refer to any instance of a request for a right of reply either. The Annual Report of 2015 refers to the scheme having been reviewed in line with the legislative requirements and also notes the 'lack of utilisation' of the scheme (at p. 46).

# Chapter 4. Political Broadcasting

*406.* Political broadcasting is covered mainly by provisions of the Broadcasting Act 2009 and the Code of Fairness, Objectivity and Impartiality in News and Current Affairs of April 2013. The Code was prepared by BAI in accordance with section 42 of the Act, which requires BAI to prepare codes of standards to be observed by broadcasters (*see* paragraph 368). The Code is accompanied by Guidance Notes. In addition, BAI published a Code of Referenda and Election Coverage in 2011, which is also accompanied by Guidance Notes. Further to Rule 27 of the Code of Fairness, Objectivity and Impartiality in News and Current Affairs, BAI has also produced Guidelines in Respect of Coverage of Referenda to be adopted by broadcasters in their coverage of referenda. All of these Codes, rules, guidance notes and guidelines are discussed in the sections which follow.

## §1. Rules on Political Independence of Broadcasters

*407.* The key provisions of the Broadcasting Act in relation to the independence of broadcasters in the context of news and current affairs programming are set out in Chapter 3 above. The BAI Code of Fairness, Objectivity and Impartiality in News and Current Affairs of April 2013 gave effect to the provisions. Among the stated objectives of the Code are:

- To promote independent and impartial journalism in the provision of news and current affairs content;
- To inform and generate awareness among citizens with regard to standards they may expect in relation to news and current affairs content;
- To protect the interests of citizens, in their right to access fair, objective and impartial news and current affairs content.

*408.* The Code contains both principles and rules. It is stated that the rules should not be taken to imply that a presenter or a reporter cannot convey critical views or pursue vigorous lines of questioning. What is necessary is that 'production, reporting and questioning on any news or current affairs item is credible, trustworthy and editorially independent'. The principles include accuracy and responsiveness, transparency and accountability.

*409.* The Broadcasting Act section 86 provides for exclusion from membership of the Boards of RTÉ and TG4 persons *inter alia* who are nominated as a candidate for election or who are elected to the Oireachtas (Parliament) or to the European Parliament. Section 87(d) further provides that each member of the Boards of RTÉ and TG4 shall perform his or her functions in such a manner as to:

> safeguard the independence of the corporation, as regards, the conception, content and production of programmes, the editing and presentation of news and current

affairs programmes and the definition of programme schedules from State, political and commercial influences.

*410.* The Guidance Notes accompanying the Code state that conflicts of interest can arise for anyone who is responsible for news and current affairs content and relevant staff and their managers need to be conscious of this possibility. It is also important that broadcasters take appropriate measures to ensure, insofar as possible, that independent producers or freelance staff do not have any interests which could undermine the fairness, objectivity and impartiality of the output they produce for the broadcasters. The Notes also reiterate that 'a news presenter and/or a reporter in a news programme may not express his or her own view on matters that are either of public controversy or the subject of current public debate' (Notes 21, 22). Furthermore, the Notes state in reference to the Code that it 'seeks to prevent a partisan position being advocated by the presenter and to guard against a presenter using his/her programme to pursue an agenda, via comments, choice of guest etc., such that a biased view on an issue is articulated'. (Note 24)

*411.* The Guidance Notes also require that 'Each broadcaster shall have and implement appropriate policies and procedures to address any conflicts of interests that may exist or arise in respect of anyone with an editorial involvement in any news or current affairs content, whether such person works on-air or off-air' (Note 25). Any personal, professional, business or financial interest of anyone with an editorial involvement in news or current affairs content that calls into question (or that might reasonably be perceived as calling into question) the fairness, objectivity or impartiality of a programme or item, shall be brought to the attention of the audience. In the case of a serious conflict of interest it might be necessary for a broadcaster to withdraw a reporter or presenter from a particular item or story, as audiences have a right to expect that editorial decisions are not influenced by the outside activities or personal or commercial interests of programme-makers or those who appear on air (*see* Note 26).

*412.* Complaints of breaches of the Code, including whether presenters expressed their own personal political viewpoint, are addressed in the first instance to the broadcaster concerned and if not resolved are dealt with by the Compliance Committee of the BAI.

*413.* In addition to the Codes and Guidelines issued by BAI, individual broadcasters, such as RTÉ, then formulate standards and steps to be taken for their own staff having regard to the BAI documents. RTÉ's Journalism Guidelines of October of 2014,[386] for instance, in addressing the issue of editorial independence and political independence, state *inter alia* that:

> RTÉ must be editorially independent of government, business interests, political parties, trade unions, and pressure groups. There is no room for any perception that presenters, reporters or producers personally benefit from their decisions as to who participates in programmes, what products are featured and what issues are discussed.

386. Available at: https://static.rasset.ie/documents/about/rte-journalism-guidelines-2014.pdf.

> Equally importantly, there must be no grounds for the perception that editorial decisions in some way reflect the personal views of production teams. As citizens, all programme□makers have rights to their own private views about topics of current debate. These views must not be seen to determine agendas, lines of questioning, or editorial decisions in programming.
>
> (Section 9: Editorial Integrity and Independence)

*414.* Among RTÉ's standards of editorial integrity and independence are that it shall 'ensure that editorial decisions are not improperly influenced by political, sectional, commercial or personal interests' (section 9.2). There are also provisions on financial journalism, acceptance of gifts and involvement in commercial activity and investments. Presenters are not permitted to wear religious or political badges or symbols on screen which could be perceived to undermine editorial independence (section 9.6).

*415.* Appendix 1, under the heading of 'RTÉ and Political Coverage/Studio Election Debates', sets out the applicable standards:

- Gather and present news and information with due impartiality
- Present a diversity of perspectives so that, over time, no significant strand of thought or belief is either knowingly excluded or disproportionately under or over represented
- Do not state or imply that any perspective is the editorial opinion of RTÉ. RTÉ takes no editorial stance other than its commitment to fundamental democratic principles including the rule of law, freedom of expression and religion, parliamentary democracy and equality of opportunity
- Do not misrepresent any perspective
- Do not unduly favour one perspective over another

*416.* Appendix 2 of the Guidelines provides guidance on reporting from the Internet and Social Media sources. It includes that programme-makers must ensure that in their use of social media they avoid damaging perceptions of their own or RTÉ's impartiality. The advice on 'biased sources' states that '[a]s with any medium, hidden commercial or political agendas can shape a Web site's content. You should check the links to and from a site as these can often reveal political or commercial affiliations'. (App. 2.3)[387]

387. RTÉ's position on election and referenda coverage, use of opinion polls and surveys is also set out, along with its position on the political activities of its staff. *See* further §2 'Fair Representation in Election Periods' below.

## §2. Fair Representation in Election Periods

*417.* The overall obligations of broadcasters in relation to news and current affairs reporting, including at the time of elections or referenda are set out in section 39(1) and (2) of the Broadcasting Act 2009:

> 39.–(1) Every broadcaster shall ensure that–
>
> (a) all news broadcast by the broadcaster is reported and presented in an objective and impartial manner and without any expression of the broadcaster's own views,
>
> (b) the broadcast treatment of current affairs, including matters which are either of public controversy or the subject of current public debate, is fair to all interests concerned and that the broadcast matter is presented in an objective and impartial manner and without any expression of his or her own views, except that should it prove impracticable in relation to a single broadcast to apply this paragraph, two or more related broadcasts may be considered as a whole, if the broadcasts are transmitted within a reasonable period of each other,
>
> …
>
> (2) Nothing in subsection (1)(a) or (b) prevents a broadcaster from transmitting party political broadcasts provided that a broadcaster does not, in the allocation of time for such broadcasts, give an unfair preference to any political party.

*418.* Party political broadcasts, referred to in (2), occur mainly during election campaigns and referendum campaigns. They consist of political parties presenting their policies and reasons to vote for them in short clips in the few minutes allocated to them. The actual time to be allocated to each registered party is decided by the individual broadcaster, based on the statutory framework and relevant BAI code and guidelines. The process of allocation has to be transparent and can be challenged on fairness grounds as a breach of statute, code or guidelines.

*419.* The BAI Code of Fairness, Objectivity and Impartiality in News and Current Affairs of April 2013, outlined above in section 1 of this chapter, is the main document in respect of news and current affairs, both generally and during election periods and the periods leading up to a referendum. BAI Guidelines specifically dealing with elections and referenda are reviewed and updated in advance of each general election and referendum.

*420.* The relevant part of the Code is Rule 27, which is headed 'Election and Referendum Coverage'. It simply states:

> Coverage of an election or a referendum shall comply with guidelines and codes of practice issued from time to time by the BAI.

The BAI issued Referenda Guidelines leading up to a referendum in May 2015 and Election Guidelines leading up to a General Election in November 2015. The details of both sets of Guidelines are set out in turn (in chronological order) below.

## I. Guidelines in Respect of Coverage of Referenda

*421.* The most recent Referendum Guidelines – Guidelines in Respect of Coverage of Referenda – were issued under Rule 27 of the Code in March 2015 in the lead-up to the marriage equality referendum. The Guidelines apply in addition to the rules in the Code and also provide guidance to broadcasters on the manner in which fairness, objectivity and impartiality may be achieved in their coverage. Having set out the legal requirements under the 2009 Act, the Guidelines go on to address how to achieve fairness, objectivity and impartiality in covering the referendum:

> Broadcasters play an important and valuable role in the manner in which information about referenda is communicated to, and discussed by, the Irish public. For this reason, broadcasters are encouraged to cover the referenda campaigns as comprehensively as possible, taking into account the resources available to them, their target audience and the type of programming that the broadcaster provides to the audience. In their approach to coverage, broadcasters are asked to have regard to the following:

- Fairness, objectivity and impartiality can be achieved by a variety of means, for example, through the selection of contributors, the airtime afforded, the scope of the debate, the structure of the programme, the presenter's handling of the topic, the make-up of audiences or through other suitable means. Broadcasters should note that the referenda are dynamic events and they should give active consideration to their approach to coverage over the duration of a campaign and amend this approach if they consider it necessary and appropriate;
- While it is important to ensure that coverage provides airtime to referenda interests[388] to set out their views on proposed changes to the Irish Constitution, broadcasters are encouraged to approach coverage with an emphasis on the issues that the public must decide upon rather than taking an approach limited, simply, to ensuring that referenda interests receive equitable airtime.

*422.* In further detailed guidance, broadcasters are *inter alia* 'encouraged to seek out the widest range of opinions on the issues raised by the proposed constitutional amendment(s)' but there 'is no obligation to automatically "balance" each contribution on an individual programme with an opposing view. Further, there is no requirement to allocate an absolute equality of airtime to referenda interests during coverage of the

388. 'Referenda Interests' includes, but is not limited to, political parties, elected representatives, the Government, organisations established specifically for the purpose of campaigning during the referenda, individuals (including those holding or formerly holding a public office) campaigning for a particular outcome to the referenda, as well as existing social and civil society groups engaging in a campaign in respect of the referenda.].

referenda. However, the approach taken must be equitable to all interests and undertaken in a transparent manner'. The Guidelines also make clear that it 'is appropriate that decisions in respect of editorial coverage of the referenda rest solely with broadcasters. In doing so, broadcasters must develop mechanisms in respect to their approach to coverage that are open, transparent and fair to all interested parties. These mechanisms should be considered and developed at an early stage and information on the approach being adopted should be available to all interested parties. Broadcasters should be in a position to demonstrate how this was achieved in the context of complaints received directly by the broadcaster or by the BAI'.

*423.* Further to the Referendum Acts (1998 and 2001) the Government appoints a Referendum Commission in advance of each referendum. The role of the Commission includes the promotion of public awareness of a referendum and the encouragement of the electorate to vote at the poll. In this context, and further to the Referendum Acts and the Broadcasting Act 2009, the Minister for Communications, Energy and Natural Resources may direct RTÉ, TG4 and the BAI to arrange for the allocation of broadcasting time to facilitate the Referendum Commission in its role.[389]The Guidelines also reiterate the provision of the Broadcasting Act 2009 that announcements by the Referendum Commission do not constitute advertisements and do not count towards the calculation of advertising airtime or the limits on such airtime in place for Irish radio and television broadcasters.

*424.* As a moratorium operates from 2pm on the day before the poll takes place and throughout the day of the poll itself until polling stations close, the Guidelines give indications of the issues that can arise and the steps to be taken to avoid infringing the moratorium. These are in similar terms to those given in the Election Guidelines and are discussed in that context below.

*425.* The Guidelines end with the necessary information on how to make a complaint. Complaints from members of the public regarding breach of the Fairness Code and Election and Referenda guidelines are made in the first instance to the broadcaster concerned and, failing a satisfactory outcome, to the Compliance Committee of BAI. Formerly, such complaints were made to the Broadcasting Complaints Commission (BCC).

*426.* A number of complaints and court challenges have been taken to the broadcast coverage of the 'yes' and 'no' sides in referendum campaigns. One case of particular relevance was *Coughlan v. RTÉ,*[390]which involved the allocation of airtime to political parties in relation to a referendum. All of the political parties were in favour of a 'Yes' vote on the issue – the removal of the constitutional ban on divorce – and all were given airtime by RTÉ. Mr Coughlan complained to the Broadcasting Complaints Commission (BCC – the forerunner of the Compliance Committee of BAI) that RTÉ had breached the statutory requirement of fairness and provided a one-sided, unbalanced presentation of the referendum issue. As the BCC found against him on the central issue, Mr Coughlan sought a judicial review in the High Court. The High Court, and subsequently the Supreme Court on an appeal by the BCC and RTÉ, held that fair

389. This provision is contained in the Broadcasting Act 2009 and is restated in the Referendum Guidelines. The relevant Minister is now the Minister for Communications, Climate Action and Environment.
390. [2000] 3 I.R.1; [2000] IESC 44 (available at www.bailii.org).

procedures required equality to each side of the argument in a referendum. Judge Denham, now the Chief Justice, while in agreement, pointed out, however, that mathematical equality was not a requirement of constitutional fairness and equality (at §81). Since then, however, the matter has been addressed by setting up an independent referendum commission, presided over by a judge, to provide the public with information on the issue(s) to be voted upon in a referendum.[391]

## II. General Election Guidelines

*427.* As stated above, BAI issues guidelines before each election and referendum. It issued guidelines on General Election Coverage in 2015 in accordance with Rule 27 of the BAI Code of Fairness, Objectivity and Impartiality in News and Current Affairs, which requires broadcasters to comply with Guidelines in respect of coverage of elections. The Guidelines deal *inter alia* with conflicts of interest, opinion polls, social media, advertising, and party political broadcasts.

In relation to conflicts of interest, the Guidelines state:

> In this context, it is the view of the BAI that it is not appropriate for persons involved with election interests to present programmes during the election campaign period. However, it is a matter for broadcasters to decide on a case-by-case basis the appropriate arrangements, in the context of the contractual, employment or volunteer relationship, between the presenter and the broadcaster and in the context of their statutory obligations.
>
> Endorsements by broadcasters of election candidates, participating political parties or election interests[392] are not permitted. In addition, endorsements on-air by staff (who are employed, contracted or who volunteer with a broadcaster) of election candidates, participating political parties or election interests, are also not permitted.
>
> Broadcasters should note that comments made off-air, for example in print publications or social media, by programme presenters in respect of the General Election, particularly presenters of news and current affairs, may have the potential to undermine the perceived impartiality of their coverage. It is a matter for

391. *See* http://www.refcom.ie. The role of the Referendum Commission is to explain the subject matter of referendum proposals, to promote public awareness of the referendum and to encourage the electorate to vote at the poll.

392. The term 'Election interests' includes, but is not limited to, political parties, elected representatives, the Government, organisations established specifically for the purpose of campaigning during the General Election, individuals (including those holding or formerly holding a public office) campaigning for a particular outcome to the General Election, as well as existing social and civil society groups engaging in a campaign in respect of the General Election.

broadcasters to deal with such issues in the context of their contractual, employment or volunteer relationship with presenters.

*428.* With regard to opinion polls during an election campaign, the Guidelines recognise their usefulness but counsel broadcasters:

> Where opinion polls are being used as part of coverage of the General Election, coverage should be accompanied by information to assist viewers/listeners to understand the significance of the opinion poll. Information on the details of the date of the poll, the name of the organisation that has commissioned and/or paid for it, the company/organisation who conducted it and the number of people polled must be provided on-air. In representing the findings of opinion polls to viewers and listeners, broadcasters are advised to take into account not only the interpretation of the findings provided by those who have undertaken the opinion poll but to also have regard to their own analysis of the results.

*429.* Social media play an important role during election periods. The Guidelines refer to the fact that broadcasters are required, under the BAI Code of Fairness, Objectivity and Impartiality in News and Current Affairs, to have in place appropriate policies and procedures for handling on-air contributions via social media. The Guidelines state that these 'policies and practices must be applied where social media is referenced on-air in the context of coverage of the General Election. Given the importance of a General Election, additional steps should be implemented by broadcasters to ensure that on-air references to social media are accurate, fair, objective and impartial'.

*430.* The kind of problems that can arise with the use of social media on-air became evident when an unverified tweet was read out by the presenter during a live televised debate between the candidates in the Presidential election, broadcast on RTÉ in October 2011. Several complaints were upheld by BAI but the Compliance Committee considered that a statutory investigation into the programme (as provided for under section 53 of the Broadcasting Act 2009) was not warranted for a number of stated reasons, including that RTÉ has taken significant steps to address the issues.[393]

*431.* The Guidelines also contain a section on advertising. It reminds broadcasters that section 41(3) of the Broadcasting Act 2009 provides that a broadcaster shall not broadcast an advertisement (i.e., a paid-for advertisement as opposed to a political party broadcast) which is directed towards a 'political end'. In the context of an election, it says:

> … broadcasters shall ensure that advertising is free of material that promotes candidates, political parties or election interests, as well as content that addresses election issues or which might be reasonably considered as being directed towards a 'political end' in contravention of Section 41(3). This prohibition also applies to advertising for events, notices regarding meetings or other events being organised by election interests as part of their activities.

393. *See* http://www.bai.ie/en/statement-by-the-bai-compliance-committee-the-frontline-presidential-debate/ The candidate took a High Court action against RTÉ: *see Gallagher v. RTÉ* [2017] IEHC 237. The case ended in an apology and damages reported to be a six-figure sum.

*432.* In determining whether an advertisement may contravene the statutory prohibition on advertising directed towards 'a political end', the BAI is of the view that it is reasonable for broadcasters to take into account the following three factors:-

- The content of the advertisement;
- The context in which the advertisement is broadcast;
- The aims and objectives of the advertiser and of the advertising campaign.

*433.* The statutory position regarding party political broadcasts is different to that of advertising during elections in that party political broadcasts are permitted during election campaigns, further to section 39(2) of the Broadcasting Act 2009. The Guidelines point out:

> While there is no obligation on broadcasters to transmit party political broadcasts, those that do so shall ensure that party political broadcasts are transmitted at times that are aimed at achieving a similar audience for all such broadcasts. Similar broadcast treatment shall be provided for all party political broadcasts, both at their introduction and at their conclusion. Such broadcasts may only be availed of by political parties included on the Register of Political Parties as provided for under Irish law.
>
> To ensure that a party political broadcast does not rank as an advertisement (which is prohibited by Section 41(3) of the 2009 Act) no payment or similar consideration shall be applied for such broadcasts.
>
> Notwithstanding the above, broadcasters should consider whether the transmission of party political broadcasts may in practice result in an imbalance in coverage of an election, including coverage of non-party political candidates who cannot avail of such broadcasts, and whether that imbalance should accordingly be addressed via other election programming.

*434.* A moratorium applies to broadcasting, both television and radio, in the run up to polling in an election. The moratorium on coverage of the election operates from 2pm on the day before the poll takes place and throughout the day of the poll itself until polling stations close. During that period, broadcasters must comply with the requirement that: 'Electioneering and/or references to issues linked to the General Election and/or references by any on-air personnel, including guests, to the merits or otherwise of an election candidate(s) and/or their policies shall not be broadcast while the moratorium is in operation.'[394]

*435.* Further detailed guidance is provided on applying the moratorium, which extends to all areas of programming, and the care and steps that should be taken. The public must be kept informed and therefore factual information on polling times and such like is permitted, as is coverage of legitimate news and current affairs stories that

394. The 2015 guidelines are available at: http://www.bai.ie/en/news-and-information/publications/.

are unrelated to the General Election. However, broadcasters should avoid airing content (including breaking news stories) that the broadcaster believes is intended and/or likely to influence or manipulate voters' decisions. Particular care has to be taken around the opinions expressed by any programme contributors during the period covered by the moratorium. Steps should also be taken to ensure that overnight programme repeats scheduled during the moratorium do not contain material that would breach the moratorium. Broadcasters are advised to either edit programmes (if practical) or schedule an alternative programme so as to avoid accidental breaches of the moratorium. Also, particular care is necessary when commenting upon or covering newspaper reviews as the print media are not subject to a moratorium. Exit polls, which are conducted outside polling stations on voting day, are to be broadcast only after the closure of the polling booths.

*436.* As in the case of the Referenda Guidelines, the Election Guidelines encourage broadcasters to provide coverage in the Irish language. Also, like the Referenda Guidelines, they set out the process for making a complaint.

## III. RTÉ's Journalism Guidelines

*437.* RTÉ's Journalism Guidelines of 2014 include a section in Appendix 1 on election coverage. The Guidelines stress *inter alia* that fairness and impartiality, as well as providing opportunities for political debate, are essential parts of RTÉ's role at election time. As the performance of presenters and reporters comes under intense scrutiny, RTÉ must be, and be seen to be, completely impartial in its handling of political debate.

*438.* The importance of monitoring of output across radio and television is also regarded as an important part of RTÉ's procedures at election and referenda times. The monitoring process is as follows:

> RTÉ puts in place for all General Elections, European Elections, Presidential Elections and Referenda a Steering Group which represents all output areas. This group co□ordinates RTÉ's coverage of the campaign and ensures that RTÉ's overall coverage is fair to all parties. Balance and fairness have to be maintained both within individual programme strands and across all output. A formal monitoring of output is put in place in the run up to elections to provide accurate information about election coverage on all RTÉ channels and to ensure that balance is achieved. Appearances by all candidates and their election teams are measured.

*439.* All programme-makers are obliged to achieve balanced coverage within their own programmes (either within individual programmes or within related programmes). Where unanticipated events occur which lead to balance not being achieved (e.g., a candidate not turning up for an interview or a link going down) the steering group must be informed at the earliest possible moment. Within News it is recognised that news values may over-ride considerations of apportioning of proportionate attention to candidates. At all times when this happens the steering group must be informed to allow full consideration of the consequences.

*440.* Specifically in relation to election debates, advice is given on format, audience selection, questions and editorial supervision. In relation to questions, for example, the advice is that:

- The range of questions selected must cover all representatives in the debate, but editorial judgment can be used to ensure key issues in the election are properly addressed through use of additional questions and presenter supplementaries.
- Potential questions should be submitted to the production team in writing. The team may discuss amendments with the potential questioner to ensure clarity or legal safety, but the final wording must be left to the questioner.
- Questions devised by contributors must not be given to other audience members to read.
- Questioners should not be connected to political parties or candidates' campaigns in an election programme.

*441.* Appendix 1 also contains a detailed approach to the use of opinion polls and surveys, the political activities of RTÉ staff and staff training. Finally, Appendix 2 provides guidance on reporting from the Internet and Social Media sources.

## §3. News and Current Affairs Programmes

*442.* As referred to above, the Broadcasting Act 2009 section 42 requires BAI to prepare codes of standards to be observed by broadcasters (*see* above). The codes envisaged in section 42(2) relate *inter alia* to objectivity and impartiality in news broadcasts; to the treatment of current affairs, including matters which are either of public controversy or the subject of current public debate, which must be fair to all interests concerned, and presented in an objective and impartial manner and without any expression of the broadcaster's own views; and to the allocation of time for transmitting party political broadcasts, which must not give an unfair preference to any political party. The relevant code, which incorporates the requirements of section 42(2) is the BAI Code of Fairness, Objectivity and Impartiality in News and Current Affairs of April 2013.[395] The provisions of the code are outlined above in the section on 'Programme Standards' in relation to 'Impartiality'.

### I. Fairness Rules

*443.* Guidance Notes, incorporating the fairness rules, supplement the code.[396] The fairness rules require broadcasters *inter alia* to deal fairly with contributors to current affairs content or with persons or organizations referred to in that content; to

395. Available at http://www.bai.ie/en/codes-standards/.
396. BAI Code of Fairness, Objectivity & Impartiality in News and Current Affairs Guidance Notes, available at: http://www.bai.ie/en/codes-standards/.

make interviewees for news and current affairs content generally aware of the subject matter and the nature and format of their contribution, so that their agreement to participate constitutes informed consent; and not to interview any person without the consent of that person. The broadcast of any news or current affairs content in the absence of consent must be editorially justified. Care must always be taken with the inclusion of interviews with children or vulnerable people in news or current affairs content. In all cases, the over-riding principle must be to avoid the broadcast of material that may be unfair or detrimental to their interest. The consent of a parent, guardian or legal representative shall generally be obtained prior to the broadcast of any interview with a child less than 16 years of age or a vulnerable person. Other principles relate to the refusal of a person or organization to contribute; secret filming; door-stepping; and fairness in the re-use of material.

*444.* The guidance notes, which accompany each of the fairness rules, are quite detailed and give useful guidance on the application of all of the fairness, objectivity and impartiality rules set out in the Code. They give concrete advice based on practical matters and examples of issues that may arise. They also make a number of useful statements in relation to the overall objectives of the Code and the principles underlying the Code. They state, for example, that in developing a set of objectives for the Code, the BAI had regard to 'the relationship between the regulator, the broadcaster and the citizen'. The objectives of the Code are therefore 'concerned with the citizen and in particular in ensuring that their right to fair, objective and impartial news and current affairs content is protected, while at the same time providing them with the necessary information to consider whether standards in relation to news and current affairs content are being met by broadcasters'.

*445.* These Guidance Notes relate specifically to the Code of Fairness, Objectivity and Impartiality in News and Current Affairs but they point out that matters of privacy, harm or offence arising in news and current affairs programming are subject to separate legislative provisions and a separate code, namely the Code of Programme Standards.

## §4. Political Advertising

*446.* The Broadcasting Act 2009 permits party political broadcasts (free airtime for advertising by political parties in election campaigns) subject to requirements of fairness in the allocation of free airtime, and concern not to give an unfair preference to any political party.[397] There is no obligation on broadcasters to allocate airtime for party political broadcasts but if they do so they must do so fairly.

*447.* With regard to paid advertising, the Broadcasting Act 2009 continues in operation a ban, which was in place in previous legislation from 1960 onwards, on

397. At s. 39(2), s. 41(5) and s. 42(2)(e)). In addition, one of the grounds for refusing to grant a right of reply is that 'the matter concerned relates to a party political broadcast' (s. 49)(21)(p)).

any advertisement which is directed towards a political end (section 41(3)).[398] This provision has been invoked on a number of occasions and has led to a small number of court challenges, including *Colgan v. IRTC,*[399] which concerned an anti-abortion advertisement. The rationale for the ban appears from the dicta in the court's judgment to be that political issues are by their nature sensitive and divisive and also that paid advertising can give an unfair advantage to 'rich men', presumably wealthy candidates and well-endowed political parties. It may be noted also that 'political end' does not refer only to 'party political' but has been interpreted more widely by the courts to include, for example, attempts to change government policy or decisions. However, as the court in *Colgan* also pointed out, the term 'political end' is not so broad as to include public affairs generally. Clearly there is an issue of freedom of expression engaged in the drawing of lines in this regard.

*448.* The ban on political advertising in broadcasting is not confined to election periods. However, during election periods other issues also arise. A number of complaints to broadcasters and, indeed, court cases have arisen in the past, for example, in relation to the allocation of airtime, both in respect of elections and referenda. For over two decades, for example, section 31 of the Broadcasting Authority Act 1960, as amended, was used to impose a ban on certain outlawed organizations involved in violence in Northern Ireland being interviewed on radio or television. The ban was extended to spokespersons for, or representatives of, Sinn Féin, which was a registered political party but was also the political wing of the IRA, which was a banned organization. The ban was challenged in the run-up to a general election in 1982 in *The State (Lynch) v. Cooney* but was ultimately held by the Supreme Court to be constitutional. A later challenge to the ban was brought before the European Commission of Human Rights in *Purcell v. Ireland* but the application was held to be 'manifestly ill-founded'.[400] Several other cases relating to the ban were heard in the domestic courts, as the ban was applied widely by RTÉ, the only licensed broadcaster at the time, including to ordinary members of Sinn Féin in their separate roles, such as in one case, a spokesperson for workers in a factory who were on strike.[401]

*449.* Other cases of advertisements being banned on radio or television because they were deemed to be directed towards a political end include a ban by the then regulator, BCI, in June 2004 on advertisements for an anti-war concert. The anti-war movement, which was promoting the concert, had recently registered its 'Stop Bush Campaign' as a political party. Separate radio advertisements urging the public to attend protests against Mr Bush were also refused by the BCI. The BCI also banned news reports of criticisms by a leading Trade Union, SIPTU, of the Government's

398. Broadcasting Authority Act 1960, s. 20(4) – this was the legislation that first provided for television broadcasting. Broadcasting Act 2009 s. 41(3).The ban extends to advertising that has any relation to an industrial dispute also. Section 41(4) bans advertising 'which addresses the issue of the merits or otherwise of adhering to any religious faith or belief or of becoming a member of any religion or religious organisation'.

399. [2000] 2 I.R. 490.

400. (1991) 12 H.R.L.J. 254. *See* discussion of this case and of *The State (Lynch) v. Cooney* [1982] I.R. 337; [1983] ILRM 89 (above at paragraphs 180–186 and 18–21 respectively).

401. *O'Toole v. RTÉ [1993]* 1 ILRM 454, 458. For this and other cases involving the broadcasting ban, *see* M. McGonagle, *Media Law*, 2003, Chapters 8 and 10.

decentralization plans. The reports were being broadcast by a number of commercial radio stations on the day before the European and local elections.[402] In a separate incident, RTÉ asked the Christian Solidarity Party to remove references to the citizenship referendum from their party political broadcasts. The referendum was held in June 2004 on the same day as the European and local elections. The request followed a number of court rulings in previous years regarding balance in referendum broadcasts.[403]

*450.* In 2007 BCI instructed commercial stations to cease broadcasting an advertisement for Trócaire, the official overseas development agency of the Catholic Church in Ireland. The issue was a reference in the advertisement to an online petition that Trócaire was running as part of its Lenten (the period before Easter) campaign, urging the government to implement UN Resolution 1325 on gender inequality. BCI stated that the ban in the Act (the Radio and Television Act 1988) was not confined to advertisements directed to a *party* political end, but also encompassed procuring a reversal of government policy or particular decisions of government. Thus, a broadcast advertisement calling on the Government to produce a National Action Plan and seeking public signatures for a petition in this regard had a political objective as contemplated under the Act.[404] BCI also banned a radio advertisement highlighting the needs of autistic children on the grounds that it too was 'political'. The BCI prohibited the advertisement as it 'could only be understood to be critical of government policy', even though the Constitution at Article 40.6.1i, expressly recognizes the right to criticize government policy, as long as it is not used to 'undermine public order or morality or the authority of the State'. The particular advertisement followed a court action taken by the family of one such child and was due to be broadcast in the month prior to a general election.[405]

402. BCI was the forerunner of BAI and the relevant legislation at the time was the Radio and Television Act 1988. *See* M. McGonagle, 'Ban on Political Advertisements and Pre-Election News Reports, IRIS 2004-8:11/23, available at http://merlin.obs.coe.int/iris/2004/8/article23.en.html; also, T. McGonagle, 'IRELAND: An Overview of Selected Issues on Freedom of Political Expression' in Susanne Nicoltchev, Ed., *IRIS Special: Political Debate and the Role of the Media – The Fragility of Free Speech* (Strasbourg, European Audiovisual Observatory, 2004), pages 89-93, available at: https://www.ivir.nl/publicaties/download/IRIS-Special-Political-Debate-and-the-Role-of-the-Media.pdf.

403. *See* IRIS 1998-6:7, IRIS 2000-2:7 and IRIS 2001-7:9; also, IRIS 2001-7:9/19.

404. *See* M. McGonagle and C. O'Malley, 'Political and Religious Advertising', IRIS 2008-5:13/22.

405. *Ibid.*

# Chapter 5. Advertising Rules

## §1. Different forms of Commercial Communications

*451.* The statutory basis for advertising rules in relation to broadcasting is the Broadcasting Act section 41. Section 41 of the Act prohibits certain kinds of advertising. It specifies that broadcasters shall not broadcast any advertisement directed to a political end, or which has any relation to an industrial dispute, or which addresses the issue of the merits or otherwise of adhering to any religious faith or belief or of becoming a member of any religion or religious organization. However, the ban on advertisements directed to a political end does not apply to party political broadcasts or advertisements broadcast at the request of the Referendum Commission in relation to a referendum.

*452.* The different forms of permitted advertising envisaged in the Act are 'advertising, teleshopping material, sponsorship and other forms of commercial promotion employed in any broadcasting service' (section 42). The term 'teleshopping material' is defined (section 42(8)) to mean 'material which, when transmitted, will constitute a direct offer to the public for the sale or supply to them of goods or other property (whether real or personal) or services'.

*453.* Section 42(2) requires that codes – which the Act requires BAI to develop – relating to broadcast advertising shall provide:

(g) that advertising, teleshopping material, sponsorship and other forms of commercial promotion employed in any broadcasting service, in particular advertising and other such activities which relate to matters likely to be of direct or indirect interest to children, protect the interests of children having particular regard to the general public health interests of children,

(h) that advertising, teleshopping material, sponsorship and other forms of commercial promotion employed in any broadcasting service, other than advertising and other activities as aforesaid falling within paragraph (g), protect the interests of the audience,

...

*454.* Provision is also made for regulation of the advertising of certain foods which are deemed harmful to children:

> (4) A broadcasting code prepared by the Authority under subsection (2)(g) may prohibit the advertising in a broadcasting service of a particular class or classes of foods and beverages considered by the Authority to be the subject of public concern in respect of the general public health interests of children, in particular those which contain fat, trans-fatty acids, salts or sugars.

In this regard, BAI in drafting a code is authorized to consult with the relevant public health authorities (section 42 (5)).

*455.* In summary, therefore, the code(s) to be prepared by BAI must protect the interests of children (persons under 18 years of age) having particular regard to the general public health interests of children (section 42(2)(g)). In other matters, not related to children, advertising, teleshopping material, sponsorship and other forms of commercial communication must protect the interests of the audience (section 42(2)(h)). A list of factors relating to the audience to which BAI must have regard in preparing or revising a code is given in section 42(3)).

## I. BAI General Commercial Communications Code

*456.* The BAI's General Commercial Communications Code of June 2017 gives effect to the provisions of the Act and definitions contained in it in respect of linear broadcasting indicate the different forms of commercial communications envisaged. They include: Commercial Communications; Advertising; Sponsorship; Misleading Commercial Communications; Comparative Commercial Communications; Cross-Promotions; Surreptitious Commercial Communications; Subliminal Commercial Communications; Teleshopping; Television Product Placement; Virtual Advertising; Interactive Advertising; and Split-Screen Techniques. Updates made in the 2017 revision of the Code include rules regarding commercial communications for financial services and products; and the provision of greater clarity on the distinction between sponsorship and product placement.

*457.* The General Commercial Communications Code also provides for certain minutage exclusions, notably self- and cross-promotions and information announcements, mainly public service announcements. While they must adhere to the principles of the code, they are not counted in the minutage allowed for commercial communications (discussed in §3 below). Examples are:

- Information announcements broadcast on RTÉ services for forthcoming concerts, recitals or performances, whether intended for broadcast or not, given by the National Symphony Orchestra, the RTÉ Concert Orchestra, and other RTÉ performing groups or of any other comparable groups which are employed by or under contract to RTÉ or employed by or under contract to a broadcaster and to which the public are allowed entry.
- Sponsorship announcements and product placements.
- Announcements of outside broadcasting events or of non-broadcast events organized in whole or in part by the broadcaster if the public are allowed entry free of charge.

'Trailers', on the other hand are excluded because they are considered to be programmes and not commercial communications once they relate to programmes carried on the same broadcasting service. Trailers for programmes on another broadcasting service, aired without payment or similar consideration, are considered cross-promotions, when the broadcasting services are owned and controlled by the same broadcaster. Likewise, charity appeals that are broadcast free of charge are excluded from the minutage. Under the revised Code, mandatory regulatory statements in radio advertisements for financial services and products are also excluded from the calculation of advertising minutage.

## II. Children's Commercial Communications Code

*458.* The children's code applies specifically to commercial communications that promote products, services, or activities that are deemed to be of particular interest to children and/or broadcast during and between children's programmes. The forms of advertising covered are: Advertising; Sponsorship; Misleading, Comparative, Surreptitious and Subliminal Commercial Communications; Teleshopping; Television Product Placement; Virtual, Interactive and Split-screen Advertising. These categories are defined in the Code in terms that relate directly to children. For instance, Children's Advertising, Children's Sponsorship and Children's Product Placement are defined as 'advertising, sponsorship and product placement (as defined in the General Commercial Communications Code) that promote products, services or activities that are deemed to be of particular interest to children and/or broadcast during and between children's programmes'. Additionally, the definitions in the Children's code include 'children's programmes', 'programme characters', and 'licensed characters'. 'Scheduling' is also defined:

> A children's programme is defined with reference to the type of programme and/or the profile of those watching or listening to that programme i.e. programmes that have an audience profile of which over 50% are under 18 years of age. When scheduling children's commercial communications, broadcasters shall comply with guidelines issued by the BAI and updated from time to time.

In addition, there are child-specific provisions in the Children's Code, such as that Christmas themed children's advertising may not be broadcast prior to 1 November each year.

## III. Other Codes

*459.* In addition to the BAI General Commercial Communications Code and Children's Commercial Communications Code, which apply to (linear) broadcasting, there are other codes that apply to advertising in audiovisual media.

*460.* The Code of Standards for Advertising and Marketing Communications in Ireland 2016 of the ASAI is outlined above under 'Ethical Codes' in the General Introduction. The Code applies to all forms of marketing but in relation to audiovisual media it applies to 'marketing communications broadcast on television or radio or screened in cinemas or with video, DVD or Blu-ray'. The code also applies *inter alia* to online advertisements in paid-for space (including banner or pop up advertisements and online video advertisements); paid-for search listings; preferential listings on price comparison sites; viral advertisements; in-game advertisements; commercial classified advertisements; advergames that feature in-display advertisements; advertisements transmitted by Bluetooth; advertisements distributed through web widgets and online sales promotions and prize promotions.

*461.* A voluntary code also applies to ODAS, and is outlined above in relation to the regulation of audiovisual media. It defines 'Advertising', 'Audiovisual commercial communication', 'Comparative audiovisual commercial communications', 'Inappropriate commercial communications', 'Misleading audiovisual commercial communications', 'Product Placement, 'Sponsorship', 'Subliminal audiovisual commercial communications', 'Surreptitious audiovisual commercial communications' and 'Teleshopping'. It sets out the requirements with regard to each category.

## §2. Restrictions on Content

*462.* The Broadcasting Act 2009 defines 'programme material' to include advertisements. It is stated to mean 'audio-visual material or audio material and includes advertisements and material which, when transmitted, will constitute a direct offer to the public for the sale or supply to them of goods or other property (whether real or personal) or services'. It follows, therefore, that the programme standards set out in section 42 of the Act apply. Indeed, it is specifically stated in section 42(2)(f) in relation to 'programme material', which includes advertising, that codes shall provide:

> that in respect of programme material broadcast by a broadcaster that audiences are protected from harmful or offensive material, in particular, that programme material in respect of the portrayal of violence and sexual conduct, shall be presented by a broadcaster–

(1) with due sensitivity to the convictions or feelings of the audience, and
(2) with due regard to the impact of such programming on the physical, mental or moral development of children, …

*463.* The BAI General Commercial Communications Code addresses the restrictions on content explicit or implicit in the statute. The Rules and Guidance are built around four main principles, namely: Legal, Honest, Decent and Truthful; Human Dignity, Offence and Harm; Transparency; and Protection of Children. There are General Rules (section 5) and specific guidance pertaining to advertising and teleshopping (section 6), specific advertising techniques (section 7), sponsorship (sections 8 and 9), product placement (section 10), and specific products and services (sections 11–22).

*464.* In relation to offence, harm and human dignity, for instance, the Code states:

- Commercial communications shall not prejudice respect for human dignity, cause serious or widespread offence, cause harm or encourage harmful behaviour.
- The manner in which persons and groups in society are represented in commercial communications shall be appropriate and justifiable and shall not stigmatize, support or condone discrimination or incite hatred against persons and groups in

society, based on sex, racial or ethnic origin, nationality, religion or belief, disability, age, sexual orientation or membership of the Traveller community.

- Broadcasters shall have due regard for the appropriateness and/or justification for broadcasting commercial communications that include, depictions and/or descriptions of violence, sexual conduct and coarse and/or offensive language.
- Commercial communications shall not encourage behaviour prejudicial to health or safety or grossly prejudicial to the protection of the environment.

*465.* Other examples of the restrictions include the following. All pertinent details of an offer contained in a commercial communication must be stated in a clear and understandable manner and shall not be contained solely in footnoted text on TV or taglines at the end of a commercial communication on radio (Code 5.1). There are also rules relating *inter alia* to disclaimers and on-screen messages (Code 5.2) and presenters and other on-air personnel shall not advertise or endorse products or services during editorial content (Code 5.3). With regard to comparative commercial communications, 'direct or implied comparisons with other products or services are permissible provided they objectively compare products or services meeting the same needs or intended for the same purpose. Points of comparison or top seller claims (e.g., claims a brand or product is number one) shall be based on facts that can be substantiated. The subject matter of a comparison shall not be chosen in such a way as to confer an artificial or unfair advantage to a promoter of a product or service'. (Code 5.4)

*466.* Among the other content provisions in the General Commercial Communications Code are that individual living persons shall not normally be portrayed or referred to in commercial communications without their permission. In general, any reference to such an individual, taking the form of a caricature or an impersonation which has not been approved by the person in question, is not permitted. However, references to living persons may normally be made in commercial communications for books, films, radio or television programmes, newspapers, magazines etc., which feature the persons referred to in the communication, provided they are not offensive or inaccurate (Code 5.7). Commercial communications shall not be calculated to induce unwarranted fear on the part of the viewer or listener (Code 5.8). Commercial communications for certain products, such as tobacco, prescription medicines and infant formula (up to six months) are not permitted, while commercial communications for other products, such as alcohol, medicines and medical, cosmetic and slimming treatments, food and follow-on infant formula are carefully circumscribed. There are rules also in relation to financial services and products, gambling, premium-rate telecommunications services, fortune tellers and psychic services. Also, in accordance with the Broadcasting Act, political and religious advertising and advertising relating to an industrial dispute are prohibited.

*467.* The Code has detailed rules and guidance on sponsorship, use of logos, and the programme material that is not permitted. In the case of medicinal products and medical treatment, for instance, only the name or the image of the undertaking may be given, but specific medicinal products or medical treatments available only on prescription may not be promoted. Certain types of programmes, such as news, current affairs, religious services, may not be sponsored. However, audience competitions may be sponsored but they must not constitute advertising, as defined in the Code,[406] and audiences must be clearly informed of the existence of a sponsorship agreement (Code 8.4). Entry mechanisms and prizes for competitions must not give undue prominence to the sponsor, in particular its facilities, products or services (Code 8.6).

*468.* In respect of children, and in addition to the provisions of the Children's Commercial Communications Code, the General Commercial Communications Code 2017 (Principle 4) states *inter alia* that 'broadcasters share a responsibility with parents and guardians for what children listen to and watch' and it is expected that broadcasters 'will protect children from material that is unsuitable or would be likely to cause physical or moral detriment', and that commercial communications:

- shall not directly exhort children to buy or hire a product or a service by exploiting their inexperience or credulity;
- shall not directly encourage children to persuade their parents, guardians or others to purchase the products or services being promoted;
- shall not exploit the special trust children place in parents, guardians, teachers or other persons;
- shall not unreasonably show children in dangerous situations.

## I. Restrictions on Content in Children's Commercial Communications

*469.* The Broadcasting Act requires BAI to develop codes that address a number of issues including that 'advertising and other such activities which relate to matters likely to be of direct or indirect interest to children, protect the interests of children having particular regard to the general public health interests of children' (section 42(2)(g)). Furthermore, a broadcasting code 'may prohibit the advertising in a broadcasting service of a particular class or classes of foods and beverages considered by the Authority to be the subject of public concern in respect of the general public health interests of children, in particular those which contain fat, trans-fatty acids, salts or sugars' (section 42(4)) and in this regard, BAI 'may consult with the relevant public health authorities' (section 42(5)).

*470.* In preparing the Children's Commercial Communications Code, which came into operation on 13 September 2013, BAI commissioned research, including a report from an Expert Working Group, and took account of the literature on health and nutrition issues. It also decided, following an extensive public consultation process from September 2011, to adopt the Nutrient Profiling Model in relation to High Fat, Salt and Sugar (HFSS) foods.[407] Following some controversy and public debate about the inclusion of cheese in the HFSS category, BAI took the recommendation of the

406. There must be a clear separation between sponsorship and advertising for the audience (Code 8.2, 8.5). Part 8 of the Code applies to television sponsorship. Similar provisions that apply to radio are set out in Part 9 but they differ in some respects to television. For instance, unlike television, current affairs and religious programmes may be sponsored (Code 9.7).

407. Details of the research and consultation process can be found by searching for HFSS foods using the search function on www.bai.ie.

Department of Health, and exempted advertisements and other commercial communications for cheese from the model. Nonetheless, on the recommendation of the Department of Health, adverts for cheese must include an on-screen message indicating the recommended maximum daily consumption limit for cheese.[408] Otherwise, commercial communications for HFSS food and drink are not permitted in children's programmes as defined by the Code. Acoustic or visual warnings are required in all children's commercial communications for fast food products, outlets and/or brands, and confectionery products, and the use of celebrities to promote such foods is prohibited.[409] There are additional content rules that apply to commercial communications for HFSS food and drink that are broadcast outside of children's programmes but which are directed at children. Such communications shall not include programme characters; licensed characters (e.g., characters and personalities from cinema releases or video games); shall not contain health or nutrition claims; and shall not include promotional offers.

*471.* The overall objectives of the Children's Commercial Communications Code, on which the content rules are based, are:

- To offer protection for children from inappropriate and/or harmful commercial communications;
- To acknowledge the special susceptibilities of children and ensure that commercial communications do not exploit these susceptibilities;
- To ensure that commercial communications are fair and present the product or service promoted in a way that is easily interpreted by children and does not raise unrealistic expectations of the capabilities or characteristics of the product or service being promoted, and;
- To provide unambiguous guidelines to broadcasters, advertisers, parents, guardians and children on the standards they can expect from commercial communications on Irish broadcasting services.

*472.* The Children's Commercial Communications Code recognizes that children are those up to the age of 18 but also that children of different ages require different levels of protection. Apart from the general protections that apply to all children, the Code therefore has a number of protections that apply to children under 6 years of age, those under 13 years of age and those under 15 years of age. For example, under the heading 'Factual Presentation' (section 6), the Code sets out the need for clarity as regards matters such as price (U/18), actual size (U/15), whether assembly is needed (U/15), and whether batteries are needed (U/15). In relation to on-screen messages or small print, there are two provisions. For children over the age of 6, the messages must be clear, simple to understand and left on screen long enough for children to read them (U/15). However, for children under the age of 6, on-screen messages or small print must be stated orally so that children who cannot read can understand them (U/6).

408. An appendix to the Children's Commercial Communications Code sets out the Nutrient Profiling Model.

409. In the case of fast foods, the message is: 'should be eaten in moderation and as part of a balanced diet' and in the case of confectionary: 'snacking on sugary foods and drinks can damage teeth'.

*473.* Various products and services are prohibited in the Children's Code, in addition to those prohibited in the General code. They are: Betting and Gaming services or products (except the National Lottery as permitted by the National Lottery Act 1986); Slimming products and services (slimming being defined as weight reduction, limitation or control); Introduction and dating services; Services of a sexual nature; Teleshopping; Paid product placement; Split-screen, interactive and virtual advertising; Surgical and non-surgical cosmetic procedures; Fortune Tellers, psychics etc.

## II. Children – ODAS Code

*474.* In relation to children and on-demand services, S.I. 258 of 2010, on which the ODAS code is based, provides that:

- Sponsorship logo shall not be displayed during children's programmes – 7.7 (Part 1, section 5 of the ODAS Code)
- On-demand audiovisual media service providers shall develop codes of conduct aimed at ensuring that on-demand audiovisual media services do not contain inappropriate audiovisual commercial communication, accompanying or included in children's programmes, of foods and beverages containing nutrients and substances with a nutritional or physiological effect, in particular those such as fat, trans-fatty acids, salt/sodium and sugars, excessive intakes of which in the overall diet are not recommended – 7.8 (Part 1, section 1 (j) of the ODAS Code)
- Product placement is not permitted in children's programmes – 8.2(a) (Part 1, section 6 of the ODAS Code)

*475.* The On-Demand AVS Code of Conduct (ODAS Code) gives effect to AVMSD. It advises service providers to take on board provisions of the BAI Code in regard to children's advertising for foods and beverages (1j). It also stipulates that in commercial communications alcoholic beverages shall not be aimed specifically at minors, and should comply with the relevant provisions of the ASAI Code, and any provisions of the voluntary industry code in place in relation to alcoholic beverages (1(e)).

## III. Children – ASAI Code

*476.* The ASAI code also contains a number of provisions relating to children. Apart from general requirements, such as the requirement that advertisers, when using media primarily targeted at children, should not promote products that are unsuitable for children (section 6.12), the Code devotes a whole section to children (section 7). Although the provisions apply more widely to all media, not just to broadcasting, they address many of the same characteristics of children as the BAI Children's Commercial Communications Code. Section 7.4, for instance states that:

Marketing communications should contain nothing that is likely to result in physical, mental or moral harm to children or that is likely to frighten or disturb them, except to promote safety or in the public interest.

*477.* It then sets out the Rules that apply. These include that: children should not be portrayed in a manner that offends against accepted standards of good taste and decency; should not be shown in morally or physically dangerous situations or behaving dangerously in the home or outside; should not be encouraged to engage in, or be portrayed engaging in, antisocial behaviour or bullying; if appearing as pedestrians or cyclists they should be seen to observe the Rules of the Road and, where relevant, should be seen wearing child car seats, seat-belts and safety helmets; and younger children, in particular, should not be shown using or in close proximity to dangerous substances or equipment without direct adult supervision. Section 7.5 then addresses the requirement not to exploit the loyalty, credulity, vulnerability or lack of experience of children. It does so in similar terms to the BAI Children's Code. Likewise, section 7.6 requires factual, unexaggerated information as to products, which should not minimize the price of products by the use of such words as 'only' or ' just' and should make it clear if extra items are needed to use the product (for example, batteries).

## §3. Time and Frequency Restrictions

*478.* The Broadcasting Act 2009, section 41 provides *inter alia* that:

(2) The total daily times for broadcasting advertisements in a sound broadcasting service must not exceed a maximum of 15 per cent of the total daily broadcasting time and the maximum time to be given to advertisements in any hour shall not exceed a maximum of 10 minutes.

BAI is required under section 43 of the Act to prepare, and from time to time as occasion requires, revise, rules ('broadcasting rules') with respect to:

(a) the total daily times that shall be allowed for the transmission of advertisements and teleshopping material on a broadcasting service, (and)
(b) the maximum period that shall be allowed in any given hour for the transmission of advertisements and teleshopping material on a broadcasting service. The Authority can make different such rules with respect to different classes of broadcasting service.

*479.* The BAI Rules on Advertising and Teleshopping (Daily and Hourly Limits) of July 2010 were developed in accordance with this statutory obligation. The rules apply to all services licensed by the BAI but do not apply to public service broadcasters, RTÉ and TG4. The maximum daily and hourly amount of advertising and teleshopping permitted on those services is determined by the Corporation, subject to the approval of the Minister for Communications, following consultation with BAI, as provided for in section 106(3) of the Broadcasting act 2009. A similar arrangement, but with the approval of the Minister for Arts, Sport and Tourism, is provided for in section 127(6) of the Act in respect of the proposed Irish Film Channel. However, film and cinema works broadcast by the Irish Film Channel shall be broadcast uninterrupted by advertisements or acknowledgements of sponsorship (section 127(7)).

*480.* The 2010 Rules provide that total daily time for broadcasting advertising and teleshopping spots shall not exceed a maximum of 18% of the total broadcast day. The time to be given to advertising and teleshopping spots in any clock hour shall not exceed a maximum of twelve minutes (Rule 4.1). The time to be given to advertising spots in children's programmes shall not exceed a maximum of ten minutes in any clock hour (Rule 4.2). As noted above, teleshopping is not permitted in children's programmes. In other programmes, teleshopping windows shall be of a minimum uninterrupted duration of fifteen minutes. With the exception of self-promotion channels and channels exclusively devoted to teleshopping, the maximum number of teleshopping windows per day shall be eight and the total daily time permitted for teleshopping windows shall be 3 hours (Rule 4.3).

*481.* As regards radio broadcasting, the Rules re-state the maximum 10 minutes per hour/15% per day for commercial radio services, which is set out in the Broadcasting Act 2009. No change was made to the 6 minutes per hour maximum for advertising and teleshopping spots on community radio and television services (4.5, 4.6). The time for teleshopping windows is the same as for commercial broadcasters, as set out above (4.7). Institutional and temporary radio broadcasters are not permitted to carry advertising or teleshopping (4.8). The Houses of the Oireachtas (Parliament) channel is not permitted to carry advertisements (Broadcasting Act 2009, section 125). A review of the impact of the rules was commenced by BAI in 2011 but because of the volatile advertising market and the impact of the economic recession on it, as well as the fact that the rules had not been long in operation, it was decided to leave them unchanged until the review of the General Commercial Code.[410]

## §4. Sponsorship

*482.* The provisions of the Broadcasting Act 2009 that apply to sponsorship of broadcast programmes refer, as they do also in relation to the other forms of commercial communication, to the interests of children and of the audience (section 42(2)(g) and (h)). Sponsorship is defined in the Code as:

> Any contribution made by a public or private undertaking or natural person not engaged in providing radio or television services or in the production of sound broadcasting or audiovisual works, to the financing of television and/or radio services or programmes with a view to promoting its name, its trade mark, its image, its activities, its products or its services.

The main aim in the revised code in relation to sponsorship was to provide greater clarity on the distinction between sponsorship and product placement. Thus, if a product

410. *See* BAI Rules on Advertising and Teleshopping (Daily and Hourly Limits) at: http://www.bai.ie/en/codes-standards./.

or service is built into the action of the programme, it is product placement; if sponsor announcements or references are shown during a programme but are not part of the plot or narrative of the programme, they qualify as sponsorship.[411]

*483.* The Rules pertaining to sponsorship on television and radio are set out in Rules 8 and 9 respectively of the General Commercial Communications Code 2017 (*see* above paragraph 467). Among the basic rules regarding sponsorship are: that it must 'not influence the content and scheduling of programmes in such a way as to affect the responsibility and editorial independence of the broadcaster'; that there 'shall be a clear separation between sponsorship and advertising for the audience'; and that broadcasters 'shall take care to ensure sufficient separation between formal programme sponsorship announcements scheduled before or at the end of advertisement breaks and advertising for the products or services of the sponsor carried in a separate advertisement break' (Code 8.1, 8.2).

*484.* Sponsorship rules applicable to on-demand services are contained in Reg. 7(2–8) of the Regulations of 2010 and section 2 of the ODAS Code. Section 2(c) states:

> Viewers shall be clearly informed of the existence of a sponsorship agreement. Sponsored programmes shall be clearly identified as such by the name, logo and/ or any other symbol of the sponsor such as a reference to its product(s) or service(s) or a distinctive sign thereof in an appropriate way for programmes at the beginning, during and/or the end of the programmes.

Later sub-sections (2.3, 2.4, 2.5) repeat the ban in the BAI codes on sponsorship by undertakings whose principal activity is the manufacture or sale of cigarettes and other tobacco products; and on the promotion of specific medicinal products or medical treatments available only on prescription in the State. Also, as in the case of linear broadcasting, news and current affairs programmes shall not be sponsored and shall not show a sponsorship logo during children's programmes, documentaries and religious programmes.

## §5. Product Placement

*485.* Product placement on television is prohibited unless permitted as specified in the BAI General Commercial Communications Code. The specific provisions are set out in Code 10.1 – 10.10. Among the provisions are that paid product placement is only permitted in cinematographic works, television films, sport, dramas, including one-off dramas, drama series and serials (excluding docu-dramas) and light entertainment programmes (excluding talk/chat shows that regularly include 20% or more of news and current affairs content). Also prop placement is permitted in all programmes but shall not affect the integrity of such programmes, in particular, news and current affairs programmes. However, prop placement in children's programmes is not permitted in the case of products/services that may not feature in children's programmes (e.g., alcohol and HFSS foods) and in the case of other relevant restrictions. The placement of products in programme content shall be editorially justified and shall not give undue

411. For further details *see* Code 8.3, 8.4.

prominence to the products or services in question. Audiences must be clearly informed of the existence of product placement, and the closing credits of a programme containing product placement must include the name of the providers and the products, services etc. provided. In addition, broadcasters shall keep a record of the programmes in which product placement occurs, the placement in each programme, the value of each individual placement and whether it is paid product placement or prop placement. This information must be available to the BAI upon request in the context of compliance monitoring or in instances where a complaint is investigated. This information must also be available in respect of any independent programmes commissioned by the broadcaster.

*486.* In the case of on-demand services the Regulations of 2010 stipulate that product placement is prohibited (Reg. 8) but they then go on to state the two sets of circumstances in which product placement is permissible:

(a) in cinematographic works, films and series made for audiovisual media services, sports programmes and light entertainment programmes but not in children's programmes, or
(b) where there is no payment for the placement of the product but only the provision of certain goods or services free of charge, such as production props and prizes, with a view to their inclusion in a programme.

*487.* The Regulations then set out the requirements that must be met. Media service providers of on-demand audiovisual media services must also, in co-operation with the BAI, and other relevant bodies develop codes of conduct relating to the above Regulations in respect of product placement (Reg. 13). The ODAS code (section 6) states that product placement shall be admissible in the above two sets of circumstances and goes on (section 7-8) to replicate the conditions that apply under the Regulations and indeed those contained in the (then) BAI code in respect of linear broadcasters. It adds (section 9) that programmes shown on an on-demand audiovisual media service shall not contain product placement of tobacco products or cigarettes or product placement from undertakings whose principal activity is the manufacture or sale of cigarettes and other tobacco products; or, specific medicinal products or medical treatments available only on prescription in the State.

# Chapter 6. Right to Information

## §1. Access to Major Events

*488.* The first piece of legislation to deal with major events was the Broadcasting (Major Events Television Coverage) Act, 1999, which was passed to give effect to the TWF Directive of 1989, as amended in 1997. The Act set out the consultative process for designating rights, the Minister's powers in that regard, broadcasters' duties and civil remedies in the event of breaches or threatened breaches. It also made provision for the High Court to determine 'reasonable market rates' with respect to television coverage of an event where broadcasters fail to agree. The list of major events to be covered was agreed and approved by the European Commission. The list was then set out in S.I. No. 99/2003 – Broadcasting (Major Events Television Coverage) Act 1999 (Designation of Major Events) Order 2003. The Order states: 'The events specified in the Schedule to this Order are designated as events of major importance to society for which the right of a qualifying broadcaster to provide coverage on a live basis on free television services should be provided in the public interest.' One further event, Ireland's games in the Six Nations Rugby Football Championship, was designated as 'an event of major importance to society for which the right of a qualifying broadcaster to provide coverage on a deferred basis on free television services should be provided in the public interest'.[412]

*489.* Television coverage of major events is now governed by the Broadcasting act 2009, Part 11, section 162–173, which gives effect to the provisions of AVMSD. Following a definitions section and another on application, section 162 of the Act grants the Minister for Communications, Energy and Natural Resources power to designate events as being 'events of major importance to society for which the right of a qualifying broadcaster to provide coverage on free television services should be provided in the public interest'. The list of events, which was not changed from the original list of 2003, consists of:

- Summer Olympics
- All-Ireland Senior Football and Hurling finals
- Ireland's qualifying games in the European Football Championship and World Cup
- The opening games, semi-finals and the final of the European Football Championship Finals and the FIFA World Cup Finals Tournament
- Ireland's games in the Rugby World Cup Finals Tournament
- The Irish Grand National and the Irish Derby
- The Nations Cup at the Dublin Horse Show

412. The 1999 Act is available at: http://www.oireachtas.ie/documents/bills28/acts/1999/a2899.pdf and the S.I. is available at http://www.irishstatutebook.ie/eli/2003/si/99/made/en/print.

*490.* The list only contains sports events. The Minister determines whether the events should be available live, deferred or both live and deferred (section 162(1)(b)). The above list contains the events which are to be broadcast live. The list of deferred events merely consists of one sporting event, Ireland's games in the Six Nations Rugby Football championship. The events list was reviewed in 2010 but no changes were made. The Minister made his decision following a detailed public consultation process and an independent report prepared by international consultants. The list was reviewed again in 2015. The Minister launched a public consultation concerning the possible designation of additional events as events of major importance to society. The three additional events were:

- Ireland's games in the Six Nations Rugby Football Championship (currently 'free-to-air' on a deferred basis);
- the All-Ireland Senior Ladies Football Final; and
- the All-Ireland Senior Camogie Final.[413]

As a result of the 2015 review, the All Ireland Senior Ladies Football Final and the All Ireland Senior Camogie Final have been added to the list.[414]

*491.* When the Minister is deciding on the events to be included on the list, s/he must have regard to 'the extent to which the event has a special general resonance for the people of Ireland, and (b) the extent to which the event has a generally recognized distinct cultural importance for the people of Ireland' (section 162(2) of the Broadcasting Act). Relevant factors which the Minister may take into account in determining the extent to which those criteria have been met are: whether a national or non-national team or Irish persons are involved in the event; and past practice or experience of broadcasting the event or similar events (section 162(3)). Further matters that the Minister must consider in deciding whether the coverage should be live or deferred in whole or in part are set out in section 162(4) and include the nature of the event, the time at which it is scheduled and other practical considerations. Before making, revoking or amending an order the Minister must consult with the Minister for Arts, Sport and Tourism and, as a safeguard, a draft of the Order must be placed before the Houses of the Oireachtas (Parliament) (section 162(5) and (6)).

*492.* Other provisions of the Act relate to: consultation (initially with the organizers of the event, broadcasters and then with the general public regarding the intended designation) and broadcasters' duties (with respect to designated events and to Member States events). Civil remedies provided for in the case of breach of duty include application to the High Court for: restraining orders; declarations that a contract is void; damages; a direction that the right to provide television coverage of the event shall be offered to the aggrieved broadcaster at reasonable market rates (section 166).

413. Camogie is a game like men's hurling (akin to hockey), which is played by women's teams. For further information on the lists, *see* http://www.dccae.gov.ie/communications/en-ie/Pages/Consultation/Review-of-Designation-of-Major-Events-.aspx. The name of the Department has now been changed to the Department of Communications, Climate Action and Environment (DCCAE).

414. *See* 'Senior ladies football and camogie finals made protected sporting events', www.thejournal.ie, 17 Oct. 2017.

The term 'market rates' is defined in section 167 and the criteria for determining 'reasonable market rates' are set out in section 170. A qualifying broadcaster may apply to the High Court to obtain rights where the event organizer has not made an agreement or arrangement with a qualifying broadcaster to enable it to provide coverage on free television services. The High Court can also fix the terms, including the fixing of reasonable market rates or may refer the computation of the rates to an arbitrator appointed by it (section 168). As well as notification requirements (section 171), the Act provides for a review of the designated events and the designation of events every three years (section 173).

## §2. Short News Reporting

### I. Introduction

*493.* The DCENR (now the DCCAE) was responsible for transposing the provisions of AVMSD, including those on short news reporting, into Irish law.

### II. Legal Provisions

*494.* There is no reference to short news reporting in the Broadcasting Act 2009. Instead, the legal provisions relating to short news reporting were contained initially in the European Communities (Audiovisual Media Services) Regulations 2010 (S.I. 248 of 2010). Regulation 17, which gave effect to Articles 3j–k of AVMSD, provided:

> 17. (1) For the purpose of short news reports, any broadcaster established in the State or another Member State shall have access on a fair, reasonable and non-discriminatory basis to events of high interest to the public which are transmitted on an exclusive basis by a broadcaster under the jurisdiction of the State.
>
> (2) If another broadcaster established in the same Member State as the broadcaster seeking access has acquired exclusive rights to the event of high interest to the public, access shall be sought from that broadcaster.
>
> (3) Access is guaranteed by allowing broadcasters to freely choose short extracts from the transmitting broadcaster's signal with, unless impossible for reasons of practicality, at least the identification of their source.
>
> (4) As an alternative to paragraph (3), the Minister may encourage or encourage the establishment of an equivalent system which achieves access on a fair, reasonable and non-discriminatory basis through other means.

> (5) Short extracts shall be used solely for general news programmes and may be used in on-demand audiovisual media services only if the same programme is offered on a deferred basis by the same media service provider.
>
> (6) Without prejudice to this Regulation, broadcasters or audiovisual media service providers may ensure, that the modalities and conditions regarding the provision of such short extracts are defined, in particular with regard to any compensation arrangements, the maximum length of short extracts and time limits regarding their transmission by the development of a self regulatory code of practice. Where compensation is provided for, it shall not exceed the additional costs directly incurred in providing access.

*495.* The above Regulations of 2010 were amended by European Communities (Audiovisual Media Services) (Amendment) Regulations 2012 (S.I. No. 247 of 2012), which provided at 2(b) that the following be substituted for paragraph (6) of Regulation 17:

> (6) Without prejudice to this Regulation, the BAI shall ensure that the modalities and conditions regarding the provision of such short extracts are defined, in particular with regard to any compensation arrangements, the maximum length of short extracts and time limits regarding their transmission by the development of a code of practice. Where compensation is provided for, it shall not exceed the additional costs directly incurred in providing access.

The experience of BAI and the feedback received by them at the time indicated that the arrangements between rights-holders and broadcasters were working effectively. Thus, the development of the new code envisaged in the S.I. was not regarded as a priority. However, the Code was eventually launched on 28 June 2017 and came into effect on 1 September 2017.[415] At its launch BAI stated that the Code of Practice 'is designed to ensure that the public are informed of major news, sporting or cultural events, regardless of who owns the broadcast rights', and that 'The provisions of the Code of Practice fully reflect the informal, co-operative arrangements which have been in place between broadcasters in Ireland for a number of years.' The Code defines the modalities and conditions regarding the provision of short news extracts and fulfils the BAI's obligation to develop a code of practice further to the AVMS Regulations of 2012 (Code 1.5). It covers: Access to short news extracts; Events of high interest to the public; General news programmes; Use of extracts; and Complaints.

## III. Case Law

*496.* There does not appear to be any reported case law on this matter to date.

415. http://www.bai.ie/en/bai-launches-new-short-news-reporting-code-practice/.

# Chapter 7. Access to Networks and Platforms

## §1. Introduction

*497.* Ireland has implemented the European regulatory framework governing the electronic communications sector by way of both primary and secondary legislation. Primary legislation consists of the Communications Regulation Acts 2002–2011. Secondary legislation consists of a number of regulations in 2011 to transpose the European reform package. The Comreg, is the body responsible for access to networks and platforms.

*498.* The most recent provisions governing access are the European Communities (Electronic Communications Networks And Services) (Access) Regulations 2011 (S.I. No. 334 of 2011), which give effect to Directive 2002/19/EC of the European Parliament and of the Council of 7 March 2002, as amended by Directive 2009/140/EC of the European Parliament and of the Council of 25 November 2009. The Regulations deal *inter alia* with the general framework for access and interconnection, rights and obligations for access and interconnection, functions of the regulator, conditional access systems, transparency and non-discrimination, price control and enforcement. Authorization is dealt with in the European Communities (Electronic Communications Networks and Services) (Authorization) Regulations (S.I. No 335 of 2011). The General Authorization for the Provision of Electronic Communications Networks and Services was last updated in August 2013.[416]The European Framework, as transposed by the European Communities (Electronic Communications Networks and Services) (Framework) Regulations 2011, governs the granting of rights of use for numbers and radio spectrum. On 22 December 2015, ComReg decision 08/15 revised the numbering conditions of use and application process. In December 2015 also, ComReg launched a consultation process in conjunction with its Draft Radio Spectrum Management Strategy 2016 to 2018. On 20 March 2017, ComReg published its consultation document and draft decision on the Mobile Satellite Services with Complementary Ground Component Authorization Regime.[417]

*499.* The Wireless Telegraphy (Broadband Wireless Access Local Area Licence) Regulations 2013 (S.I. No. 214 of 2013), which have effect until 2017, apply to licences granted (under section 5 of the Wireless Telegraphy Act of 1926) to keep, have possession of, install, maintain, work and use Broadband Wireless Access apparatus in accordance with the terms and conditions, as set out in Regulation 11, to be observed by the holders of such licences subject to which such licences are deemed to be granted.

*500.* The European Communities (Electronic Communications Networks And Services) (Universal Service And Users' Rights) Regulations 2011 (S.I. No. 337 of

416. Reference Number: 03/81R4, available at http://www.comreg.ie/publications/general_authorisation.
417. For further information on ComReg's activities in these and other related matters, *see* www.comreg.ie and Helen Kelly and Simon Shinkwin, 'Telecoms and Media', Matheson solicitors, Dublin, September 2017, available at: https://gettingthedealthrough.com/area/39/jurisdiction/14/telecoms-media-ireland/.

2011) provide *inter alia* for access at a fixed location and provision of telephone services; measures for disabled end users; costs; quality of service; facilitating change of service provider; dispute resolution and enforcement. On 29 June 2012, following a public consultation, ComReg designated Eircom as the 'universal service provider' (USP) for a period of two years, from 1 July 2012 to 30 June 2014, and continued it until the end of 2015.[418] However, Eircom brought a court case against ComReg in October 2014, claiming that ComReg's decision extending Eircom's designation as USP, without first carrying out a review of whether such a designation is necessary, was flawed. Eircom claimed that it imposed on the company obligations for which no appropriate justification had been advanced, including the requirement to provide fixed phone line connections, which was unfair.[419]

*501.* A High Court appeal was taken by Vodafone in 2013 against a decision of ComReg (Decision D11/12), which designated six Mobile Service Providers, including Vodafone, with SMP. Vodafone appealed insofar as the decision imposed a cost orientation obligation on Vodafone; and appealed also against Decision D12/12, which further specified the detailed nature of the cost orientation obligation imposed under Decision D11/12. In its judgment of 14 August 2013 the High Court found in part in favour of Vodafone.[420]

*502.* While some issues proceed to court therefore, others are handled via notifications from ComReg. On 9 September 2013, for example, ComReg notified Meteor Mobile Communications Limited ('Meteor', now re-branded as 'Eir') of a finding that Meteor had not complied with its statutory obligations regarding the notification of its customers of modifications to contractual conditions and was not compliant with the Universal Service Regulations.[421] On 19 February 2013, ComReg notified Eircom of its finding following an investigation that Eircom had not complied with its obligation to meet reasonable requests from other authorized operators for the provision of access, including associated facilities. This obligation was imposed in ComReg Document No. 10/39, Decision No. D05/10.[422] In January 2013 ComReg issued new decisions also on the regulation of next generation access for more high-speed broadband.[423] The last-mentioned examples illustrate that as well as issuing notifications and taking enforcement actions and court proceedings, ComReg also publishes decisions. For example, in 2016 ComReg published its decision (D03/16)

418. The provision of telephony services under Universal Service Obligations (ComReg Decision No: D07/12, ComReg Document No: 12/71). For further details of the situation of telecoms in Ireland, *see* Helen Kelly, Nina Cummins and Darach Connolly, chapter on Ireland, pp. 141–146, in Laurent Garzaniti and Natasha Good, eds, 'Telecoms and Media in 38 jurisdictions worldwide', 2015, available at: http://www.matheson.com/images/uploads/documents/Telecoms_Media_2015.PDF.

419. The matter was settled but an issue of costs was brought before the court. *See Eircom Limited v. Commission for Communications Regulation* [2015] IEHC 51, available at: http://www.bailii.org/ie/cases/IEHC/2015/H51.html.

420. *Vodafone Ireland Limited v. Commissioner for Communications Regulation* [2013] IEHC 382, available at: http://www.bailii.org/ie/cases/IEHC/2013/H382.html. *See also* ComReg, Information Notice, Reference; ComReg 13/80.

421. Reference: ComReg 13/85.

422. ComReg, Information Notice, Reference; ComReg 13/16.

423. ComReg, Information Notice, Reference; ComReg 13/11.

on the revised prices for Eir's (formerly Eircom) current generation wholesale access services. The document sets out prices *inter alia* for wholesale line rental (WLR), local loop unbundling and civil infrastructure access (access to ducts and poles). WLR is the principal means by which alternative operators who use Eir's network provide fixed voice services in Ireland. Comreg also publishes quarterly market reports.[424] ComReg also has the power to issue Fixed Payment Notices (FPNs) under the Consumer Protection Act 2007 (section 85) for breaches of the Consumer Information Regulations 2013. The first time that ComReg imposed FPNs was in September 2016 when it imposed a EUR 255,000 penalty on Virgin Media Ireland Limited ('Virgin Media'), after an investigation found that Virgin failed to provide 26,046 of its customers with a contract in a durable form. This was in contravention of the Consumer Information Regulations 2013.[425]

## §2. Must-Carry Rules

*503.* Must-carry rules are set out in the Broadcasting Act 2009 in relation to MMD services. These services must carry the national public service channels and the national commercial television channel, TV3 (section 76(1)(b), Broadcasting Act 2009). They must carry 'each free-to-air service' provided by RTE, TG4 and TV3. Furthermore, BAI may 'require the holder of a licence referred to in subsection (1) to distribute as a broadcasting service, by means of the MMD system concerned, the whole or part of the programme material supplied under one or more specified community content provision contracts the holders of which are members of the local community or community of interest … '. (section 76(4)).

*504.* Must-carry and must-offer rules pertaining to an 'appropriate network' are contained in section 77 of the Broadcasting Act. An 'appropriate network' is defined as an electronic communications network provided by a person ('appropriate network provider') which is used for the distribution or transmission of broadcasting services to the public. Where such an appropriate network is a digital provider, it 'shall ensure the re-transmission, by or through his or her appropriate network, of the Houses of the Oireachtas Channel and the Irish Film Channel'.[426] It shall also ensure the re-transmission of each FTA television service provided by RTÉ, TG4 and TV3. Similarly, an appropriate network provider shall re-transmit each national sound broadcasting service provided by RTÉ and each sound broadcasting contractor. The term 'appropriate network provider', however, excludes a multiplex contractor, or the holder of a licence for MMD transmission, or the holder of a broadcasting licence (under section 59 of the Act) or a PSB licence (under section 121 of the Act), the terms of which authorize the transmission of programme material. In addition, BAI may require an appropriate network provider to transmit as a broadcasting service, the whole or part of the

424. For decision D03/16 *see* https://www.comreg.ie//csv/downloads/ComReg_1639.pdf. Details of Comreg's various actions and publications are available at: http://www.comreg.ie/category/consumer-news/.

425. *See* : http://www.comreg.ie/publication/virgin-media-pay-e255000-penalty-failure-provide-durable-contracts/.

426. At the time of writing, the film channel has not yet been established.

programme material supplied under one or more specified community content provision contracts. All of these services must be carried without any additional charge.

*505.* The corollary of the must-carry requirements are the must-offer requirements. A must-offer service is defined as 'a free-to-air television service provided for the time being by RTÉ, TG4 and the free-to-air service provided under *section 70* by the television service programme contractor', i.e., TV3. RTÉ, TG4 and TV3 must offer their services for re-transmission (subject to agreement as to fair, reasonable and non-discriminatory terms of use) by means of any appropriate network that is available for reception in an intelligible form by members of the public in the whole of or in part of the State. They must ensure that their must-offer services are available at all times for broadcast or re-transmission (subject to agreement as to fair, reasonable and non-discriminatory terms of use) by means of every satellite television service at no additional charge. Must-offer services must be on electronic programme guides, by which members of the public access the satellite television service, for the purposes of that satellite television service and for the purposes of any other satellite television service which also utilises the same electronic programme guide.

## §3. Obligations for Conditional Access Providers

*506.* The regulator in relation to conditional access in Ireland is the ComReg.

*507.* The relevant European Directives on conditional access were transposed into Irish law by means of two Statutory Instruments, S.I. 333 of 2011, and S.I. 334 of 2011, which replaced earlier Regulations made in 2007 and 2002.[427] The first Statutory Instrument, S.I. 333 of 2011, the European Communities (Electronic Communications Networks and Services) (Framework) Regulations 2011, dealt *inter alia* with appeals against decisions of the Regulator (Part 2) and tasks and objectives of the Regulator (Part 4). The term 'conditional access' is specifically referred to in the definition of 'access', and the term 'conditional access system' is defined as 'any technical measure or arrangement whereby access to a protected radio or television broadcasting service in intelligible form is made conditional upon subscription or other form of prior individual authorisation'.

*508.* The second Statutory Instrument, S.I. 334 of 2011, the European Communities (Electronic Communications Networks and Services) (Access) Regulations 2011, has a full Regulation (No. 7) devoted to conditional access systems and other facilities, and also includes within the definition of 'access', access to 'conditional access systems for digital television services and access to virtual network services'. Regulation 7 is headed 'Conditional access systems and other facilities' and deals *inter alia* with: technical capability; offering the service to all broadcasters on a fair, reasonable and non-discriminatory basis; not prohibiting, deterring or discouraging a common interface allowing connection with other conditional access systems; consideration of SMP on the relevant market and other competition issues. It places obligations on operators of a system for conditional access to digital television and radio services, and upon whose

427. S.I. 333 of 2011 is available at: http://www.irishstatutebook.ie/eli/2011/si/333/made/en/pdf and S.I. 334 of 2011 is available at: http://www.irishstatutebook.ie/eli/2011/si/334/made/en/print.

access services broadcasters depend to reach any group of potential viewers or listeners, to ensure that:

> the system has the necessary technical capability for cost-effective transcontrol at redistribution system head-ends allowing the possibility for full control by operators of redistribution systems at local or regional level of the services using any such conditional access system.

*509.* An operator, upon whom access service broadcasters depend to reach potential viewers, must offer all broadcasters technical services enabling such action on a fair, reasonable and non-discriminatory basis 'enabling the broadcasters' digitally-transmitted services to be received by viewers or listeners authorized by means of decoders administered by the service operator (Regulation 7(2)(a)). The operator must also keep separate financial accounts regarding his or her activity as a provider of such a service (7(2)(b)).

## §4. Other Access Obligations for Network Operators

*510.* S.I. 334 of 2011 (above) imposes a number of other access obligations on network operators. First of all, the term 'access' is defined as:

> the making available of facilities or services to another undertaking, under defined conditions, on either an exclusive or non-exclusive basis, for the purpose of providing electronic communications services, including when they are used for the delivery of information society services or broadcast content services. Among other things, it covers–

(a) access to network elements and associated facilities, which may involve the connection of equipment, by fixed or non-fixed means (in particular this includes access to the local loop and to facilities and services necessary to provide services over the local loop),
(b) access to physical infrastructure including buildings, ducts and masts,
(c) access to relevant software systems including operational support systems,
(d) access to information systems or databases for pre-ordering, provisioning,
(e) ordering, maintaining and repair requests, and billing,
(f) access to number translation or systems offering equivalent functionality,
(g) access to fixed and mobile networks, in particular for roaming, and
(h) access to conditional access systems for digital television services and
(i) access to virtual network services.

*511.* The rights and obligations of operators are set out in Regulation 5. While an operator has the right to negotiate interconnection with another operator for the purpose of providing publicly available electronic communications services in order to ensure provision and interoperability of services throughout the EU, the operator must negotiate interconnection for the purpose of providing publicly available electronic communications services when requested to do so by another authorized undertaking, and must offer access and interconnection to other undertakings on terms and conditions consistent with any obligations imposed by the Regulator (Regulation 5(1)–(3)).[428] An operator of a public electronic communications network established for the distribution of digital television services shall ensure that the network is capable of distributing wide-screen television services and programmes (Regulation 5(4)). If such an operator receives and redistributes wide-screen television services or programmes, the operator must not alter a signal that it receives in wide-screen format, and must ensure that the signal is redistributed in the same format (Regulation 5(5)). Further obligations relate to the confidentiality of information acquired by one undertaking from another (Regulation 5(6)). Breach of the above obligations constitutes an offence.

*512.* Other obligations may be imposed if an operator is designated as having a SMP on a relevant market as a result of a market analysis carried out in accordance with Regulation 27 of the Framework Regulations, i.e., S.I. 333 of 2011 (paragraph 507 above). Such obligations may include a requirement to ensure transparency in relation to access or interconnection, or to publish a reference offer that is sufficiently unbundled to ensure that undertakings are not required to pay for facilities which are not necessary for the service requested, or directions requiring an operator to make changes to a reference offer. Failure to comply constitutes an offence (Regulation 9). Other obligations relate to non-discrimination; accounting separation; access to, and use of, specific network elements and associated facilities; cost recovery and price controls; functional separation; and notification of voluntary separation by vertically integrated undertakings designated as having SMP in one or several relevant markets (Regulations 10–15).

428. The functions of the Regulator in this regard are set out in Regulation 6.

# Chapter 8. Standards and Interoperability

*513.* The functions of the Regulator, ComReg, as set out in S.I. 334 (*see* paragraphs 507–509 above) require the Regulator to encourage and, where appropriate, ensure adequate access, interconnection and the interoperability of services in such a way as to promote efficiency, sustainable competition, efficient investment and innovation, and give the maximum benefit to end users (Regulation 6(1)). Indeed, the Explanatory Note that accompanies the Regulations states: 'These Regulations establish a regulatory framework for the relationships among suppliers of networks and services that will result in sustainable competition, interoperability of electronic communications services and consumer benefits.'

*514.* S.I. 333 of 2011 (paragraph 507 above) deals with the interoperability of digital interactive television services (Regulation 29). The Regulator must encourage providers of such services to use an open application program interface; encourage providers of all enhanced digital television equipment deployed for the reception of digital interactive television services on interactive digital television platforms to comply with an open application program interface in accordance with the minimum requirements of the relevant standards or specifications; and encourage providers of digital television services and equipment to co-operate in the provision of interoperable television services for disabled end users. Furthermore, the Regulator must encourage proprietors of application program interfaces to make available on fair, reasonable and non-discriminatory terms, and against appropriate remuneration, all such information as is necessary to enable providers of digital interactive television services to provide all services supported by the application program interface in a fully functional form.

# Part IV. Cross-Ownership Regulation

## §1. Introduction

*515.* Following decades of a monopoly enjoyed by RTÉ, the regulation of cross-ownership became an issue as a result of the introduction of commercial broadcasting in 1989 – *see* above. The Radio and Television Act 1988 established the IRTC as the regulatory authority and set out its composition, powers and duties. The relevant sections in relation to ownership issues were sections 6(2) and 14(2), which were imperative in the sense that they required the IRTC to have regard to certain matters, but non-directive in the sense that they did not lay down precise steps that the IRTC must take. Section 6(2) required the IRTC to have regard *inter alia* to:

(g) the desirability of allowing any person, or group of persons, to have control of, or substantial interests in, an undue number of sound broadcasting services …
(h) the desirability of allowing any person, or group of persons, to have control of, or substantial interests in, an undue amount of the communications media in the area specified …

Section 14(2) concerned the assignment of a contract or any interest therein. It empowered the IRTC to prohibit an assignment or any material change in the ownership of a company.

*516.* In the start-up period of commercial broadcasting, the situation of cross-ownership was very simple and straight-forward, involving only cross-ownership between newspapers and broadcasting. The IRTC's focus was on ownership, both within the sector itself and within each franchise area. It was concerned that newspaper owners in a particular area should not also own what in all probability would be the only local radio station. It introduced a 25% ceiling on the share that newspapers could have in a local radio station. That percentage was later raised to 27% to meet certain exigencies that presented themselves. In time, it also became reciprocal, in that a radio station was permitted to hold a maximum interest of 27% in a newspaper, and/or in one other local sound broadcasting service.

*517.* As subsequent licensing rounds took place and cross-ownership grew more complex, involving a greater variety of operators and structures, the policy was developed incrementally: percentages were determined for single interest holdings (40%, 46%); categories were drawn up of 'Relevant Persons' and 'Media Operators', who fell within the restrictions. 'Media Operators' included radio and television broadcasters, cable operators, those engaged in retransmission and satellite services, programme and advertising production companies, newspapers, magazines, advertising agencies, those involved in communications or telecommunications enterprises. 'Relevant Persons' included all of the above as well as political parties, public representatives, the churches, clergy, ruling or representative bodies of the churches and non-EU nationals. All contractors were required to disclose in full the manner and degree to which Relevant Persons had an interest in the contractor and the Contractor (and any shareholder, officer or employee of the contractor) had an interest in a Media Operator.

*518.* Over time, however, it became expedient to allow certain exceptions to the percentage rules, sometimes by reference to the expertise of particular applicants, or by reference to existing holdings, in the case of certain mergers and acquisitions. The difficulties experienced in getting an independent television station up and running, allied with the high level of investment and degree of skill and expertise required, resulted in the percentage share allotted to investors in television stations being set at 45% in the case of CanWest and TV3. The Commission also adopted the policy of requiring the appointment of all senior management in stations to be approved by the Commission.

*519.* By the time the Broadcasting Act 2001 was passed, regulations of the above type that restricted ownership to one (or two) television and/or radio channel(s) were related to a situation where radio spectrum was scarce. Such regulations were difficult to justify in the new digital environment, where spectrum scarcity was no longer an issue. The 2001 Act was intended to provide for the introduction of DTT and therefore made provision for new digital services, including EPGs. The policy on ownership and control was revised, therefore, following a process of research and public consultation, in October 2001.

*520.* When introducing the Ownership and Control Policy (2001), the Commission committed to undertake a review of its impact and effectiveness after three years. This was primarily due to the fundamental nature of some of the changes introduced in 2001. In particular, the 2001 policy removed the necessity for local ownership of stations, abolished percentage limits to be held in stations licensed under the 1988 Act by any one individual or company and provided definitions and guidelines in relation to specific statutory terms. It also permitted the sell-on of radio stations two years following the award of a contract. The policy was revised again in 2005 and has been revised at intervals since, most recently in 2012, following the enactment of the Broadcasting Act 2009. A revised policy was due to be published in 2017 but is now scheduled for 2018. Pluralism and diversity in the broadcast media remain a key objective in the BAI Strategy Statement and one of the key deliverables for 2017–2019 is to 'Continue to articulate an informed policy position on Media Plurality in Ireland that is supported by relevant research, and provide advices to the Minister as required.'

*521.* The relevant legislation is the Broadcasting Act 2009 but the regulation of ownership in the Act needs to be considered in conjunction with the Competition and Consumer Protection Act 2014, which makes changes to the regulation of media mergers and acquisitions. The relevant provisions of the Broadcasting Act 2009 are, first of all:

> 66.–(1) The Contract Awards Committee shall, in accordance with this Part, consider every application received by it–

(a) for a sound broadcasting contract made under *section 65(8)*, or
(b) for a television programme service contract, for the purpose of determining the most suitable applicant, if any, to be awarded a broadcasting contract.

(2) In the consideration of applications referred to in subsection

(1) received by it and in determining the most suitable applicant to be awarded a broadcasting contract, the Contract Awards Committee shall have regard to–

(inter alia):

(f) the desirability of having a diversity of services in the area specified in the notice catering for a wide range of tastes including those of minority interests,
(g) the desirability of allowing any person, or group of persons, to have control of, or substantial interests in, an undue number of sound broadcasting services in respect of which a sound broadcasting contract has been awarded under this Part,
(h) the desirability of allowing any person, or group of persons, to have control of, or substantial interests in, an undue number of sound broadcasting services in the area specified in the notice,
(i) the desirability of allowing any person, or group of persons, to have control of, or substantial interests in, an undue amount of the communications media in the area specified in the notice,

*522.* Section 69 of the Act states that: 'Every broadcasting contract may contain such terms and conditions as the Authority thinks appropriate and specifies in the contract.' Among the conditions that BAI may specify is a condition 'prohibiting any alteration in the Memorandum or Articles of Association of the company … or prohibiting any material change in the ownership of the company'. If no such condition is specified in the contract, the position is that any such alteration can only be made with the previous consent in writing of BAI. A similar situation applies to multiplex contracts (section 138). Among the functions of BAI as set out in section 25(2) is to 'promote diversity in control of the more influential commercial and community broadcasting services'. The Act also makes reference to the provision of 'open and pluralistic broadcasting services' (section 25(1)(c)). Also, in the case of a proposal to vary or add channels, one of the considerations is 'the contribution of the proposal to media plurality' (section 103(8)(h)).

*523.* The Competition and Consumer Protection Act 2014 (outlined above) updates the process and criteria for determining whether media mergers should be permitted as they arise or whether they pose a threat to pluralism and diversity and should therefore not be permitted in the public interest. In 2016, the Competition and Consumer Commission, established under the Act, approved the acquisition by Liberty Global Plc, through Virgin Media Limited, of sole control of UTV Ireland Limited from UTV Limited (which was an indirect wholly owned subsidiary of ITV Plc).[429] It also more recently approved (10 November 2016) the acquisition by Independent

429. M/16/038 – Liberty Global/UTV Ireland, available at: http://www.ccpc.ie/enforcement/mergers/merger-notices/m16038-liberty-global-utv-ireland.

News and Media (INM), the largest newspaper group in the State, of a number of local newspapers comprising the Celtic Media Group.[430] It decided, despite opposition from the National Union of Journalists, that 'the transaction would not lead to a substantial lessening of competition' in the areas of business concerned. However, the Commission decides purely on competition grounds, so the Minister for Communications had to decide whether the INM deal had implications on the grounds of media plurality. The process and criteria as set out in the Act are considered above at paragraph 126. In the event, the Minister, having received the BAI's report, which had also taken account of the views of an Advisory Panel appointed by the Minister, decided that the acquisition of the local newspapers by INM could go ahead with certain conditions or undertakings attached. However, INM decided, before the Minister had announced his decision, not to proceed with the deal.

## §2. Monomedia Ownership Restrictions

*524.* Monomedia ownership restrictions were understandable pre-1988 when the Irish media consisted only of print media and public service broadcaster, RTÉ. Concentration of ownership, while desirable to some extent in order to achieve economies of scale, particularly in a small media market, had to be monitored so as not to endanger pluralism and diversity of sources and output. The body that dealt with issues of mergers and acquisitions within the print industry was the Competition Authority (now the Competition and Consumer Commission). The Authority decided, for example, in 1995 that regardless of how the market was viewed, Independent Newspapers had a dominant position and was clearly capable of inflicting considerable harm on most of its rivals and could force them out of the market altogether.[431] The acquisition by Independent Newspapers of a stake in the Irish Press national newspaper group prevented competition in the market and therefore amounted to an abuse of a dominant position. Likewise, a proposal by Independent Newspapers to increase their stake in the *Sunday Tribune* newspaper was deemed to be likely to prevent or restrict competition and to be an abuse of a dominant position.[432]

*525.* After the introduction of commercial broadcasting in 1989, the main focus turned from monomedia ownership issues to issues of cross-ownership between print and broadcast media. Successive Broadcasting Acts contained requirements to ensure a pluralism of ownership and diversity of services within broadcasting and between broadcasting and print media. The desire was to ensure the availability of a number of distinct providers of news and current affairs, and a diversity of media offerings at national and regional levels. However, with some of the fledgling radio stations finding it difficult to survive in the early years, consideration had to be given also to trying to

430. M/16/044 – INM/CMNL, available at: http://www.ccpc.ie/enforcement/mergers/merger-notices/m16044-inmcnml.
431. Competition Authority, Interim Report of Study on the Newspaper Industry, Dublin: The Stationary Office, 1995.
432. Competition Authority, Report of the Investigation of the Proposal whereby Independent Newspapers plc would Increase its Shareholding in the Tribune Group from 29.9% to a possible 53.09%, Dublin: the Stationary Office, 1992.

ensure viability and sustainability in the sector. The advent of cable and satellite and newer forms of broadcasting, along with related activities, meant that attention moved also to consideration of vertical, horizontal and diagonal integration and the effects they would have on markets and on media pluralism and diversity. The Competition Authority was the body with responsibility for monitoring media mergers and acquisitions up to 2014.[433]

*526.* The BAI, on the other hand, was and remains responsible for ensuring pluralism and diversity. Its Ownership and Control Policy in 2012, grounded on the Broadcasting Act 2009, sets out a number of factors that are considered by BAI in applying the statutory criteria. For example, as stated above, section 66(2)(g) of the Broadcasting Act requires BAI to have regard to: 'the desirability of allowing any person, or group of persons, to have control of, or substantial interests in, an undue number of sound broadcasting services'. In this regard, BAI operates four thresholds designed to ensure that a reasonable range and number of different voices are available to the public:

(1) A number equivalent to 15% or less of the total number of commercial sound broadcasting services licensed under the Act is considered an acceptable level for any one entity. In applying this threshold, the BAI shall not differentiate between whether an entity has 'control' or 'substantial interests' in a service when making a determination with regard to the number of sound broadcasting services held by that entity.

(2) A number equivalent to between 15% and 20% of the total number of commercial sound broadcasting services licensed under the Act requires additional consideration by the BAI. The BAI shall take such consideration with reference *inter alia* to a Compliance Audit, submitted by the entity, in respect of all of its sound broadcasting services over a two-year period. This period shall commence twelve months in advance of the date on which the application is received. The Compliance Audit shall set out the relevant contractor's compliance with regard to all of the statutory, policy and contractual provisions. Guidelines for the submission of a Compliance Audit are available from the BAI. …

(3) A number equivalent to between 20% and 25% of the total number of commercial sound broadcasting services licensed under the Act requires further additional consideration by the BAI. The BAI shall give such consideration with reference *inter alia* to a Compliance Audit, submitted by the entity, in respect of all of its sound broadcasting services over a two-year period, as set out in 2 above. In addition the BAI shall have regard to the following five factors:

    (1) The number of services where an entity has control rather than a substantial interest.
    (2) The extent to which the relevant services are operating in common or separate franchise areas.

433. For instance, in 2012 the Competition Authority cleared the creation of a joint venture between Raidió Teilifís Éireann (RTÉ) and Teilifís na Gaeilge (TG4) to create Multiplex Broadcasting Services N.I. Limited. Decision reported at: www.bbc.com/news/uk-northern-ireland-17154065 and https://ukfree.tv/article/1107052031/Northern_Ireland_RTE1_RTE2_TG4_special_minimultip.

(3) The relative audience shares of the relevant services when compared with all sound broadcasting services licensed under the 2009 Act.
(4) The extent to which the relevant services have a common target audience focus.
(5) The extent to which the relevant services represent a concentration of the supply of news and information taking into account all communications media.

(4) A number equivalent to over 25% of the total number of commercial sound broadcasting services licensed under the Act would be unacceptable; regardless of whether an entity has control of, or substantial interests in, the relevant services.

## §3. Cross-Media Ownership Restrictions

*527.* Cross-media ownership in the early days of commercial broadcasting has been outlined in the introduction to this section. As the media sector developed, it was inevitable that it would wish to expand and to build further on its experience and expertise. With technology offering the possibility of a range of new services, new players emerged and, as a result, further and more complex forms of cross-ownership presented themselves. Risks and levels of investment were higher. There was pressure on companies to grow, to be able to compete with outside interests and to withstand predators. The local radio industry became part of a much broader industry. Some level of cross-ownership was and is inevitable. There is no doubt that cross-media ownership can provide strategic advantages but it can also subject audiences to the likelihood of receiving similar content in different markets. It is the impact of cross-ownership on the audience that is significant, not necessarily the fact of cross-ownership in itself.[434]

*528.* Sections 66(2)(i) and 137(2)(i) of the Broadcasting Act require the BAI to have regard to: 'the desirability of allowing any person, or group of persons, to have control of, or substantial interests in, an undue amount of the communications media in' a specified area. The term 'communications media' is defined in the Ownership and Control Policy 2012 as encompassing:

(a) the provision of a broadcasting service,
(b) the provision of a broadcasting services platform, or
(c) the publication of newspapers or periodicals consisting substantially of news and comment on current affairs.

*529.* The term 'media business', which is used in the Competition and Consumer Protection Act 2014 in relation to media mergers, is now defined as:

> 'media business' means the business (whether all or part of an undertaking's business) of– (a) the publication of newspapers or periodicals consisting

434. Thomas Gibbons, 'Concentrations of Ownership and Control in a Converging Media Industry', in Chris Marsden & Stefaan Verhulst, *Convergence in European Digital TV Regulation,* Blackstone Press Ltd., London (1999), p. 155.

substantially of news and comment on current affairs, including the publication of such newspapers or periodicals on the internet, (b) transmitting, re-transmitting or relaying a broadcasting service, (c) providing any programme material consisting substantially of news and comment on current affairs to a broadcasting service, or (d) making available on an electronic communications network any written, audio-visual or photographic material, consisting substantially of news and comment on current affairs, that is under the editorial control of the undertaking making available such material;

*530.* The Competition and Consumer Protection Act (section 74) further defines 'plurality of the media' as including 'both diversity of ownership and diversity of content'. Diversity of ownership in turn is defined as meaning 'the spread of ownership and control of media businesses in the State linked to the market share of those media businesses as measured by listenership, readership, reach or other appropriate measures'; and diversity of content is defined as meaning 'the extent to which the broad diversity of views (including diversity of views on news and current affairs) and diversity of cultural interests prevalent in Irish society is reflected through the activities of media businesses in the State including their editorial ethos, content and sources'. Under the Act, the Competition and Consumer Protection Commission has a role in relation to notifications and certain determinations of proposed media mergers, although it is the Minister for Communications who, on the basis of specified criteria, ultimately makes a determination as to whether the result of the media merger is likely to be contrary to the public interest in protecting plurality of the media in the State. The whole process is set out in detail in the Act at section 74.

*531.* The BAI has a role in respect of cases in which a full media merger examination is deemed necessary. In cases which require a full media merger examination, that is, where the Minister, having applied the criteria, is 'concerned that the media merger may be contrary to the public interest in protecting plurality of the media in the State', he or she shall request the BAI to carry out an examination of the proposed merger. BAI must then publish the request on its website, invite submissions to be made not later than twenty working days from the date of publication of the request, send a copy of the request to the Joint Oireachtas Committee and invite a submission from that Joint Oireachtas Committee within twenty working days. It must then report in writing to the Minister within eighty days and then to the undertakings involved. The report must contain a recommendation, based on specified criteria, as to whether the media merger should be put into effect with or without conditions or should not be put into effect. Further provision is made for BAI *inter alia* to enter into discussions with the undertakings involved. Also, where the Minister deemed it necessary in specific cases, he or she may appoint an advisory panel to provide a reasoned opinion to BAI.

## §4. Restrictions of Board Member Positions

*532.* The relevant statutory criteria relating to ownership are 'control of' and 'substantial interests in'. Both of these and other relevant terms are examined and explained in the preceding paragraphs. The terms 'control' and 'substantial interests' are defined in the BAI Ownership and Control Policy 2012 as:

> 'Control' – is in a position proprietarily, financially or in terms of voting rights to determine or direct the policy of the company, with regard in particular to programme output, that is, sourcing, production, supply or delivery to the audience.

> 'Substantial interests' – has sufficient proprietary, financial or voting strength within a relevant company or companies to be able to influence directly or indirectly to an appreciable extent the strategic direction or policy (which shall include editorial policy) of the company (companies), with regard in particular to programme output, that is, sourcing, production, supply or delivery to the audience.

*533.* The 2009 Act (section 66(2)(a) and section 137(2)(a)) also requires the BAI, when awarding certain broadcasting contracts or multiplex contracts, to have regard to: 'the character, expertise and experience of an applicant or, if the applicant is a body corporate, the character, expertise and experience of the body and its directors, manager, secretary or other similar officer and its members and the persons entitled to the beneficial ownership of its shares'.

*534.* In this regard, the BAI applies a number of tests relating to character at the application stage for a licence, during compliance reviews and when considering proposals for changes to the ownership and control of contractors. The tests apply *inter alia* to Directors, management positions approved by the Authority and shareholders whose shareholding constitutes a substantial interest, or control, as defined in the Policy. The tests include whether the applicant has ever been convicted of a range of offences; whether the applicant has ever been restricted or disqualified as a Company Director, or convicted of any offence under the Companies Acts in Ireland or under equivalent legislation in any other jurisdiction; ever been adjudicated a bankrupt, become insolvent or entered into a voluntary arrangement with creditors, or had a receiver appointed to any of its assets, in Ireland or any other jurisdiction; ever had a licence or contract issued by a broadcasting licensing body or any other statutory body suspended or revoked in this or any other jurisdiction.

*535.* In relation to experience and expertise, the BAI applies tests relating to the Board of Directors and the management structure. In applying the tests, BAI examines *inter alia* the proposed arrangement in terms of the relevant individuals within the structure, (e.g., is there an over-reliance on one individual in the corporate and/or management structure) and the overall membership and structure of the Board and management team (e.g., are there any independent directors).

*536.* With regard to financial resources, BAI examines whether the applicant has available to it adequate financial resources and does its approach accord with good business and economic principles, having regard to the nature of the service proposed.

*537.* Overall, therefore, in assessing applications for changes in the ownership and control of an entity, and in making its determination in this regard, BAI has regard to the statutory, contractual and policy framework set out in section 1 of its Ownership and Control Policy 2012 and the role and powers of the Competition and Consumer Protection Commission (formerly the Competition Authority) and of the Minister pursuant to the provisions of the 2014 Act.

## §5. Restrictions of Co-operation Agreements

*538.* Sections 69 (regarding broadcasting) and 138 (regarding multiplexes) of the Broadcasting Act 2009 provide that the BAI may prohibit the assignment of, or any material change in, the ownership of an applicant, either by specifying a condition in the contract itself or by making the assignment subject to the previous consent in writing of the BAI, in which case the BAI shall have regard to the ownership and control provisions set out in sections 66(2) and 66(4) or 137(2) of the Act as appropriate. When changes in ownership are contemplated, the tests set out in the Ownership and Control Policy 2012, as outlined in the preceding paragraph, are applied by BAI.

*539.* In the case of broadcasting contracts entered into under sections 63 (sound broadcasting) and 70 (television broadcasting) of the Act, the BAI generally looks unfavourably upon proposed changes in ownership structures within a two-year period after the award of a contract. It does so on the basis that a change in ownership within a two-year period would be likely to undermine the integrity of the licensing process itself and be unfair to unsuccessful applicants. BAI operates a level of flexibility, however, where an application for such change is from an applicant whose contract has been renewed. An application in such case should satisfy the following criteria:

- There were no other applicants for the contract;
- The shareholders who are disposing of their interest were also shareholders of the applicant over the period of the first contract; and
- The proposed new shareholders have undertaken to comply with all of the contractual obligations arising from the contract concluded between the BAI and the original applicant.

*540.* The BAI does not apply any specific moratorium on changes in the ownership and/or control of multiplex contractors appointed under section 137 of the Act. Contractors are, however, subject to statutory and contractual provisions in relation to any changes proposed.

*541.* RTÉ and TG4, the public service broadcasters, have certain powers that they can exercise with the consent of the Minister for Communications and the Minister for Finance. Under the Broadcasting Act 2009 (section 104(2)–(5)), they may, with the necessary consents, the Minister for Communications having also consulted with BAI, 'promote or take part in the formation or establishment of a company, and enter into joint ventures or partnerships in pursuance of its objects'. Similarly, they may 'acquire, hold and dispose of shares or other interests in a company and become a member of a company'. They may also determine the form of the memorandum and articles of association of a subsidiary with the consent of the two Ministers. In granting consent to any of these actions by RTÉ and TG4, the Minister may attach 'particular terms or conditions as he or she considers appropriate in the circumstances'.

*542.* In relation to mergers, the Competition and Consumer Protection Act 2014 makes provision in certain instances for the Minister for Communications to consult with BAI. One such instance is with regard to levels of media ownership, including across different sectors of the media that would, subject to the particular circumstances of each media merger, be regarded as contrary to the public interest. Another such instance is with regard to indicators of diversity of content and diversity of ownership and control of media businesses that would be used in determining whether a media merger would be regarded as contrary to the public interest (section 28L(a) and (b)). The Act (section 28M (1)) also requires BAI to prepare for the Minister 'a report which shall describe the ownership and control arrangements for undertakings carrying on a media business in the State; describe the changes to ownership and control arrangements of such undertakings over the past three years; and analyse the effects of such changes on plurality of the media in the State'.

## §6. Transparency Obligations

*543.* Transparency requirements of various types and at various levels permeate broadcasting legislation. They range from requirements on BAI under the Broadcasting Act 2009 to collect and disseminate information to the public on broadcasting generally and on specific aspects of it, to requirements on broadcasters to keep records and accounts and to supply relevant documentation in response to complaints or investigations. Provision of false or misleading information of a material nature by a broadcaster can lead to a contract being suspended or terminated (section 51). The allocation of public funding to RTÉ and TG4, the public service broadcasters, carries with it a number of accountability and transparency duties detailed in the Broadcasting Act. Also, as noted in the previous paragraph, the Competition and Consumer Protection Act (section 28M (1)) requires BAI to prepare for the Minister every three years 'a report which shall describe the ownership and control arrangements for undertakings carrying on a media business in the State; describe the changes to ownership and control arrangements of such undertakings over the past three years; and analyse the effects of such changes on plurality of the media in the State'. This report serves the goals of both transparency and monitoring of media pluralism and diversity.

*544.* In the specific case of media mergers or acquisitions, the Competition and Consumer Protection Act 2014 provides a detailed system for notification and examination. In the case of a merger or acquisition that is a media merger, the undertakings involved that notified the Commission under section 18(1), or that notified the European Commission, as the case may be, shall notify the Minister for Communications, Energy and Natural Resources in writing, and shall provide him or her with full details, of the proposal to put the merger or acquisition into effect (section 28B(1)). When making a notification under subsection (1), each of the undertakings involved in the media merger must provide full information to the Minister on all circumstances in relation to the media merger concerned that may impair plurality of the media in the State and shall notify the Minister of any changes in the information (section 28B(3)). If any of the information supplied is false or misleading or full details have not been provided the application will be void (section 29(7)). Failure to supply the information is an offence and may be subject to a fine not exceeding EUR 250,000 (section 29(8)). For the purposes of section 29(8) the person in control of an undertaking is: (a) in the case of a body corporate, any officer of the body corporate who knowingly and wilfully authorizes or permits the contravention, (b) in the case of a partnership, each partner who knowingly and wilfully authorizes or permits the contravention, (c) in the case of any other form of undertaking, any individual in control of that undertaking who knowingly and wilfully authorizes or permits the contravention.

## §7. Monitoring of Ownership and Pluralism

*545.* The obligations of BAI in relation to ownership and control are explained in the preceding paragraphs. It may be recalled that section 69 of the Broadcasting Act 2009 states that: 'Every broadcasting contract may contain such terms and conditions as the Authority thinks appropriate and specifies in the contract.' Among the conditions that BAI may specify is a condition 'prohibiting any alteration in the Memorandum or Articles of Association of the company … or prohibiting any material change in the ownership of the company'. If no such condition is specified in the contract, the position is that any such alteration can only be made with the previous consent in writing of BAI. The statutory criteria and the BAI rules on changes of ownership, therefore, ensure ongoing monitoring of ownership and pluralism by BAI. The process now embodied in the Competition and Consumer Protection Act 2014, as outlined above, gives the Competition and Consumer Protection Commission a role in assessing media mergers and acquisitions in terms of Competition law and gives BAI a distinct and expanded role in relation to ensuring pluralism and diversity in proposed merger and acquisition situations. All such changes in ownership are monitored in the context of proposed mergers and acquisitions.

*546.* An example of an inquiry by BAI in a non-merger situation occurred in 2012. Following the restructuring of Independent News and Media (INM), the largest newspaper group in the State, Denis O'Brien emerged as the major shareholder. As Denis O'Brien's company, Communicorp, controls, and/or has substantial interests in, six independent radio services in Ireland, the Broadcasting regulator, BAI, examined his position in INM under its Ownership and Control Policy (2012), pursuant to its statutory obligations, in particular its obligation to consider 'the desirability of allowing any person, or group of persons, to have control of, or substantial interests in, an undue amount of communications media' in an area. However, it determined that Mr O'Brien did not control INM but rather that he had 'a substantial interest in the Company (INM)'. As he owned 29.9% of INM, BAI said, he had not reached the 30% threshold at which he would be obliged to make a bid for the remaining shares of the Company. Among the other factors taken into account by BAI was the fact that he did not own shares which would give him more than 50% of the voting rights exercisable at meetings of INM's shareholders. However, as further appointments were due to be made to the Board of INM, Communicorp was requested to ensure that it kept the Authority fully informed of all developments in this regard.[435]

435. *See* http://www.bai.ie/en/bai-statement-on-the-media-interests-of-mr-denis-obrien/.

*547.* As outlined above (paragraph 523), a further issue arose in 2016 in relation to the extent of Denis O'Brien's media interests. INM, in which he has a 'substantial interest', reached a deal to buy seven regional newspapers, owned by the Celtic Media Group. The matter was examined by the Competition and Consumer Protection Commission under the Competition and Consumer Protection Act 2014.[436] The proposed buy-out was approved by the Commission on competition grounds, and then came before BAI for examination on pluralism grounds.[437] The Minister established an Advisory Panel in accordance with the Act to advise BAI, which then reported to the Minister, as provided for in the Act. However, the outcome was that just before the Minister announced his decision, INM decided not to proceed but did not give reasons. The new process for approaching and public interest proofing proposed mergers and acquisitions has therefore been put into operation and the criteria set out in the Act applied, although the final decision in this instance was rendered unnecessary.

*548.* In addition to the domestic monitoring processes, the EUI media monitoring project has also reported on media pluralism in Ireland. In 2015, Ireland was included in the second pilot project as one of the nineteen countries not examined in the first pilot.[438] The report on Ireland identified concentration of ownership as a high risk, although there appeared to be some confusion as to the statutory basis and the thresholds applied. In reference to one of the 'relevant criteria' that the Minister is to have regard to in assessing proposed media mergers or acquisitions, namely 'the undesirability of allowing any one undertaking to hold significant interests within a sector or across different sectors of media business in the State', the suggestion is that the Competition and Consumer Protection Act 2014 specifies that the threshold for this should be 20%. The Act does not specify any such figure and the only reference to such a figure is in the Ministerial Guidelines, which were issued in conjunction with the Act:

> 'significant interest' means
>
> Has sufficient voting, financial or ownership strength within the relevant media business or media businesses to influence directly or indirectly, to an appreciable extent, the direction or policy of the media business or media businesses with regard in particular to news, current affairs or cultural content. This includes sourcing, production, supply or delivery of such content.
>
> The following thresholds in relation to voting power at a general meeting of the media business, or the nominal value of the shareholding, are provided by way of guidance in terms of what constitutes a significant interest:

---

436. *See* http://www.ccpc.ie/enforcement/mergers/merger-notices/m16044-inmcnml.

437. At the same time, an attempt was being made to sell the radio station, Newstalk, owned by Mr O'Brien, to INM in which he is the main shareholder. (Reported in *The Irish Times* 5 Nov. 2016). However, the sale did not proceed.

438. http://monitor.cmpf.eui.eu/mpm2015/results/ireland/.

- A holding or voting strength of between 10% and 19% (directly or indirectly) may constitute a significant interest.
- A holding or voting strength of more than 20% or more of the voting power (directly or indirectly) will generally constitute a significant interest.

Thus, according to the Ministerial Guidelines, all holdings or voting strengths of less than 10% and above will not constitute a significant interest and therefore will not be scrutinized, while those above 20% will 'generally' constitute a significant interest.

# Part V. Supervision: Media Regulator

## Chapter 1. Organization

*549.* There is no single over-arching regulator for the whole media and communications sector in Ireland, although the BAI is arguably the primary one. The Government Minister and Department of Communications, Climate Action and the Environment have overall responsibility for the Telecommunications and Broadcasting sectors. The regulator for the broadcasting sector is the BAI, while the regulator for the communications sector is the ComReg. Other bodies, such as the Competition and Consumer Protection Commission, also have regulatory roles in relation to specific areas of media activity. There is no regulator for the print sector, although the independent Press Council has a quasi- or co-regulatory role (*see* discussion of the Press Council (paragraphs 299–309, and paragraph 274 above).

### §1. Department of Communications, Climate Action and Environment

*550.* The DCCAE, formerly the DCENR, has a Communications Division, which deals with: Broadcasting and Media; Broadband; Digital Strategy; Postal Matters; Internet Policy; Spectrum and Digital Agenda for Europe.[439] The Department oversees the work of a number of State agencies, which include ComReg, RTÉ, TG4, BAI.

### §2. Broadcasting and Media Division

*551.* The Department is responsible for the development of the legislative and regulatory framework for broadcasting and for certain other media in Ireland. That includes both domestic legislation, primary and secondary, and the overseeing of the transposition of relevant EU Directives. The Department is responsible also for developing policy in relation to the funding of the public service broadcasters, RTÉ and TG4, and the development of the broadcasting sector in general. It forms policy on new media, oversees the media mergers process and interacts with the EU and Council of Europe on broadcasting and media matters. It also handles issues such as the setting of the television licence fee for PSB and arranges for the collection of the

439. For further information on the organisation of the Department as a whole, *see* the Freedom of Information 'Section 15 and 16 Guide' available at: http://www.dccae.gov.ie/.

fee by An Post (the postal service) and the making of payments to RTÉ. It manages Exchequer and TV Licence payments to TG4 and payments of 7% of the TV Licence Fee to the BAI-operated Broadcasting Fund. The Department also has corporate governance responsibilities in relation to RTÉ, TG4 and the BAI. It is the Department also that handles the list of designated events.[440] It has commissioned a number of reviews of the designated events since 2009, in accordance with section 173 of the Broadcasting Act 2009 (*see* above paragraph 491).

## §3. Broadcasting Authority of Ireland

*552.* The Broadcasting Authority of Ireland (BAI), was established in October 2009 under the Broadcasting Act 2009, and replaced the BCI and the Broadcasting Complaints Commission. The BAI consists of the Authority itself (the Board) and two Committees, the Contract Awards Committee and the Compliance Committee, the latter replacing the former Broadcasting Complaints Commission but with a wider remit. The Authority is a body corporate, with perpetual succession and the power to sue and be sued and to acquire, hold and dispose of land and other property (section 7, 2009 Act).

*553.* The Authority has nine members, one of whom is the Chairperson. Five of the members are appointed by the Government on the nomination of the Minister (section 8(1) of the 2009 Act), as are the other four but, in the case of the four, the Minister must first inform the Joint Oireachtas Committee that has responsibility for broadcasting matters of the proposed appointment and the Minister 'shall have regard' to the Committee's reasoned advice (section 8(2), 2009 Act). Not less than four of the members of the Authority shall be men and not less than four of them shall be women (section 8(3), 2009 Act).

*554.* The Contracts Awards Committee comprises eight members, four of whom are appointed by the Government, with the remaining four being appointed by the Authority, two of whom are Authority members, and two of whom are members of staff of the BAI. The Compliance Committee likewise comprises eight members, four of whom are appointed by the Government, with the remaining four being appointed by the Authority, two of whom are Authority members, and two of whom are members of staff of the BAI. In the case of each Committee the Government and the Authority are required, insofar as is practicable, to endeavour to ensure that there is an equal balance between men and women. A person may be appointed to either the Contracts Awards Committee or the Compliance Committee, but not both.

*555.* The criteria for membership of the Authority or either committee relate to experience of or shown capacity in one or more of a list of areas set out in section 9 of the Act, which comprises a wide range of media, legal, regulatory, cultural and social affairs. Section 9 states:

440. Broadcasting Act 2009, s. 162. The Irish list was adopted in 2003 following approval from the European Commission in accordance with the then Television without Frontiers Directive (97/36/EC).

> 9.–(1) A person shall not be appointed by the Government to be a member of the Authority or a statutory committee unless he or she has had experience of or shown capacity in one or more of the following areas–

(a) media affairs,
(b) public service broadcasting, commercial broadcasting or community broadcasting,
(c) broadcast content production,
(d) digital media technologies,
(e) trade union affairs,
(f) business or commercial affairs,
(g) matters pertaining to the development of the Irish language,
(h) matters pertaining to disability,
(i) arts, music, sport or culture,
(j) science, technology or environmental matters,
(k) legal or regulatory affairs, and
(l) social, educational or community affairs or Gaeltacht affairs.

*556.* The term of office is five years (with the possibility of one further term) and the role of members is to represent the public interest in respect of broadcasting matters. It is for the Minister to determine any remuneration and expenses payable to members. A member may be removed from office by the Government if, in the Government's opinion, the member has become incapable through ill-health of performing his or her functions, or has committed stated misbehaviour, or his or her removal appears to the Government to be necessary for the effective performance by the Authority or committee of its functions. However, this can only be done if resolutions are passed by each House of the Oireachtas calling for his or her removal. This condition operates as a safeguard for the independence of the Authority. Section 10(6) provides that:

> (6) A member of the Authority or a statutory committee shall cease to be and shall be disqualified from being a member of the Authority, or the statutory committee where such member–

(a) is adjudicated a bankrupt,
(b) makes a composition or arrangement with creditors,
(c) on conviction on indictment by a court of competent jurisdiction is sentenced to a term of imprisonment,
(d) is convicted of an offence involving fraud or dishonesty, or
(e) is disqualified or restricted from being a director of any company.

*557.* Failure to attend meetings may result in removal from office in accordance with section 10(8):

> (8) Where a member of the Authority or a statutory committee fails–

(a) for a consecutive period of 6 months, to attend a meeting of the Authority or the statutory committee, as the case may be, unless the member demonstrates to the Minister's satisfaction that the failure to attend was due to illness,
(b) to comply with the requirements of section 21,[441] or
(c) to make a declaration in accordance with the requirements of section 17 of the Ethics in Public Office Act 1995,

the Minister may, with the consent of the Government, by order remove the member from membership of the Authority or the statutory committee, as the case may be.

*558.* Sitting politicians may not hold office as a member of the Authority:

12.–(1) Where a member of the Authority or a statutory committee is nominated as a candidate for election to the European Parliament, or to either House of the Oireachtas, he or she shall thereupon stand suspended from membership of the Authority or the statutory committee, as the case may be, and shall not be entitled to participate in meetings of the Authority or the statutory committee or receive from the Authority any remuneration or allowances in respect of the period commencing on such nomination and ending when such person is so regarded as not having been elected as the case may be.

(2) Where a member of the Authority or a statutory committee is–

(a) nominated as a member of Seanad Éireann,
(b) elected as a member of either House of the Oireachtas or the European Parliament, or
(c) regarded pursuant to Part XIII of the Second Schedule to the European Parliament Elections Act 1997 as having been elected to that Parliament to fill a vacancy, he or she shall thereupon cease to be a member of the Authority or the statutory committee, as the case may be.

*559.* A person who holds employment or an interest in a broadcasting undertaking, including but not limited to a public service broadcaster, or an undertaking holding a contract under the Act, shall be disqualified from becoming or cease to be a member of the Authority or a statutory committee (section 12(6)). Similarly, a person who holds an interest in an undertaking which publishes a newspaper in the State shall be disqualified from becoming or cease to be a member of the Authority or a statutory committee (section 12(7)). A member of the Contracts Committee may not also be a member of the Compliance Committee and vice versa (section 12(8) and (9)).

*560.* The Broadcasting Act 2009 (section 21(1)) also requires a member of BAI or of either of its statutory committees to make a declaration of interests. A member must disclose any interest s/he has in any body or concern with which BAI has made a contract or proposes to make a contract; or any interests s/he has in any contract

441. Section 21 deals with disclosure of certain interests. *See* para. 560.

which BAI has made or proposes to make. Section 21 also provides for disclosure of conflicts of interest that may arise during meetings. Section 23 requires the Authority to draw up and adopt a code of conduct in respect of controls on interests and ethical behaviour to apply to each member of the Authority and its committees. The term 'interests' is defined in the Act (section 2) to include:

(a) employment by or on behalf of–

  (1) any business related to the functions of the public body concerned,
  (2) any organization representative of any business related to the functions of the public body concerned,

(b) ownership of any business related to the functions of the public body concerned,
(c) shares in, bonds or debentures of, or other like investments in any business related to the functions of the public body concerned, where the aggregate of such holdings exceeds EUR 13,000,
(d) a directorship or shadow directorship (within the meaning of the Companies Acts) in any business related to the functions of the public body concerned, held currently or during the previous two years, or
(e) gifts of travel, holidays, transport or other benefits (more than EUR 650), including benefits from any beneficial interest in or connected with any business related to the functions of the public body concerned, during the previous two years which were received by the person concerned or by his or her spouse.

## §4. The Commission for Communications Regulation

*561.* ComReg is the statutory body responsible for the regulation of the electronic communications sector (telecommunications, radio-communications and broadcasting transmission) and the postal sector. It is responsible for facilitating competition, for protecting consumers and for encouraging innovation.

# Chapter 2. Tasks

*562.* The tasks assigned to the BAI and its two Committees are set out in the Broadcasting Act 2009, sections 25–29 under the headings of 'Objectives' and 'Functions'. Their 'Powers' are set out in section 31 and 'Duties' in section 32.

## §1. Objectives

*563.* The 'Objectives' set out in section 25 are very wide-ranging. They have been discussed elsewhere in this text and therefore will just be summarized here. The objectives are concerned with providing a pluralistic and diverse broadcasting sector that will deliver high-quality programming that will cater to the needs of all the people of the island of Ireland, adults and children, whatever their religions, languages, cultures, or disabilities. The guarantee of freedom of expression in the Constitution must be upheld, PSB must be facilitated and the regulatory environment must sustain independent and impartial journalism. Measures taken by BAI must be proportionate to its objectives, must produce regulatory arrangements that are stable and predictable and must accommodate and encourage technological development.

## §2. Functions

*564.* The 'Functions' of the BAI, as stated in section 26 of the Act, include the preparation of a strategy for broadcasting services additional to the PSB channels, and to issue a strategy statement (under section 29(1) of the Act); to liaise and consult with the Communications Regulator (ComReg) in the preparation of the allocation plan for the frequency range to be dedicated to sound and television broadcasting; to make a levy order under (section 33(1) of the Act), imposing a levy on public service broadcasters and broadcasting contractors, for the purpose of meeting expenses properly incurred by BAI and its committees in the performance of their functions; and to prepare broadcasting codes and rules and a right of reply scheme. Other functions relate to rules and contracts for electronic programme guides; the provision of new broadcasting channels (the Houses of the Oireachtas Channel and the Irish Film Channel); and the provision of multiplexes other than the RTÉ multiplex services. The remaining functions relate mainly to reports, reviews, consultations, advice and guidance and other such matters referred to in various sections of the Act.

*565.* The principal functions of the Contract Awards Committee, as set out in section 27 relate to broadcasting and content provision contracts, digital broadcasting and multiplex services, and to make recommendations on these matters to the Authority. The functions of the other Committee of BAI, namely the Compliance Committee, are set out in section 28. They concern primarily monitoring and enforcement issues but also include investigating and deciding on complaints; and reporting on compliance, including by public service broadcasters. Interestingly, the Compliance Committee 'shall review on an ongoing basis the extent to which the television broadcasts of broadcasters under the jurisdiction of another Member State which are wholly or mainly directed towards audiences in the State comply with broadcasting codes, in particular the codes referred to in section 42(2)(g) and (h)'.[442] The Compliance Committee may delegate some of its functions to a member of staff of the Authority, who is not a member of the Compliance Committee, or to a sub-committee of the Compliance Committee, subject to such conditions as the Compliance Committee considers appropriate.

## §3. Powers

*566.* The 'Powers' accorded to the BAI and its Committees under section 31 of the Act are 'all the powers necessary, incidental or conducive to their functions'. In other words, they extend to the making of contracts, agreements and arrangements; requiring contractors to enter into financial bonds with the Authority; acquiring and making use of copyrights, patents, licences, privileges and concessions; compiling, preparing, publishing and distributing, with or without charge, printed, audio and audiovisual material; subject to the consent of the Minister, arranging for the provision of broadcasting and related services for and on behalf of any Minister of the Government; and undertaking, sponsoring or commissioning research. The Authority may also invest any of its funds in any manner in which a trustee is empowered by law to invest trust funds.

## §4. Duties

*567.* As regards the 'Duties' of the BAI and its committees, section 32, having first defined the term 'commercially sensitive information' in subsection (1), elaborates as follows:

> (2) It is the duty of the Authority to so conduct its affairs as to secure that its revenue becomes as soon as possible, and thereafter continues to be, at least sufficient to meet its expenses.
>
> (3) The Authority and its statutory committees shall have a duty to keep the performance of their functions under review with a view to securing that regulation by the Authority and its statutory committees does not involve–

(a) the imposition of administrative burdens which are unnecessary, or
(b) the maintenance of administrative burdens which have become unnecessary.

> (4) In reviewing its duty under subsection (3) the Authority and its statutory committees shall, from time to time, publish a statement setting out how they propose, during the period for which the statement is made, to ensure that

442. The codes referred to are the commercial communications codes.

regulation by the Authority and the statutory committees does not involve the imposition or maintenance of unnecessary administrative burdens.

[(5)-(9) concern such 'statements', when they are due, revision, etc.]

(10) The Authority shall not disclose commercially sensitive information obtained from a corporation or the holder of a contract under Part 6 or 8 [regarding contracts] in pursuance of the Authority's functions under this Act.

(11) The Authority is not contravening subsection (10) if the disclosure–

(a) is made with the consent of the corporation or the holder of a contract under Part 6 or 8 to which it relates, or
(b) is required by law.

# Chapter 3. Sanctioning Powers

## §1. Financial Sanctions

*568.* The sanctioning powers of the BAI are set out in the Broadcasting Act 2009. Chapter 2, sections 52–56, deal with 'financial sanctions'. They include monetary fines up to EUR 250,000, withdrawal or suspension of licences. The term 'financial sanction' is defined as 'a specified amount to be paid by a broadcaster for a breach by the broadcaster as directed by the Court under section 55(1) or the Authority (i.e., BAI) under section 55(3)'. The potential for financial sanctions to be imposed arises when the Compliance Committee is of the opinion that there are circumstances suggesting that it is appropriate to investigate and report on any apparent breach by a broadcaster of a requirement laid down by the Act or of a broadcasting code or rule drawn up in accordance with the Act. The Compliance Committee may appoint an investigating officer to investigate and report on the apparent breach following the procedure set out in section 53 (3)–(7) and section 54.

*569.* Where it emerges that (a) there has been a breach by the broadcaster concerned, or (b) the broadcaster concerned has failed to co-operate in an investigation, the Committee may recommend to the Authority that the Authority notifies the broadcaster concerned in accordance with the procedure set out in section 54(4). In the notification, it must be stated *inter alia* that the Authority intends to apply to the Court for a determination that there has been a breach or a failure to co-operate with an investigation, unless the broadcaster concerned requests, in writing within fourteen days of the date of the notification or such further period as the Authority allows, that the Authority deal with the matter itself under section 55(2). The notification must also indicate the amount of the financial sanction (not exceeding EUR 250,000) that is proposed, if the matter is dealt with by the Authority itself under section 55(2). The Authority may indicate in the notification the amount of the financial sanction (not exceeding EUR 250,000) that it intends to recommend to the Court if the matter is dealt with by the Court under section 55(1).

*570.* The Authority must, however, ensure that any financial sanction imposed is appropriate and proportionate to the breach or the failure to co-operate with the investigation, and will act as a sufficient incentive to ensure future compliance in respect of the requirement breached. It must also take into account the seriousness of the breach; the turnover of the broadcaster in the financial year ending in the year previous to the breach and the ability of the broadcaster to pay the amount; the extent of any failure to co-operate with the investigation; any excuse or explanation by the broadcaster for the breach or failure to co-operate with the investigation; any gain (financial or otherwise) made by the broadcaster or by any person in which the broadcaster has a financial interest as a consequence of the breach; and a number of other considerations relating to the nature of the breach, its duration, etc. (section 56). The broadcaster concerned has a right to be heard at various stages of the process and a right of appeal to the court. All payments made to the Authority under this section shall be paid into or disposed of for the benefit of the Exchequer in such manner as the Minister for Finance may direct (section 55(7)).

## §2. Suspension or Termination of Contract

*571.* Section 51 of the Broadcasting Act 2009 makes provision for the suspension or termination of a licence contract in certain circumstances, subject to a number of considerations and caveats. The Compliance Committee may recommend to the Authority that the Authority terminate or suspend a contract entered into by the Authority: (a) if any false or misleading information of a material nature was given to the Contract Awards Committee by or on behalf of the holder of the contract before it was entered into; or (b) if the holder of the contract has, upon a finding by the Compliance Committee following an investigation (under section 50(7)), 'failed on one or more occasions to comply with a term or condition of the contract and the nature of that failure is of such seriousness as, in the opinion of the Compliance Committee, warrants the termination or suspension of the contract'. In such circumstances, the Committee must notify the holder of the contract of an opportunity to make submissions at a hearing before the Committee. A decision to suspend or terminate a contract may be appealed by the holder of the contract to the High Court.

*572.* Under the Broadcasting Act 2009, certain powers are reserved to the Minister for Communications. For example, during the continuance of any national emergency, the Minister may suspend any broadcasting licence or multiplex licence as defined in section 129 and, while any such suspension continues, the Minister may operate any service which was provided under the suspended licence or requires such service to be operated as he or she directs (section 61(2)). The Minister may also suspend any PSB licence and any licence under section 132(1) or (2) or section 133(1) or (2), (i.e., licences issued by the Communications Regulator, ComReg) during the continuance of any national emergency (section 122(1)).

# Selected Bibliography

Books


Adams, Michael, *Censorship: The Irish Experience* (The University of Alabama Press, Alabama, 1968).

Carolan, Eoin and Ailbhe O'Neill, *Media Law in Ireland.* (Dublin: Bloomsbury Professional, 2008).

Cassidy, Eoin, and McGrady, Andrew G., *Media and the Marketplace: Ethical Perspectives* (Institute of Public Administration, Dublin, 2001).

Cox, Neville, and McCullough, Eoin, *Defamation Law and Practice* (Clarus Press, Dublin, 2014).

Delany, Hilary and Carolan, Eoin, *The Right to Privacy* (Thomson Round Hall, 2008).

Hazelcorn, Ellen and Smyth, Patrick (eds), *Let in the Light: Censorship, Secrecy and Democracy* (Brandon Books, Dingle, 1993).

Horgan, John, *Irish Media: A Critical History Since 1922* (Routledge, London and New York, 2001). (new edition in preparation)

Horgan, John, *Broadcasting and Public Life: RTÉ News and Current Affairs 1926–1997* (Dublin: Four Courts Press, 2004).

Inglis, Brian, *Freedom of the Press in Ireland 1784–1841* (Faber and Faber, London, 1954).

Jones, Derek (ed.), *Censorship: A World Encyclopedia* (Fitzroy Dearborn, London and Chicago, 2001), 4 volumes.

Keogh, Dermot (ed.), *Irish Democracy and the Right to Freedom of Information (Ireland: A Journal of History and Society)* (Dept of History, UCC, Cork, 1995).

Kiberd, Damien (ed.), *Media in Ireland: The Search for Diversity* (Open Air, an imprint of Four Courts Press, Dublin, 1997).

Kiberd, Damien (ed.), *Media in Ireland: The Search for Ethical Journalism* (Open Air, an imprint of Four Courts Press, Dublin, 1999).

Kiberd, Damien (ed.), *Media in Ireland: Issues in Broadcasting* (Open Air, an imprint of Four Courts Press, Dublin, 2002).

McDonagh, Maeve, *Freedom of Information Law in Ireland,* 2nd ed.(Round Hall Sweet & Maxwell, Dublin, 2006).

McDonald, Marc, *Irish Law of Defamation,* 2nd ed. (The Round Hall Press, Dublin, 1989).

McGonagle, Marie (ed.), *Law and the Media: The Views of Journalists and Lawyers* (Round Hall Sweet & Maxwell, Dublin, 1997).

McGonagle, Marie, *Media Law,* 2nd ed.(Thomson Round Hall, Dublin 2003) (new edition in preparation)

Morash, Christopher *A History of the Media in Ireland*(CambridgeUniversity Press, 2010).

Murphy, Yvonne, *Journalists and the Law,* 3rd ed. (Dublin: Round Hall, 2011).

Pine, Richard, *2RN and the Origins of Irish Radio* (Four Courts Press, Dublin, 2002).

Savage, Robert J., *Irish Television: The Political and Social Origins* (Cork University Press, Cork, 1996).

Woodman, Kieran, *Media Control in Ireland*(Galway University Press, Galway, 1985).

Articles

Brennan, Gerard 'The Third Branch and the Fourth Estate' (1997) xxxii *Irish Jurist* 62.

Carolan, Eoin 'The Implications of Media Fragmentation and Contemporary Democratic Discourse for 'Journalistic Privilege' and the Protection of Sources' (2013) *Irish Jurist*, 49: 182–192.

Carolan, Eoin 'Stars of Citizen TV: Video Surveillance and the Right to Privacy in Public Places', (2006) 28 DULJ 326

Cox, Neville 'Sacrilege and Sensibility: The Value of Irish Blasphemy Law' (1997) 19 *Dublin University Law Journal*, 87.

Cox, Neville 'Public Figures and Defamation Actions Following the Reynolds Case', *DublinUniversity Law Journal*, 21, 1999, 206–219

Delany, Hilary 'Prior Restraint Orders and Freedom of Expression', (2005) 40 *Irish Jurist* 138

Hogan, Gerard 'Free Speech, Privacy and the Press in Ireland' (1987) *Public Law* 509.

Kelleher, Denis 'Social Networking, Privacy and the Future of News', (2011) *Irish Jurist* 46 (1) 191

Kennedy, Rónán 'Was it Author's Rights All the Time? Copyright as a Constitutional Right in Ireland' (2011) 18(1) *DublinUniversity Law Journal*, 253

**Selected Bibliography**

Komorek, Ewa, 'Legal Protection of Media Pluralism at National Level. An Examination of the United Kingdom and Ireland' *Hibernian Law Journal* 9, no. 1 (2010): 92.

McCormack, Gerard 'Corrupting the Criminal Process' (1985) 1 *Irish Law Times* 6. 'The Right to Jury Trial in Cases of Contempt' (1983) *Gazette of the Incorporated Law Society of Ireland* 177 and 209.

McDonagh, Maeve 'Freedom of Information in Ireland and Europe: Progress and Regression' (2001) 29(2) *International Journal of Legal Information* 256.

McDonagh, Maeve 'The Interaction of European Community Law and National Access to Information Laws: An Irish Perspective' (2000) 9(2) *Irish Journal of European Law* 216.

McDowell, R. B. 'Irish Newspapers in the Eighteenth Century' (1984) 8(2) *Media and Popular Culture, The Crane Bag* 40.

McGonagle, Tarlach, 'Wresting (Racial) Equality from Tolerance of Hate Speech' (2001) 23 D.U.L.J. 21.

Ní Raifeartaigh, Úna 'Fault issues and Libel Law: A Comparison between Irish, English and United States Law' (1991) 40 *I.C.L.Q.* 763.

Ní Raifeartaigh, Úna 'Defences in Irish Defamation Law' (1991) 13 *Dublin University Law Journal*, 76.

O'Callaghan, Jerome 'Censorship of Indecency in Ireland: A View from Abroad' (1998) 16 *Cardozo Arts and Entertainment Law Journal* 53.

O'Dell, Eoin 'Does Defamation Value Free Expression?' (1990) *Dublin University Law Journal*, 12 50. 'Reflections on a Revolution in Libel' (1991) *I.L.T.* 181.

O'Neill, Ailbhe 'Defamation by Hyperlink and the Publication Rule', (2012) 19 (1) DULJ 317

Pollard, M. 'Control of the Press in Ireland through the King's Printer's Patent 1600-1800' (1978–1980) 14 *Irish Booklore* 79.

Reports

Broadcasting

Broadcasting Authority of Ireland (BAI), *Representation and portrayal of people with disabilities in Irish broadcasting* (November 2011).

Broadcasting Authority of Ireland (BAI), *Prompting cultural diversity in the Irish broadcasting sector: an assessment of international standards and best practices with a view to their operationalization in an Irish context* (March 2010).

Report of the Forum on Broadcasting, August 2002. www.dcmnr.gov.ie/files/FINLREPT3.DOC

Department of Arts, Culture and the Gaeltacht, *Clear Focus: The Government's Proposals for Broadcasting Legislation* (Pn 3648, Stationery Office, Dublin, 1997).

Competition

Report of the Advisory Group on Media Mergers, June 2008: http://www.dbei.ie/en/Publications/Publication-files/Advisory-Group-on-Media-Mergers ...

Competition and Mergers Review Group, *Final Report* (Pn 8487, Department of Enterprise, Trade and Employment, Dublin, 2000).

Competition Authority, *Interim Report of Study on the Newspaper Industry* (The Stationery Office, Dublin, 1995).

Competition Authority, *Report of the Investigation of the Proposal whereby Independent Newspapers plc would increase its shareholding in the Tribune Group from 29.9% to 53.09%* (Stationery Office, Dublin, 1992).

Miscellaneous

Copyright Review Committee, 'Copyright and Innovation: A Consultation Paper', 29 February 2012, available at http://www.djei.ie/science/ipr/crc_consultation_paper.pdf

Report of the Advisory Group on Privacy, 31 March 2006, available at: http://www.justice.ie/en/JELR/WkgGrpPrivacy.pdf/Files/WkgGrpPrivacy.pdf

Report of the Legal Advisory Group on Defamation, March 2003. www.justice.ie under 'publications'.

Report of the Commission on the Newspaper Industry, (Pn 2841, Stationery Office, Dublin, 1996).

Constitution Review Group, *Report of the Constitution Review Group* (Stationery Office, Dublin, 1996).

Law Reform Commission: www.lawreform.ie, under 'Publications':
Law Reform Commission: Consultation Paper on the Civil Law of Defamation (March 1991)

Law Reform Commission: Report on the Civil Law of Defamation (LRC 38–1991)

Law Reform Commission: Consultation Paper on the Crime of Libel (August 1991)

Law Reform Commission: Report on the Crime of Libel (LRC 41–1991)

## Selected Bibliography

Law Reform Commission: Consultation Paper on Contempt of Court (July 1991)

Law Reform Commission: Report on Contempt of Court (LRC 47–1994)

Law Reform Commission: Consultation Paper on Privacy: Surveillance and the Interception of Communications (September 1996)

Law Reform Commission: Report on Privacy: Surveillance and the Interception of Communications (LRC 57–1998)

Useful Websites

www.asai.ie (Advertising Standards Authority for Ireland)

www.bailii.org, www.irlii.org (British and Irish legislation, case law, journals)

www.bci.ie, www.bai.ie (Broadcasting Commission of Ireland, now the Broadcasting Authority of Ireland)

www.comreg.ie (Commission for Communications Regulation)

www.dataprotection.ie (Data Protection Commissioner)

www.dcenr.gov.ie/ (Department of Communications); now http://www.dccae.gov.ie/

www.iab.ie (Internet Advisory Board)

www.irishstatutebook.ie (Irish Statute Book, Acts and Bills 1922 – present)

www.ispai.ie (Internet Service Providers Association of Ireland)

www.hotline.ie (Hotline regarding child pornography on the Internet, supervised by the Internet Advisory Board.)

www.ifco.ie (Irish Film Classification Office)

www.lawreform.ie (Law Reform Commission)

www.nationalarchives.ie (National Archives of Ireland)

www.nuj.org.uk (National Union of Journalists in Britain and Ireland)

www.oic.gov.ie (Office of the Information Commissioner)

www.oireachtas.ie (Acts and Bills passed since 1998)

www.tca.ie (The Competition Authority)

# Index

*The numbers here refer to paragraph numbers.*

www.ingramcontent.com/pod-product-compliance
Ingram Content Group UK Ltd.
Pitfield, Milton Keynes, MK11 3LW, UK
UKHW020140290926
15471UKWH00003B/614

9 789403 500232